WHICH? WAY TO A HEALTHIER DIET

WHICH? WAY TO A HEALTHIER DIET

Judy Byrne

Published by Consumers' Association
and Hodder & Stoughton

Which? Books are commissioned and researched by The Association for Consumer Research and published by Consumers' Association, 2 Marylebone Road, London NW1 4DF and Hodder & Stoughton, 47 Bedford Square, London WC1B 3DP

First edition June 1993
Copyright © 1993 Consumers' Association Ltd

British Library Cataloguing in Publication Data
Byrne, Judy
Which? Way to a Healthier Diet: easy healthy options for all kinds of lifestyle.
– (Which? Consumer Guides)
I. Title II. Series
613.2

ISBN 0–340–59101–3

Typographic design by Paul Saunders
Illustrations on pages 26 and 39 by Andrew Bezear
Cover photographs by Pictor International Ltd; Loisjoy Thurston, Bubbles Photo Library; John Walmsley
Index by Marie Lorimer

Much of this book is based on research carried out for *Which?* and *Which? way to Health* magazines, both published by Consumers' Association. See also page 229 for other sources.

Typeset by J&L Composition Ltd, Filey, North Yorkshire

Printed and bound by Firmin-Didot (France)
Groupe Herissey
Nº d'impression: 23967

Contents

Other books from Consumers' Association

Understanding Headaches and Migraines – A practical guide to avoiding and coping with all forms of headache

Understanding HRT and the Menopause – Managing 'the change' with or without hormone replacement therapy

Understanding Stress – The causes and symptoms, and the most effective methods of stress management

Understanding Back Trouble – How to prevent, treat and cope with back trouble

Preventing Heart Disease – Understanding and taking care of your heart

Caring for Parents in Later Life – The practical, financial, legal and emotional issues

Which? Medicine – The essential consumer guide to over 1,500 medicines in common use

All are available from bookshops, including the *Which?* shop at 359–361 Euston Road, London NW1 (telephone: 071–486 5544); and by post from Consumers' Association, Castlemead, Gascoyne Way, Hertford X, SG14 1LH.

Access/visa cardholders can phone FREE on (0800) 252100 to place their order.

Free Trial Subscription to Which? way to Health

Whether you want positive advice on staying fit, a healthy diet or detecting health problems at an early stage, *Which? way to Health* is for you. Published every two months, it gives you the results of tests on health products, and practical advice to help you to take control of your own health and to lead a lifestyle that will cut down health risks and keep stress levels in check.

Written in a clear, uncomplicated way, *Which? way to Health* gives you the plain facts without scientific jargon or marketing hype. It is truly independent: it takes no advertising, so it can tell you the things you want to know, not what advertisers want you to know. For details of our *free* trial subscription offer write to Dept. E6, Consumers' Association, FREEPOST, Hertford X, SG14 1YB.

INTRODUCTION

THIS book is for busy people. It is for everyone who cares about good health. It is for those who want to enjoy the energy, vitality and resistance to illness that a healthy diet promises but who may not have much time in which to find out how to achieve it and put it into practice. *Which? Way to a Healthier Diet*, with its emphasis not on guidelines but on actual foods, is for everyone who believes that life is too short to spend a large proportion of it at the kitchen sink.

Our eating patterns are changing. We now eat out more than ever before. According to recent studies, men on average now get at least a third of their calories and women at least a quarter from eating out. Unfortunately, food eaten outside the home is more likely to have a high proportion of fat than food cooked at home. Hot dogs, chips and hamburgers topped with hefty dollops of mayonnaise, relish or cheese have helped to see to that. We increased the amount we spend on eating out by more than 200 per cent from the mid-1970s to the mid-1980s. Take-aways now account for more than a quarter of our food – in Britain we eat more than 4,000,000 takeaway meals a year between us.

About 40 per cent of what we eat at home is in the form of snacks, and the younger you are the less likely you are to cook and the more likely to buy convenience foods or eat out.

This book is dedicated to everyone juggling long or erratic working hours and a family life. It is dedicated to single parents on the treadmill of running a household unaided, to people living alone and tempted to ignore the food-health link because they are 'only' caring for themselves, and to all carers every-where who shoulder the burden of looking after the elderly and the unwell. It is for people who have retired from work and want to enjoy their leisure and for the unemployed who need to keep their spirits as well as their energy levels high. It is for everyone who refuses to be obsessed by a quest for the 'perfect' diet but who still wants what they eat to contribute to glowing good health.

Healthy eating is for you if you want to know how to make healthy eating choices at the sandwich bar or the take-away, in the restaurant and when you go on holiday. It is about healthy eating that will last you for the rest of your life.

It will be especially helpful for you if you know that your genes and history have already put you in a particularly high-risk group for diet-related illness and your doctor has spelled out strict guidelines within which you must learn to eat.

Few of us have the time or the inclination to plough through the small print of each new report on nutrition, to analyse the research design, to compare its findings with other work in the field. Few of us want to become so immersed in studying nutrition that we need to submit the week's menus to a computer program to check whether we are getting it all absolutely right. And few of us have the time or the energy to become involved in cooking meals every day.

Here is the good news: most people could achieve ample improvement in their diet just by making a few quite simple changes. This book, with its emphasis on practical hints and tips, helps you to discover how. You don't have to be fanatical. There is no need to go overboard. The chapters that follow bring better health within the reach of everyone who puts into practice just some of the ideas and changes it suggests. And that is the spirit in which the tips are intended. They are not tablets of stone to be ignored at your peril. They simply highlight the many different ways in which you can make your diet healthier – choose the ones that suit you best.

And there is more good news: not only can healthy eating be simple and easy to adapt to your own lifestyle but it is not expensive. For example, with its increased emphasis on pasta, rice and bread and a corresponding reduction in the consumption of red meat, a 'healthier' supermarket trolley can actually help your budget, too.

Healthy eating is not dieting. But the guidelines are similar for people who want to stay healthy and people who want to get and keep their weight down. Healthy eating may change your size and shape only slowly but it can do so forever, while crash dieting simply triggers the next phase of the yo-yo cycle as soon as you stop. Healthy eating re-educates your palate and your body. Crash dieting builds up a backlog of craving that can break out as soon as you reach your target weight and call a halt. Most crash dieters go straight back afterwards to the old eating habits that made them fat before, so it is hardly surprising that the weight goes back on.

What a healthy diet cannot promise is that it will keep you the shape you want to be and it will not guarantee you fashion-model skinniness. The way your body stores fat is partly inherited. For many of us 'healthy' means a little more upholstery than we wish we had. But scientists have been discovering interesting – and for many of us comforting – relationships between health and shape, which are discussed in more detail later in this book.

Health does not have to be bought at the expense of taste, either. A healthy diet can be delicious, as you will discover if you try out the suggestions in this book.

Chapter 1 outlines current thinking about **healthy eating** and looks at the problem of whom to believe when you are confronted with contradictory views. *Chapter 2* explains the components of a healthy diet and goes into more about which foods contain them.

In *Chapter 3* you will find all you need to know about **healthy shopping**. If you were to do nothing more than use it to make more informed choices at the supermarket you would become a healthier eater straight away. This section contains tips on **safe storage**, too.

Chapter 4 highlights **healthy cooking**. It compares the advantages and drawbacks of different cooking methods and gives you dozens of fatbuster ideas for making healthier versions of favourite dishes. And as fewer children eat school dinners nowadays, it offers tips for lunchboxes and suggestions for healthier snacks for people on the move.

Chapter 5 examines the guidelines for **sensible drinking**. In *Chapter 6* the focus is on **health hazards** that can make your kitchen a breeding ground for illness, while *Chapter 7* provides advice for making informed choices when you are **eating out**. *Chapter 8* covers **special tips** for the overweight, and more tips for parents who despair of getting children to eat what – and when – they want them to, together with hints on how to spot eating disorders and where to turn to for help.

Health warning

Of course, it would be wrong to suggest that food alone holds the key to good health. Improving your diet can do most for the quality of your life and health if it is part of an all-round strategy that also includes regular exercise, not smoking and learning to manage stress. Following this holistic approach to health gives benefits greater than the sum of the parts.

To see how the factors interact, let's look, for example, at heart disease. Smokers are twice as likely as non-smokers to suffer from coronary heart disease (CHD). To get the feel of the scale of the risk involved, we can consider the fate of 1,000 young men in the UK who are regular smokers. If they are an average sample, one will be murdered and six killed on the roads. And 250 of them will die of tobacco-related illnesses, including strokes, cancers, bronchitis and emphysema and, above all, CHD.

But what determines which of them will be the unlucky one in four for whom smoking signs a death sentence? Research has found that they are more likely to be the ones with a high level of blood cholesterol or high blood pressure, and both blood cholesterol and blood pressure can improve in response to changes in diet – see the first two chapters.

That is not the end of the story. Exercise has also been found to reduce the risk of CHD in at least three different ways. It, too, can reduce the total of cholesterol in the blood a little, and that reduction is more in the 'bad' low-density lipid than in the 'good' high-density lipid type of cholesterol (explained in detail in Chapter 2). Exercise has been found to reduce the level of high blood pressure and seems to help prevent the increase in blood pressure with age that doctors once thought was inevitable. Studies have found that people who exercise are more likely to succeed if they try to give up smoking, so young smokers who exercise are, for a number of reasons, more likely to end up in the lucky 750 than in the unlucky 250.

But this web of factors that determines the exact risk for any individual is yet more complex. Stressful events trigger a quite predictable series of reactions in the body, which include causing the blood pressure to rise and releasing extra fats, such as cholesterol, into the bloodstream. Both responses are useful if the cause of the stress is an attacking tiger. They help the body to fight back or take flight. However, they have become redundant in modern man and woman with no tiger to fight. The persistence of these primitive physiological responses now simply increases the risk that stress will lead to CHD. In addition, some people feeling stressed reach for a cigarette, which they mistakenly believe helps relax them, or for something sweet to eat, increasing the dangers of obesity and the health risks associated with that (discussed in greater detail in Chapter 1).

Healthy eating, exercise, smoking and stress are inter-related in these and other subtle ways in determining who does and does not die from a range of illness, of which CHD is just one. But it is the one that is most common in Britain, killing an average of 460 people a day. It kills one in three of the men who die under the age of 65 and one in seven of the women.

There is evidence that starts from the other end of the equation and comes up with the same conclusions about how smoking, lack of exercise and poor diet contrive to cause fatal coronary heart disease. Since 1968, deaths from CHD in US citizens between the ages of 35 and 74 have gone down by 53 per cent. In Australia the improvement is 48 per cent and in Finland 27 per cent. All three countries started with worse rates than Britain. During the same period, the improvement in England and Wales has been only 12 per cent, in Scotland only 9, and in Northern Ireland an even poorer 7 per cent.

So why the difference? Studies suggest that while half the

11

improvement in the US is thanks to improved surgery and drugs, the other half has come about through a changed climate of prevention in which people are smoking less, eating healthier diets and taking more exercise.

If you want to learn more about avoiding CHD and managing stress you might like to know of two other **Which? Consumer Guides**, *Preventing Heart Disease* and *Understanding Stress*, which deal with these topics in more detail.

The healthy eating debate

Much scientific enquiry has been dedicated since the 1970s to refining our understanding of exactly what constitutes a healthy diet and why. There has been progress – but at a price. Sometimes when findings seem to overturn the previous generation's orthodoxy we are tempted to suspect that no one really knows the answers and ignore any nutritional advice. But there are two important considerations.

First, because newspapers and magazines know they have a better-informed readership nowadays they report the results of studies they think will be of interest. But they often report naïvely – for example, without making clear the distinction between the findings of a meticulously designed piece of major research and a small pilot study which could at best show only that a full study might well be worthwhile. Unlike the scientific journals, most publications do not see it as part of their role to worry about whether the results of an experiment have been replicated by other investigators or not. Nor would they necessarily be aware if half a dozen similar studies had previously come up with exactly the opposite result.

Secondly, not only are newspapers and magazines catering for a more health-conscious readership avid for snippets of research information but the pressures on scientists themselves have changed. Once they waited to publish in their own trade press. Now, as competition for funding increases, they are having to learn to play the public relations game, where publicity for early results can improve the chances of getting funding for the next phase of a project. And when, as is often the case with food research, the work is actually sponsored by one of the food lobbies, then sales rather than the pursuit of knowledge for its own sake can be the driving force.

Going to your family doctor is unlikely to solve your problems. No medical degree examination in Britain includes a paper on nutrition. And research done by Dr Jan Francis in 1988 was anything but reassuring: Dr Francis monitored how 128 doctors and nurses dealt with patients at risk from heart disease because they had high levels of blood cholesterol and found that 37 of them did not understand that polyunsaturated fats needed to be increased as a proportion of total fat intake. The same number advised these patients what not to eat but made no suggestions about eating healthier diets by including foods such as fruit and vegetables.

Nevertheless, the best available advice about diet has been more consistent over recent years than many people think. For example, the basic message for some time has been 'more fibre, less fat', though nutritionists have carried on refining their understanding over the years of different types of fibre and fats and their effects. We have known for ages that sugar is bad for our teeth and our weight, even if it is only more recently that scientists have begun to look at its other effects on our bodies. Salt has had a black mark for people with blood pressure problems for decades. Only more recently have scientists begun to query whether a link between more salt and higher blood pressure might also be true for the rest of us.

So, while there might yet be much to learn it is still worth putting into practice all that we already know for the sake of our health. This book will help you discover how. It could just change your life.

WHICH? WAY TO A HEALTHIER DIET QUIZ

1. If you were at an Indian restaurant and wanted to pick the healthiest choices, which of each pair of foods would you go for: (a) a meat or a vegetable curry? (b) a chapati or a poppadum? (c) a tandoori dish or a korma?

2. Which of the following can help reduce blood cholesterol levels? (a) a moderate intake of alcohol (b) stewed coffee (c) vitamin C (d) lentils

3. If your teenage son or daughter decides to become vegetarian, which two minerals should you aim to boost in his or her diet?

4. What is the legal definition of 'low fat'?

5. All apple varieties have the same vitamin C content – true or false?

6. Which method of cooking bacon is the healthiest: frying in a teaspoonful of hot oil, frying in a quarter-inch of hot oil, frying in a quarter-inch of cold oil, grilling or microwaving?

7. Like the microwave, it cooks with little liquid and no added fat, is good for cooking fresh fruits in their own juices, and cooks in a short time so that fewer nutrients are lost. What is 'it'?

8. What is labna?

9. How long does it take the liver to process one unit of alcohol (e.g. one small glass of wine or half a pint of beer)?

10. What are the best and worst places to store bread?

For the answers, see page 228.

CHAPTER 1

WHAT IS A HEALTHY DIET?

A HEALTHY diet is one that provides the body with everything it needs to grow, to repair its tissues, and to produce just the amount of energy it needs. But it is much, much more. A healthy diet is also one that gives a feeling of vitality and well-being, maximum resistance to illness, and protection against such conditions as heart disease and cancer in which diet may be a factor. With one person in five in the UK dying of diet-related disease, do we owe ourselves anything less?

Healthy eating does not have to be complicated. This chapter explains the guidelines, but if you prefer to move straight on to the basic facts, the building blocks of a healthy diet are described in the next chapter. If you are already familiar with both you might prefer to skip to **Chapter 3**, which explains how to put the guidelines into practice with minimal effort.

But to make sound decisions about what we and our families eat, it helps to be familiar with where the recommendations come from and how the whole nutrition process works.

The digestive system

The digestive system breaks down the food we eat with the help of various chemical substances it secretes into the mouth, stomach and bowels. Other chemicals carry the digested materials into the bloodstream. There they are used either for maintenance work on the body itself or to provide the energy we use when we breathe, sleep, move and even think. If we make more energy than we use, we store it as fat. So we need our food to provide both energy and a tissue repair kit, plus small but essential amounts of chemicals that the body must have but cannot manufacture for itself. When the body does not get what it needs from food, the result can be anything from feeling a bit under the weather to major breakdown.

Over most of this century there has been a shift in the more developed countries towards a diet that includes more meat, fish, poultry, eggs and dairy products, along with an increased tendency to refine and purify food, to add sugar and salt to manufactured foods to increase their taste appeal, and away from the old staples like grains and vegetables that used to make up the bulk of most people's diets. Refining starches robs them not only of valuable fibre but of essential nutrients as well.

Our health has paid a price for our affluence. Over the same period cancer, diabetes, high blood pressure and heart and kidney diseases have increased in the West, while in poorer countries where most people still eat a simpler, less refined diet these diet-related conditions continue to be comparatively rare.

The evidence of history is echoed by geography. The major and influential Seven Country Study led by the American Professor Ancel Keys set out in the 1950s to compare lifestyles across the world and their links with local diseases. The countries studied were Finland, Yugoslavia, the Netherlands, Greece, Italy, the United States and Japan.

The simply perfect diet

The Study's findings and subsequent follow-up studies put the spotlight on the unassuming Mediterranean hilltop village of Celso, nestling among Italian olive groves. There, the inhabitants, who live off the fruit of the land and trees in the surrounding fields, have been tested for diet-related disease every ten years in a study coordinated by the Institute of Nutrition in Rome. They have been found to be among the least likely people in the world to die of diet-related disease. They eat plenty of home-made pasta, bread, soup, fruit, vegetables and olive oil and they drink red wine. It turns out that they have been eating for centuries just what the World Health Organization (WHO) now says we all should. A healthy diet includes not only carbohydrate, protein and some fats but vitamins and minerals as well – and in the right proportions.

The WHO laid down its guidelines on what the proportions are in its 1990 report *Diet, Nutrition and the Prevention of Chronic Diseases*. It was written by a group of international scientists who were brought together specifically to consider the whole body of research on nutrition, to examine all the available findings and to set out the current scientific consensus on diet and health.

The report stated that eating well can help prevent coronary heart disease, hypertension, stroke, gallstones and tooth decay as well as obesity and can give some protection against cancer. It also said that what we eat may contribute to the incidence of osteoporosis (brittle bones), diabetes in middle age, and intestinal and bowel problems.

But how can we be sure that the experts' advice is worth following? How, with so many opposing views and so much conflicting advice in the media, can we be sure that anyone really knows?

Between the lines

Stories in the newspapers about how one expert disagrees with another tend to give scientific research a bad name. Doesn't that mean, we grumble, that it is a waste of time taking notice of any of them? The trouble is that journalists are rarely trained to read scientific reports critically and, when they are, ifs, buts, maybes and similar qualifications don't make for eye-catching headlines or snappy copy. So we need to learn to read between the lines. The temptation to oversimplify must be almost overwhelming when a journalist has a ration of just a few hundred words at his or her disposal to report the design and findings of a complicated piece of research. And scientists who agree aren't usually as newsworthy as scientists who disagree. If one says that fat should be no more than 25 per cent of our daily diets and another is happy with 30, to a journalist that spells disagreement. The *real* story is that there is agreement among scientists that most of us are getting far too much of our daily energy input in the form of fat for the good of our health.

Building up a jigsaw

Actually, orthodox medical research is like a jigsaw with one little piece after another fitting into place, and sometimes being displaced when another bit that fits even better comes along. Nutritional research has rarely overturned the previously accepted wisdom. Rather, it has refined. And research into healthy eating rarely *proves*. Usually at best it *appears* to show.

It is worth bearing in mind, too, that newspapers will publish research reports if the results make a good headline. Respected scientific journals, on the other hand, publish only if they have satisfied themselves that the research is well designed and the results are statistically significant – in other words that they have been subjected to mathematical tests to check that the probability of the result occurring by chance is extremely small. Leading journals such as the *British Medical Journal* and *The Lancet* have results checked by statisticians, so if you are not a maths expert yourself you can rely on the findings.

Questions to ask

But if you want to know how seriously to take the results of any study there are still a number of questions you might want to ask. They could include:

- Was there a control group – a group of similar people used as a comparison – as well as an experimental group involved? For example, if a drug was tested, there should have been a control group taking a placebo (a dummy pill) or given the same amount of advice and attention but no medication, so that the results of the two groups could be compared.
- Was it a double blind study – that is, one in which neither the researchers/observers nor the subjects knew who was in the experimental group and who in the control group? If not, the outcome might have been influenced by the experimenters' or subjects' expectations.
- Were other factors such as general diet, exercise, environment, family history and even personality adequately taken into account in the experiment design?

- How many people were involved in the study? The larger the number the more reliable the result.
- Did the study take place over a reasonable period of time? The longer it took, the more dependable the results are likely to be. If long-term illness is being considered the timescale should be in years.
- Who paid for the research? If a manufacturer or lobby with a special interest in the outcome sponsored the study the results need to be read with that in mind.
- If the report is in a newspaper, was it picked up from a journal like *The Lancet* or the *BMJ* or has a reporter got hold of previously unpublished and possibly unverified findings?

When you consider the evidence in the light of these tests, there is far more consensus among the experts than reading newspapers would ever lead you to believe. They might disagree about the relative importance of different elements. Some might think that smoking and exercise matter more than diet, for example, while others put more emphasis on what we eat. But there is a consensus that eating the right way is important to health and broad agreement about what healthy eating is.

Russian roulette

One frequent objection comes from sceptics who advance arguments along the lines of 'But I know a woman who had bacon, fried eggs and fried bread for breakfast every morning, smoked 40 a day and never took exercise, and she lived to be 99 . . .' It may even be true that she did. But it misses the point about probability and probability is the name of the research game. No one can tell you that if you eat too little fibre all your life you will die of cancer of the colon. What they *can* say is that if you eat too little fibre all your life, you are putting yourself in the group more likely to get cancer of the colon. Instead of your chances depending on the throw of a straight dice, you are putting your money on a loaded one – one you have loaded against yourself. The 'I know a woman . . .' sceptics may also know someone who survived playing Russian roulette six times. But how many times does that make it a risk worth taking to hold a revolver to your head and pull the trigger to see if the barrel has a bullet in it? And does your answer depend on whether it is your head or mine?

The healthy eating guidelines are not about the inevitable outcome for a particular individual but about what gives us all the best possible chance, in the light of current knowledge, of good health. And there is less disagreement about that than you might think.

The evidence

At the outset, we have to accept that, with many suspected causes of disease, there will probably never be absolute proof. Sometimes the research needed to establish, beyond question, that a link exists is never carried out because it would be unethical. Would you want to volunteer to be on the losing team given the diet expected to cause heart disease or cancer? There are various methods for gathering evidence that are more ethically acceptable but they are less scientifically rigorous and more fraught with practical difficulties. What they do is build up a picture, clue by tiny clue, that gradually becomes clearer and more precise. New studies are unlikely to change the picture. What they aim to do is improve the sharpness of focus all the time.

Epidemiology

As direct experiment is rarely appropriate, knowledge about nutrition often progresses by epidemiology – the study of the distribution of diseases – by comparing what happens to one group of people with what happens to another within a population or across populations. For example, studies have attempted to tease out why the incidence of coronary heart disease and cancers of the breast and bowel, three of the five diseases most generally thought to be related to diet, are high in the West but low in Japan, while the other two, cerebrovascular disease (stroke and high blood pressure) and cancer of the stomach, are more common in Japan and less in America. One possible explanation is differences in diets. (Another explanation might have been a genetic difference, but it has been possible to rule that out by studying what happens to the pattern when Japanese people migrate to America. Their children, we now know from studies of Japanese migration to Hawaii and San Francisco, leave behind the disease pattern of their parents and move on to that of their new country.)

So that narrows the possibilities down to environmental, occupational, lifestyle- or diet-related or an interaction between two or more of them. Such studies are invaluable, but they are not a fast track to instant insights. And epidemiology is complicated by difficulties in collecting dietary data everywhere and lack of uniformity from place to place about diagnosis, categorisation and record-keeping.

Retrospective studies

Practical difficulties also bedevil retrospective studies, studies which attempt to find out how a group of people who now have a particular disease differed in their diets from another group, matched as closely as possible on other non-diet factors, who have not. The reliability of such studies has to be questioned because they depend so heavily on people being able to remember what they were eating 10 or even 20 years ago. But they have their role.

Intervention trials

More can be gleaned from intervention trials, though they are discouragingly expensive and even when the money is spent the results can disappoint. A five-year study in the North Karelia province of Finland in the 1970s, for example, set out to encourage people to reduce their risk of coronary heart disease by reducing their intake of saturates, cutting smoking, and taking other health measures such as identifying and treating high blood pressure. The area had the highest incidence of CHD in the world at the time, and it did go down. It would have been a good, clear-cut result except that the incidence also dropped in the neighbouring province, which was being used as a control group. The explanation may be that the North Karelia propaganda effect spilled over the border, but that is only guesswork. If it was good news for the residents, it was not for the advancement of nutritional knowledge.

Ethical factors can come into play in intervention trials, too. For example, a massive $115,000,000 was poured into what was called the Multiple Risk Factor Intervention Trial carried out at the University of Minnesota, which ended in the early 1980s with an inconclusive result on diet. The problem was that there was no adequate control group because it was considered unethical to identify the individuals at highest risk of developing heart disease within a population and then not to tell them so and give them appropriate advice to help them reduce that risk.

Laboratory tests and animal studies

Two other means of studying diet also contribute only indirect evidence. Laboratory tests can study the way in which, for example, different chemicals react together in a test tube, or how cells taken from a body respond to changed conditions or the presence of other substances. But all they prove is what happens in a test tube. Such tests can suggest to scientists what *could* happen in the human body; that is not necessarily the same thing as what actually does. Animal studies are similarly inconclusive. They have the advantage that several generations can be studied over a condensed timescale compared with humans but they have two major drawbacks. Many people are unhappy on moral grounds about using animals in this way, and in any case what happens to humans in the same situation is not necessarily the same thing.

Building up the evidence

Another reason that research reports may seem to invite scepticism is that clear-cut single causes of death or disease would be helpful to keep the books tidy but they are probably rare in real life. A diet too high in fat might be bad for your heart, for example, but your risk of dying of a heart attack would be worse if you inherited susceptible genes, smoked heavily and took no exercise into the bargain. The more factors that can interact to cause disease, the harder it is to tease out statistically how much is attributable to what.

Despite the difficulties and the drawbacks inherent in each research method, approaching the same subject from a number of different angles can gradually build up a useful picture, piece by piece, as research into the role of certain essential fatty acids in diet illustrates.

A tale of fatty acids
An epidemiological approach first put scientists on to the trail of the role of the omega-3 essential fatty acids (see under **Fats** in the next chapter) in offering protection against the risk of CHD.

Omega-3 fatty acids first came under scrutiny with the discovery that heart disease is rare among Eskimos who eat fatty fish and whale blubber in a big way. The story began with the work of two Danish medical researchers, John Dyerberg and H.O. Bang, who were working at the Alberg Hospital in the Netherlands and became interested in Eskimos, whose diet was a cardiologist's nightmare. The name by which Eskimos prefer to be called is Inuit, which actually means 'raw meat eater'. They lived on raw seal and raw fish, had the highest consumption of fat in the world and ate virtually no fresh vegetables, fruit or complex carbohydrates. Yet they confounded the predicted consequence of that by their low rates of heart and arterial disease and they also had a low incidence of other degenerative diseases, including cancer, gallstones, diabetes and rheumatoid arthritis. Again, genetic inheritance was ruled out by the fact that those who migrated from their native land to Eastern Canada seemed to lose their apparent immunity to heart disease.

The role of raw fish
The two doctors decided to turn the usual research paradigm on its head. Instead of asking why so many people in other cultures died of heart disease, the question they posed to themselves was why so few of the Inuit did. To find out they set out in the winter of 1976 to live in Greenland and study their diet at first hand, along with a British nutritionist, Dr Hugh Sinclair, who had been an expert on Eskimo nutrition from before the time when contact with the outside world began to change their ways. The three made a number of intriguing discoveries, including the fact that despite the huge amounts of

fat in their diet, the Inuit had a low blood level of triglyceride (see under **Cholesterol** in the next chapter) and one thing they had in common with the Japanese was a high consumption of raw fish. Epidemiological studies within Japan seemed to confirm this finding. The inhabitants of Okinawa Island were eating about twice as much fish as people on the mainland, and they had the lowest death rate of all.

Dr Sinclair decided on a remarkable next step. In March 1979, he began a six-month diet of nothing but seal, fish and shellfish. Because of the apparent risk to his health in the light of what was then known about health and diet, he decided to allow no volunteer to join him. It was a courageous move because not only was nothing known about how the change of diet would affect a Westerner but he was sentencing himself to a relentlessly boring menu. But by the end of it he had begun to have an idea why the Inuit were so free from heart attacks and circulatory problems and which essential fatty acids might hold the key. A number of other studies followed. For example, Dyerberg and Bang put volunteers on a diet consisting largely of mackerel and found a significant reduction in their blood cholesterol.

Meanwhile, Dr Daan Kromhout had also been intrigued by the suggestion that it was the large quantity of fish in their diet that was protecting the Greenland Inuit from heart disease. He and his colleagues began in 1960 to organise a 20–year trial in the old industrial town of Zutphen in the eastern Netherlands to investigate the relationship between fish consumption and coronary heart disease there. They studied 852 men between the ages of 40 and 59, about 20 per cent of whom ate no fish and whose average intake overall was 20g a day, about a third of which was oily fish such as herring and mackerel. Both participants and their wives were interviewed about their eating habits. During the 20 years over which they were monitored 78 of the men died of CHD.

When the findings were published in May 1985 in the *New England Journal of Medicine* analysis of the results had found an inverse relationship between fish consumption and CHD deaths – more dietary fish equalled less risk of fatal CHD. The death rate was actually 50 per cent lower among the men who had 30g of fish a day than among those who had none. The paper concluded with a recommendation that we should all have one or two fish dishes a week for the health of our hearts.

And yet more fish

And the story did not end there. More Dutch research published in July 1992 showed that people who eat fish once or twice a week have a decreased risk of dying from a stroke. Research into fish oils continues to yield promising (though not yet conclusive) results in other areas. They begin to look useful not only in protecting against cardiovascular disease and high blood pressure but in the treatment of arthritis and other inflammatory disorders, and in psoriasis and other skin problems. Animal studies have suggested that fish oils can prevent and/or inhibit some cancers and successfully treat kidney disease in some animals.

Further research will now need to confirm these animal findings and check whether they extend to humans, too. Professor Michael Tisdale, head of a team at Aston University, Birmingham, is working on the possibility that fish oil may be able to shrink solid tumours and halt the dramatic weight loss often seen in cancer victims. Laboratory work on eicosapentaenoic acid or EPA – the most promising-looking of the omega-3 essential fatty acids to date – is beginning to unravel how EPA could block the release of the unique hormone-like proteins produced by some tumours and so shrink the tumour by starving it. Some patients at Edinburgh Royal Infirmary are to have the chance of taking part in trials before the end of 1993 and the Medical Research Council is seeking to patent EPA's use as a tumour treatment. There are hopes, too, that EPA could hold the key to a new and earlier test for many types of cancer.

So, far from being a closed book, research into the potential contribution to healthy eating of oily fish is still causing research excitement.

The guidelines

The World Health Organization guidelines that point the way to the prospect of a healthier future for us all were drawn up after considering all the research available. More recently, the Committee on Medical Aspects of Food Policy (COMA) made an up-to-date assessment of the current state of research, particularly as it is relevant to the UK, and published its recommendations in 1991. And reassuringly straightforward the combined guidelines are.

♥ The WHO recommends that we eat at least five portions of fruit and vegetables (besides potatoes) a day. That's not as difficult as it may at first sound. If you drink a glass of orange juice with your breakfast, have a side salad and a banana with your lunch and beans and carrots with your evening meal, for example, you are there. It doesn't matter nutritionally if the vegetables are frozen and the fruit canned – though whenever you opt for cans it is better to avoid those with added salt or sugar and to choose fruit canned in juice rather than in syrup. (As a rough guide, you can count each of the following as a portion: one cup of leafy salad, one cup of cooked vegetables, half a cup of chopped raw vegetables, a medium banana, an apple, an orange.)

♥ COMA recommends that we get an average of 18g of fibre (an individual minimum of 12g and maximum of 24g) a day, measured by the New Englyst method. The equivalent figures under the older Southgate method are 30g (20–40g). The new method has Government backing, but manufacturers can choose to use either on packaging.

♥ COMA recommends that we get nearly half our daily calories from complex carbohydrates found in starchy foods such as bread, potatoes, rice, pasta and breakfast cereals.

Most of us in the UK currently get a little over a quarter of our intake that way. Perhaps part of the reason is that these foods have had an undeserved reputation for being fattening when the blame really belonged to the fatty spreads and sauces we often served with them. In fact, if you take the same weight of starchy foods and fat, the fat has about twice the calories.

Wholemeal bread and cereal foods are better than white or refined because they contain more vitamins, minerals and essential fatty acids. But it is more important to eat plenty, whether white, brown or wholemeal, than to insist on wholemeal only.

Adding neat bran to our food is no substitute for getting fibre from the food itself. The bran layer of cereals contains phytate, which reduces our absorption of minerals like iron and zinc from food. Wholemeal foods are rich enough in them to compensate so it does not matter, but bran alone has the phytate without the extra minerals.

♥ COMA recommends that fat should not make up more than a third of our daily calories. That's a maximum 90g for men and 70g for women and means a cut of about a sixth of our average present intake. The guidelines are more stringent still on saturates (see **Chapter 2**), which should go down to no more than 10 per cent, an average cut of nearly a third.

The good news here is that when we start to increase our intake of bread, potatoes and cereals we will probably find we automatically cut down on more fat-laden options. In addition, we can reduce fat by choosing lean **meat** and leaving uneaten the fat on red meat and the fatty skin on **chicken**. Meat products like pies, burgers and sausages often conceal high fat levels. So do cakes and biscuits.

White fish is low in fat but high in vitamins and minerals and **oily fish** has lots of the essential fatty acids our bodies need. But we should ease up on fried or salted fish.

Milk and dairy products are important sources of calcium and going for the skimmed or semi-skimmed option does not significantly reduce the vitamins and minerals. Only the fat is lower.

♥ COMA recommends that we let the protein take care of itself. Most of us in the UK get more than enough already.

There are plenty of suggestions for easy ways to start putting the advice into practice from **Chapter 3** onwards and more detailed information about and descriptions of the building blocks of a healthy diet in the next chapter.

Vegetarianism

Vegetarianism means different things to different people. To some, it is just giving up red meat and poultry. Others say that is only demi-vegetarianism and that you are not vegetarian until you also renounce fish. Some give up cow's milk because they believe it is cruel to take calves away from their mothers and either bring them up artificially or kill them for veal in order to take for human consumption the milk on which they would have been raised.

Vegans are even stricter in their definition and usually exclude all food of animal origin including eggs and honey and anything processed using animal products. They usually also reject fur, leather shoes and cosmetics with ingredients of animal origin or that have been tested on animals. Most extreme are those vegans who believe it is also wrong to uproot living plants and so go further and become fruitarians. They eat only fruit, nuts and berries. A fruitarian diet is unlikely to be nutritionally adequate and is not recommended.

It is difficult to be as clear-cut about the relative merits of non-vegetarian, vegetarian and vegan diets. There have been a number of studies but the results are difficult to interpret, partly because people who are vegetarian are often also non-smokers who do not drink alcohol and who are more health-conscious than average. Some actually become vegetarian for health reasons because they want to cut the risk of, or attempt to cure, a particular illness. So it is hard to make a straight comparison with the general population.

We do know that prostate cancer is rare in developing countries and those where the diet is mainly vegetarian or fish-based. Meat-eaters are almost twice as likely to get cancer of the prostate as vegetarians. And at the halfway point of a ten-year study of 88,000 nurses being carried out by Professor Walter Willett of Harvard University he says that he has found a highly significant link between meat consumption and cancer of the colon, which confirms results from a number of retrospective studies. Vegetarians and vegans are also less likely to be obese, with the attendant health risks (see below). On the other side of the scales, vegetarians and vegans are more at risk from deficiencies of vitamin D and vitamin B12 if they don't take care (see under **Vitamins** in the next chapter).

Vegetarians and meat-eaters seem to have about the same average life expectancy. It may be that they have a slightly different distribution of diseases rather than one being more illness-prone overall than the other.

Obesity

We live in a diet-obsessed society, in which the non-verbal message 'Thin Is Beautiful' leaps out of almost every page of every glossy magazine. Stop a dozen average-sized women in the street and ask if they are happy with their weight and ten of them will probably tell you that if only they were between half a stone and a stone lighter, they would be happier not just with their bodies but with their entire lives. Recent surveys suggest that at any given time one in three or four men and women in the UK is on some sort of weight-loss diet. That represents a considerable triumph of optimism over experience when you consider that two-thirds of successful dieters put back most or all of what they have lost within a year.

For a tragic but not insignificant minority, mainly female and in their teens and twenties, vague discontent with the size of their bodies crystallises into something more serious. Three women in 100 have or have had a serious eating disorder. The lure of being twig-thin goes so deep that it feeds into other psychological problems and they become victims of these life-blighting or even life-threatening eating disorders. (For more about recognising and dealing with them see **Chapter 8**.)

Healthy eating is *not* dieting. But if you enjoy good general health, get plenty of exercise and follow the healthy eating guidelines on reducing fat and sugar and filling up with carbo-hydrates your weight should stay within medically acceptable limits. You will not become seriously overweight or obese.

The Body Mass Index

Obesity means the *excessive* accumulation of body fat. It is a condition that puts your health at risk. It is not just being a little on the plump side. Weight is no longer considered a good guide to size status – not least because muscle weighs more than fat. A fit woman may weigh a lot more than another who takes a dress size up but gets no exercise. A better way to tell if you are obese is to use the Body Mass Index, which is not a direct measurement of fat but gives a good working indication of your fat status.

To find out how you rate, divide your weight in kilogrammes by the square of your height in metres. For example, if you are 5ft 4ins (1.63 metres) and weigh 9st 13lbs (63kg), you multiply 1.63 by 1.63, which gives 2.66, and divide 63 by 2.66 to give 23.68 – below the threshold for even slight obesity.

If you score under 25, you are at a lower risk of a heart disease and a number of other health threats. If you score 25 to 29.9 you are rated slightly fat and the risk is beginning to rise. From 30 to 40 you are rated as moderately obese. And if you come out at more than 40, your health is in jeopardy.

But it is not a case of the lower the better, either. A BMI

under 20 also spells a higher risk of diseases such as reproductive organ malfunctions, fertility problems, severe depression, brittle bones and osteoporosis.

The healthy way to lose weight

If you do need to lose weight, the healthy way to do it is to adjust the input/output equation to take in a bit less energy from food and increase the exercise you do to use up a bit more until your weight reduces. For permanent results without harm to your health you should ensure you lose no more than one or two pounds a week and be prepared to change your eating patterns permanently to stay there. Go for more and risk both your health and running into the yo-yo effect – you stop dieting and watch it all bounce right back. A recent study that followed 3,000 people over 14 years found that yo-yo dieters who keep climbing back on the weight-loss treadmill become more prone to heart disease – and more likely if they get it to die of it – than people who don't keep jumping through the diet hoop.

When you cut your calorie intake drastically, your body slows down its metabolic rate to try to protect its fat store, making it harder and harder to lose weight anyway – and easier to put it back again the minute you relax your vigilance and go back to the eating pattern that made you overweight in the first place. Appetite suppressant pills might sound like the answer to a dieter's prayer but they can be addictive and can have side-effects, including raising blood pressure. And the magical cures you will see advertised from time to time that promise to help you lose weight without dieting will part you from more £££s than lbs. Every one so far investigated has been found to be ineffective.

There are more hints on how to lose weight healthily in the following chapters. Every suggestion for cutting fat and reducing sugar will be doubly helpful for you. Remember the guideline of no more than a third of your calories from fat is a *maximum*. It is not an allowance or recommendation. We actually need only very small amounts of essential fatty acids and a small amount of fat for the fat-soluble vitamins in our diet.

Research is continually refining our understanding of health risks and it now appears that there is an 'apples and pears' relationship between excess weight and risk. Being overweight is more dangerous for your health if you carry most of your stored fat around your waist, the apple-shaped pattern of many chubby men and often an indication of a high level of cholesterol in the blood (see under **Cholesterol** in the next chapter), than if it comes to roost more on your hips, the pear-shape that so many overweight women settle into.

There is a measure you can apply, called the Waist-to-Hip Ratio or WHR. To find out how you rate, measure your waist at the level of your navel and your hips at the widest point around the bottom. Divide the waist measurement by the hip. For example, a woman with a waist of 28ins and hips of 38ins has a WHR of 0.74. A WHR higher than 0.8 for females and 0.95 for men means too much intra-abdominal fat and an increased risk of early death.

But obesity is still a major health hazard for both sexes. It:

☹ considerably increases the likelihood of a number of diseases, including diabetes, especially above a Body Mass Index of 28
☹ shortens and/or reduces the quality of life by raising blood pressure, increasing the incidence of heart disease, especially for overweight men, and causing gout and hiatus hernia
☹ increases the risk of gallstones, osteoarthritis, and cancers of the uterus, gall bladder and breast.

Calories

One term about which many of us still seem confused, according to surveys, is the dieter's dirty word – calorie. A calorie is a unit of the energy into which food can be converted by our bodies to be either used or stored. A calorie is the same 'size' whether it comes from a fat, protein or carbohydrate source, and if it is not used for fuel, growth or repair it ends up the same way, however it started out – as fat.

How the different groups of food fit together into an overall picture of healthy eating is explained in more detail in the next chapter.

CHAPTER 2

THE BUILDING BLOCKS

IT MAY help you to put the healthy eating guidelines into practice if you understand what the different constituents of foods are and how they all fit together into the overall picture of good nutrition. Although the guidelines generally apply right across the age range, there are a few differences for children and the elderly – see **Chapter 8** for more detail.

Carbohydrates

The main source of energy in most people's diets is the sugar and starch from the carbohydrates that green plants make out of carbon dioxide and water with the help of sunlight. The plants make both the sugars and starches that they store for their own energy supply and their supporting structures – the plant equivalent of the human skeleton. In general, we get sugar from fruits and starch from seeds and roots, although there is an animal sugar source. The milk of mammals, including humans, contains lactose or milk sugar.

All carbohydrates are made up of the same atoms – carbon, hydrogen and oxygen – but different carbohydrates combine them in different ways. Starches, also called complex carbohydrates to distinguish them from the more chemically straightforward sugars, consist of chains of glucose linked together. They break down to yield glucose (and a fibre residue) when they are digested.

Carbohydrates are an important part of our daily diet. They are what we should eat to fill up. Happily, starchy foods like bread, rice, potatoes and cereals are also relatively inexpensive, and they are good sources of other nutrients. Potatoes, for example, also provide vitamin C while pulses, nuts and seeds are good providers of protein and vitamins E and B (for more details see under **Vitamins** below).

There is research evidence to suggest that:

☺ A diet rich in fruit and vegetables reduces the risk of some cancers; broccoli and cauliflower look particularly promising.

☺ Fruits and vegetables can give at least some protection against cancers of the lung, colon, breast, cervix, oesophagus (gullet), oral cavity, stomach, bladder, pancreas and ovaries.

☺ Fruits and vegetables may protect against cancer because they are good sources of antioxidant vitamins (see under **Vitamins** below) and may also contain other specific anti-cancer compounds. They are high in nutrients, low in calories.

☺ Starchy, fibre-rich foods can help in controlling hyperlipidaemia (high blood fat levels) and adult diabetes.

Sugar

Sugar, on the other hand, provides energy but no other nutrients – hence its reputation as 'empty calories'. If you are overweight, cutting down on sugar is one of the surest ways of cutting down on overall calorie intake without losing out on the nutrient front. Sugary foods such as cakes and chocolate are often high in fat, too, so cutting down on sugar tends to have the beneficial spin-off of reducing consumption of fat at the same time.

Another minus is that sugar also feeds acid-producing bacteria that damage the surface of teeth. The enamel on teeth can stand a certain amount of acid bombardment but if they are subjected to too much too often the enamel eventually wears through. The result is tooth decay. So it is best to confine to mealtimes what sugary foods and drinks you do have or give to children, rather than spreading them through the day.

Research shows that:

☹ Dental disease is actually the most widespread nutrition-related condition in Britain.

☹ Obesity rates in Britain shot up by 50 per cent in the 1980s:

twelve per cent of women and eight per cent of men are now rated seriously overweight.

☹ The British have a notoriously sweet tooth – we chomp our way through 10 kilogrammes or so of bought sweet biscuits a head every year, and the industry is confident that the figure will continue to rise (we get through less than a sixth as many savoury biscuits as sweet).

Fibre

The indigestible structural material from plants is fibre, and it is important for maintaining a healthy digestive system. All fibre passes through the mouth, stomach (or small intestine) and into the large intestine virtually unchanged. What happens to it there determines to which of two categories it belongs.

If it is **soluble** it dissolves in water to form a gooey liquid or gel and is fermented by bacteria. It is thought to have a role in helping delay the absorption of sugar and other nutrients from the small intestine. If it is **insoluble**, or what used to be called roughage, it passes out from the body unchanged. Getting plenty of it prevents constipation and may help prevent other disorders of the intestine.

Research evidence shows that:

☺ Soluble fibre in oat bran, and to a lesser extent pulses and lentils, can bring down high cholesterol levels (see under **Cholesterol** below).

☺ Insoluble fibre (plentiful in wheat and bran breakfast cereals, wholegrain bread, brown rice, wholemeal pasta and the skins of fruits and root vegetables) may help prevent constipation and piles. Undigested fibre attracts and holds water as it passes through the body, making stools bulky and soft so they move more quickly along the bowel and are usually passed with less strain.

☺ Fibre helps prevent diverticular disease, which is caused when small pouches develop in the wall of the large intestine and become infected and inflamed – usually as the result of straining.

☺ A high-fibre diet is sometimes successful in treating irritable bowel syndrome, which causes a change in bowel habit and discomfort or pain in the stomach.

☺ There is some evidence that a high-fibre diet is linked with a lowered rate of colon cancer and may help reduce the risk of bowel cancer, one of the most common cancers in Britain. Because fibre speeds up the rate at which food passes through the body, contact between the gut lining and any carcinogenic (cancer-causing) substance in food is reduced. More bulky and watery stools may also have the effect of diluting toxins.

☺ Fibre may be helpful for anyone needing to reduce weight, and for everyone who wants to ensure that they don't become overweight. Fibre needs so much chewing that it has a built-in rationing system, reducing the temptation to eat too much. Increasing the fibre in the diet helps to make meals feel satisfying and to keep hunger pangs at bay between them.

☺ Fibre may impede the absorption of fats into the digestive system.

☺ Getting the full benefit of fibre depends on drinking enough (non-alcoholic) liquid each say – see **Chapter 5**.

Everyone who decides to increase his or her fibre consumption needs to remember that a sudden spike in intake will throw the whole digestive system off-balance. Better to make the change in easy stages than to throw caution literally to the wind and go overboard overnight – easy definitely does it here. But if you find even a small increase causes wind problems, persevere. It is your body's way of asking for time to adjust.

Fats

Fats are compounds of glycerol (or common glycerine) and fatty acids and come in two main types, **saturates** and **unsaturates**. The fatty acid molecules are made up of carbon, oxygen and hydrogen atoms and when no chemical process can add more hydrogen to the molecule, the fat is called saturated. Unsaturated fats, which can be either **monounsaturates** or **polyunsaturates**, are the ones that could take up more hydrogen in some chemical reaction. As a rough rule of thumb, you can recognise saturates because they are solid at room temperature, while unsaturated fats are liquid. But it gets a little more complicated than that. The industrial hardening of fats to make some cooking fats and margarines involves hydrogenation (a reaction between hydrogen and a metal catalyst, often nickel); this converts unsaturates into either saturates or transsaturates, which behave in our bodies like saturates.

Our bodies can make from carbohydrates and protein all but those polyunsaturated fatty acids known as essential fatty acids, so we have little nutritional need of fats from our diets. But fats often act as carriers of flavours and aromas and make food more palatable. Foods rich in fat can help prevent us feeling hungry for longer than others because they are digested slowly. And we need some fat to carry the fat-soluble vitamins A, D, E and K into and around the body.

Essential fatty acids

The essential fatty acids, which were originally called vitamin F, belong to two groups: the omega-6 family, which come from vegetable oils like sunflower; and omega-3, which come from some vegetable oils such as soya-bean and rapeseed and from oily fish. We need essential fatty acids to aid digestion and vitamin absorption and for growth. Actual deficiency of essential fatty acids is rare except in babies given skimmed milk and some people with a fat absorption problem.

Although very high intakes of essential fatty acids may be harmful, there is now some evidence that more than a bare minimum, especially of omega-3 fatty acids, may offer some protection against heart and other diseases, as was discussed in the first chapter.

We now know that:

☺ Two of the omega-3 fatty acids reduce levels of triglycerides (fats that contribute to heart disease) in the blood and make the blood less sticky, thereby reducing the tendency to form blood clots, which can trigger a heart attack.
☺ Fish rich in omega-3 fatty acids include salmon, mackerel, sardines, pilchards, herrings, kippers and (uncanned only) tuna.

Although COMA recommends a significant reduction to around a third for average overall fat intake and to about 10 per cent for saturates, many nutritionists think that even this is too much to be good for us.

The American magazine *Consumer Reports*, for example, did a survey among 94 nutrition professionals – scientists, clinicians, registered dieticians and so on. Of the 68 who filled in and returned their questionnaire, most felt that the limit on fat intake should be lowered to 25 per cent of calorie intake and two-fifths wanted to see the figure reduced to just 20 per cent.

They were particularly concerned about saturates, which they blamed for:

☹ Being a significant cause of weight gain.
☹ Increasing the risk of heart disease.
☹ Possibly (although the evidence is still more unclear about this) increasing the risk of cancers of the breast, colon and prostate.

Cholesterol

Cholesterol has become something of a dirty word in healthy eating circles because high levels of it in the blood can be a warning of an increased risk of coronary heart disease (CHD). It is actually a soft, white, powdery substance with no smell, and like fat, does not mix with water. It is an important component of all the body's tissues. It forms part of the cell membranes and of the sheaths which protect nerve fibres and is involved in the manufacture of hormones, particularly sex hormones and those which regulate the body's metabolism. It is also important in digestion and is a constituent of vitamin D, which the body manufactures from the action of sunlight on skin. The body makes all the cholesterol it needs, mainly in the liver and, in smaller quantities, in the wall of the small intestine. Unfortunately, too much of it forms plaque, which clogs the coronary arteries and causes heart disease.

Cholesterol's bad reputation stems from the association between too high levels of cholesterol in the blood and the increased risk, for men, of dying from coronary heart disease,

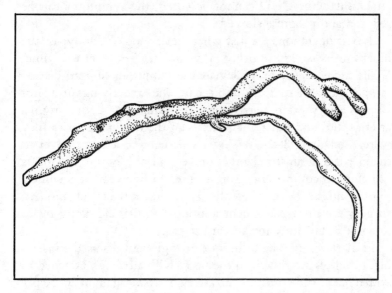

Plaque that acquired the shape of the coronary artery that it completely blocked (drawn from a photo by Maggie Moore which originally appeared in *Eater's Choice*, by Dr Ron Goor and Nancy Goor)

which accounts for more than one in four deaths in the UK and is the country's most common single cause of death. (The level of cholesterol in the blood is not an accurate predictor of risk in women.)

The heart is a muscle that pumps blood around through an extensive network of arteries, capillaries and veins, delivering nutrients to all the cells in the body and removing waste materials. It beats between 70 and 80 times a minute and pumps around 1,800 gallons of blood a day. During vigorous exercise, blood can get from heart to big toe and back in less than a minute. But it can only keep this up if it gets a constant supply of oxygenated and nutrient-rich blood via the coronary arteries. CHD begins when the coronary arteries, which branch off from the aorta (the main trunk artery), start to clog up.

Having CHD means that your arteries have narrowed so that the blood supply to your heart muscle is impaired. This can cause chest pains (angina) when you exercise, or a heart attack, because the heart muscle has been damaged by going short of blood. Between one in three and one in four heart attacks is fatal. But while CHD cannot be cured, the symptoms can be relieved and progress slowed.

Bypass operations are just what they sound – they bypass the blockage by artery grafting. But all they really buy is time. While such surgery may alleviate the symptoms of heart disease in the short-term, they don't cure the underlying problem. Bypass artery grafts narrow just the same way as the original arteries did, and can do it faster than the original arteries they were used to replace. As bypass patients' doctors explain to them, without drastic changes of diet and/or lifestyle such grafts can clog up completely again in three to five years. So while a bypass might be one of the apparent miracles of modern surgery it is not a permanent solution, just first aid. Long-term, it is not a substitute for healthy eating.

Similarly, when the technique of angioplasty is used – inserting a thin plastic tube into the body with a balloon attached to widen narrowed arteries – the artery narrows again in 20–30 per cent of patients.

Lipoproteins
The underlying mechanism is that cholesterol is transported around the body hitched up to proteins called lipoproteins ('lipo' means fat). Lipoproteins are divided, according to their density, into low-density lipoproteins (LDL) and high-density lipoproteins (HDL). LDLs carry most of the cholesterol in the blood and HDLs carry both the rest of the cholesterol in the blood and cholesterol from tissues to the liver, which turns it into bile and disposes of it. There is also very low-density lipoprotein (VLDL), which does not have any effect on blood cholesterol levels but carries blood triglycerides or fats, high levels of which make the blood more likely to clot.

LDLs are the cholesterol bad guys. (People with higher HDL levels are at lower risk of heart disease.) The LDL particles stay in the bloodstream for different lengths of time in different people; the longer they are there the greater the chance that they will become oxidised and taken up by cells called monocytes. It is monocytes engorged with LDL-cholesterol that become lodged in the artery walls, making the artery channel narrower and narrower. This accumulation of plaque on blood vessel walls both restricts the flow of blood to tissues and enables clots to attach to the walls more readily. When the deposits of fatty streaks build up into hard fibrous lumps big enough to block an artery they will cause a heart attack or a stroke, depending on which artery is blocked.

Unfortunately, the relationship between diet and cholesterol is not a straightforward one. Generally, the more cholesterol we eat the less our bodies produce. This feedback mechanism helps keep blood cholesterol at a reasonable level, but for one person in five that process doesn't work efficiently. Nutritional experts advise that we all eat less. Cholesterol is present in all food of animal origin but is virtually absent from food of plant origin. Its highest concentration is in egg yolk, fish roe and offal such as liver, kidney and brain.

Even more important than how much cholesterol there is in the food we eat, however, is the effect on cholesterol of total fat consumption and, particularly, of saturates intake. The underlying mechanism here is believed to be that high levels of LDL and cholesterol are the product of a defect in the receptor that removes LDL from the blood, and a diet high in saturated fat is thought to make this receptor even less active, thereby worsening the problem. People whose family and medical history put them at especially high risk – particularly heart attack and bypass survivors – may have already been told by their doctors that they must give themselves an even stingier fat budget than the guidelines for the general population.

Studies show that:

☺ Cutting total fat intake to 30 per cent of calories or less can reduce blood cholesterol levels by about 10 per cent, which translates into a 20 per cent reduction in heart disease risk.

☺ A moderate intake of alcohol seems to help increase the HDL level of people who are not overweight (but go easy – more is definitely not better).

☺ X-rays have been able to measure directly changes in the size of artery blockage in people eating a low-fat diet. People on a low-fat diet also had significantly fewer new blockages.

☺ Replacing saturated with monounsaturated fat, by using more olive oil and less butter, for example, helps lower blood cholesterol, but that alone is not enough – total fat needs to be reduced, too.

☺ Some types of fibre, for example in foods like lentils and rolled oats, can help lower blood cholesterol (see under **Fibre** above).

☺ Vitamin C also helps to control cholesterol deposits; eating plenty of fresh fruit and vegetables provides both vitamin C and fibre (see under **Vitamins** below).

☺ Studies show that people with diets rich in fruit and vegetables have lower cholesterol levels.

☺ A diet assault on high cholesterol levels takes about six months to have an effect and the older you are the longer it takes, so the sooner you get started the sooner you reduce your risk.

☺ Even if you know you are in a high-risk category, take heart. A Californian study of men aged 40 to 59 who had had bypass surgery for severe coronary artery disease showed no further damage or some reverse of previous damage over two years on a low-fat diet. And that was equally true both of the half on the anti-cholesterol drugs being tested in the study and the other half on the placebo (dummy) drugs.

☺ The ratio of HDL to LDL is increased by brisk exercise.

On the other hand:

☹ Obesity decreases the level of HDL.

☹ Coffee that has been boiled and let stew with the grounds can raise harmful LDL levels. One or two cups a day won't do much damage but half a dozen can have a significant effect. Filtered and instant coffee are less of a problem.

Protein

Protein is obtained from a range of foods including meat, fish, eggs, cheese, nuts, cereals and pulses, and consists of large molecules made up of smaller units of amino acids. When we eat protein, the digestive system breaks it down into its constituent amino acids and absorbs them. Then, as it needs them, the body can synthesise from these amino acids its own new proteins – a bit like threading different coloured beads on strings to form different patterns – for growth, for tissue repair, and in the manufacture of some chemical messengers (such as adrenalin), of enzymes needed for digestion, and of the antibodies with which to ward off infection. One type of 'string' is needed to build muscle, for example, while another grows hair.

Although there are hundreds of amino acids, there are about 20 most commonly found in protein from plant and animal sources. The human body has only a limited ability to convert one amino acid into another and certain amino acids must be provided in a healthy diet because the body either can't produce enough of them from others or can't make them at all. The body can make protein only when it has all the animo acids it needs present. If one is missing, no protein synthesis at all occurs. However, protein deficiencies do not occur in Britain because protein can be obtained from such a wide range of foods.

Research shows that:

☺ Most people with a varied diet get more than enough protein without having to worry about it. Pregnant women, nursing mothers, people recovering from surgery or injury and young children need a little more than healthy adults but even for them it is not usually a problem.
☺ Protein from vegetables and cereals such as pulses, lentils, brown rice and other wholemeal grains is rich in dietary fibre and low in fat.
☺ Cereal and vegetable protein sources are, in general, less expensive than animal protein.

Salt

We eat, on average, about 13g (two and a half teaspoons) of salt a day. We need some salt but we can always get enough from the foods we eat. The WHO says we should not exceed 6g a day. Two-thirds of our current average intake is accounted for by salt added to manufactured food. About half the rest is added in cooking or at the table and the other half is naturally present in foods we eat. On food labels the sodium content of salt rather than salt itself is listed: 6g of salt is the equivalent of 2300mg of sodium.

The bad news is:

☹ High blood pressure can lead to heart disease, kidney disease and strokes.

The good news is:

☺ Reducing your salt intake may lower your blood pressure.

Vitamins

Vitamins are organic substances which are chemically unrelated to one another but are all needed in small amounts in our diet to promote good health because the body is unable to manufacture them, or enough of them, for itself. They have an important role in the growth and repair of body tissues, in growing and maintaining healthy skin, in good vision and strong teeth and bones. Unlike proteins, carbohydrates and fats they do not supply the body directly with energy but some enable energy to be released to the body from the food we eat. And, though we now know much about the biological and physiological functions of vitamins, much is still to be understood. More vitamins may also remain to be discovered.

The letter by which each vitamin is known is of no significance beyond denoting the order in which they were discovered. Vitamin A was identified first, in 1911, and so on. There are 13 major vitamins A, C, D, E and K, and eight B vitamins which work together and are known as the B complex. Thiamin or B1 was the first of the B vitamins to be discovered and was originally called 'water soluble factor B'. As more B vitamins were discovered they were numbered 2 to 15, but seven were eventually disqualified because they were found not to be essential or to be the same as other existing vitamins – hence the missing numbers in the current classification.

Vitamins are divided into two major groups – water-soluble and fat-soluble. The **water-soluble** B vitamins and vitamin C are easily lost in cooking because they dissolve in water and the body does not store them in significant quantities, so we need to eat foods containing them every day in order to keep our blood and cells supplied with as much as the body needs all the

Vitamins and minerals

Vitamins & minerals	Function in body	Main sources
A	growth, night vision, healthy skin	liver, green leafy veg, carrots, eggs, cheese, milk
B1: thiamine	release of energy from foods	potatoes, wholemeal and white bread, veg, milk, breakfast cereals, pulses, nuts
B2: riboflavin	release of energy from foods	liver, meat, milk and cheese
B3: niacin or nicotinic acid	release of energy from foods	pulses, liver, meat, bread, cereal
B5: pantothenic acid	energy production	liver, kidney, eggs, peanuts, mushrooms, cheese, pears
B6: pyridoxine	metabolism of proteins	liver, cereals, pulses, poultry
B12: cobalamin	formation of red blood cells	meat, milk, cheese, eggs
B: folic acid	formation of red blood cells	green leafy veg
B: biotin	energy production from fat	liver, pork, kidneys, nuts, cauliflower, lentils, cereals
C: ascorbic acid	healing wounds, aids iron absorption	citrus fruits, blackcurrants, green leafy veg, potatoes, tomatoes
D	helps body use calcium for healthy bones and teeth	sunlight, margarine, fatty fish, eggs, butter
E	protects against harmful substances in your blood	vegetable oils, nuts, eggs, butter, wholegrain cereals
Calcium	builds bones and teeth	milk, cheese, sardines, yogurt
Iron	prevents anaemia	red meat, liver, beans, dried fruit, nuts, bread
Zinc	helps cells to divide and grow	meat, liver, herring, milk, turkey, wholegrain foods, pork

Most people get all the vitamins and minerals they need from a healthy diet; they don't need to take supplements.

time. The **fat-soluble** vitamins A, D, E and K are stored in the liver, so a good rich source of them about once a week is usually enough. In fact, liver is such a rich source of vitamin A that a single portion is enough to supply a body's needs of it for a month. (But liver is not recommended for pregnant women – see opposite.)

The antioxidants

The darlings of vitamin and mineral research in recent years have been the antioxidant beta-carotene, which is a precursor of vitamin A, vitamin C and vitamin E (the ACE vitamins as a memory aid), plus the mineral selenium. They now seem to offer some protection from illnesses, and particularly from cancers and heart disease. Their apparent role is to prevent fat from going rancid in the body by mopping up destructive oxidation agents called free radicals. These are the unstable molecules which can damage the cells in our bodies in their attempt to replace the electrons missing from their own structures by taking them from other molecules. It is now believed that heart disease and cancers may begin with such cell damage. Antioxidants seem to have the ability to donate electrons to complete the free radicals' structures for them, without becoming unstable themselves.

Fruit and vegetables are the main sources of the antioxidant vitamins and eating plenty of them seems to offer protection against heart disease and some cancers. What we don't yet know for sure is whether the protection comes from these antioxidant vitamins or whether there is something else in fruit and vegetables rather than the vitamins themselves that is having this effect. The Government has funded a three-year research programme to find out more about antioxidants and how they work and at the end of 1992 the World Health Organization decided there is now enough evidence from surveys and test tube and animal studies to justify a large-scale randomised-control trial. Whatever the exact mechanism they will eventually discover, the healthy eating message will remain unchanged – including lots of fruit and vegetables in your diet is good for you.

Vitamin A

Vitamin A is manufactured in the body from carotenoids –
chemicals found in plants which give coloured vegetables and
fruit their yellowy-red colour. The most important of the
carotenoids is beta-carotene, which the body converts into
retinol, the chemical name for vitamin A, in the small intestine.
Vitamin A can also be obtained direct in the form of retinol
from animal foods where the animal has already done the
manufacturing from carotenoids.

A large intake of retinol in early pregnancy is to be avoided
because there is some evidence that it can cause birth defects.
The Ministry of Agriculture, Fisheries and Food is researching
the effect of vitamin A in animal feed on the amount in liver
when it reaches the shops and has a voluntary code to govern
maximum levels until the results are available. For the moment,
the Government has advised pregnant women and those intend-
ing to become pregnant not to eat liver at all. But they can eat
beta-carotene, which converts to only a sixth of its own volume
of retinol, without restriction. Excess retinol stored in the body
can be poisonous and retinol poisoning has been reported in the
United States in children as young as three given daily doses of
between 30 and 150mg as a supplement for several months. But
the reason there is no risk of getting too much retinol from beta-
carotene is that if your liver stores are full of retinol, the body
won't convert any more.

NEEDED: For normal growth, healthy skin and immune system,
good vision and for renewing body tissues.

FOUND: Already as retinol in liver, egg yolks, butter, cheese,
milk (but not skimmed milk), kidney and cod liver oil, herring
and mackerel; and as beta-carotene in leafy green, yellow and
red vegetables including spinach, Chinese leaves, watercress,
carrots and tomatoes; also yellow sweet potatoes and pumpkin;
and fruits, including mangoes, apricots and cantaloupe melons.
Vitamin A is added, by law, to margarine.

LOST: Through light and air exposure, cooking at high temperatures in fats.

The vitamin B complex

Each of the B complex vitamins has a slightly different role to
play (outlined below). However, the members of the group also

work together to produce energy from food by metabolising fats and protein and to ensure good brain and nervous system functioning, an efficient digestive system, and healthy skin, hair, eyes, mouth and liver. They are usually found together in foods.

Besides the natural sources of B vitamins listed below, many breakfast cereals are fortified with thiamin, riboflavin, niacin, B6 and B12 and sometimes folate – the label on each packet will give details. White and brown flours are fortified with thiamin and niacin, which wholemeal flour contains naturally.

Vitamin B1: Thiamin

It is lack of vitamin B1 that causes beriberi in some underdeveloped countries and can cause alcoholics living rough to lose the sensation of touch and become mentally disordered. Alcoholic down-and-outs get a lot of sugars from alcohol and a high sugar intake means they need more thiamin to release the energy from it but they may not eat enough to get it.

NEEDED: For the release of the energy from starches and sugars. The more carbohydrates we eat the more B1 we need.

FOUND: In breakfast cereals, potatoes, vegetables, wholemeal and white bread, milk, meat and poultry, meat and yeast extracts, fish, eggs, pulses (especially red kidney beans) and nuts.

LOST: B1, of all the B vitamins, is the one that is most affected by cooking and especially by the addition of bicarbonate of soda or baking soda. It is also leached into cooking water and lost in drips from thawed frozen food but some can be recovered by using the cooking liquid, for example in stock or soup.

Vitamin B2: Riboflavin

NEEDED: Essential for healthy skin and eyes. Releases energy from other foods.

FOUND: In meat (especially liver and kidney), milk and milk products, meat and yeast extracts, eggs, vegetables and new potatoes, breakfast cereals.

LOST: By exposure to light (which is why it is better not to leave milk on the doorstep, even in cold weather).

Vitamin B3: Niacin
Niacin is the generic name for nicotinic acid and nicotinamide. Nicotine in tobacco has a similar chemical structure, but little similarity beyond that.
NEEDED: For the release of energy from foods.
FOUND: In meat and meat products, poultry, meat and yeast extracts, bread, breakfast cereals, vegetables, milk and milk products, and fish, peanuts, eggs.
LOST: Tends to be leached into cooking fluids.

Vitamin B5: Pantothenic acid
NEEDED: For energy production.
FOUND: Mainly in meat, milk, vegetables and eggs, but also in so many foods that hardly anyone gets too little.
LOST: Dissolves in cooking water and is easily lost by heat, freezing, milling and canning, and in contact with bicarbonate of soda.

Vitamin B6: Pyridoxine
Some people report having found this vitamin helpful in treating premenstrual syndrome. In 1991, Dutch scientists published a review of 12 studies that had looked at the link between B6 and PMS and found no conclusive evidence for that or for claims that B6 counteracts side-effects of being on the contraceptive pill.
NEEDED: For healthy body tissue and immune system, nerves and skin. It converts protein into energy, plays a role in the production of red blood cells and the cells of the immune system, as well as in the multiplication of all cells, and is used in hormone production. But too high doses, from supplements, can be dangerous.
FOUND: Meat (including bacon), poultry, potatoes, vegetables, eggs, bread, breakfast cereals, fish, dairy produce, oranges, bananas.
LOST: Leached into cooking water but not destroyed, so it can be reused, as for vitamin B1. Destroyed by light.

Vitamin B12: Cobalamin
Vegetarians who have milk and eggs regularly can obtain enough vitamin B12 but vegans who have neither meat nor

food products of animal origin must include in their diet foods to which it has been added, or take vitamin B12 as a supplement, or both. A number of recent studies have refuted claims that soya products (including unpasteurised miso) are the source of B12, which were long thought to be for people on a microbiotic diet. Vegan foods with added vitamin B12 include yeast extracts, such as Marmite, Tastex and Barmene, and soya milks, including Granogen and Plamil. Some breakfast cereals and, in Britain, all meat substitutes also have added B12.

Unlike the other water-soluble vitamins, the body can store excess vitamin B12 in the liver. It takes years for a deficiency to show up because the body would take four to five years to use up completely its stored B12. Symptoms of deficiency depend on the presence or absence of another B vitamin, folate or folic acid (see below), of which vegetarians and vegans tend to have a high intake. This makes anaemia symptoms unlikely for them.

However, they are likely to develop neurological symptoms, starting with a tingling sensation in the hands and feet, followed by a loss of the sense of touch. In these early stages, treatment with vitamin B12 can still reverse the symptoms. If the deficiency continues to go untreated, the progression is through degeneration of the spinal cord to paralysis and possibly death. Vegan mothers who do not take additional vitamin B12 will also have too low a concentration of it in their breast milk.

NEEDED: For the formation of red blood cells and by all rapidly dividing cells such as those in bone marrow and intestines. Also for maintaining the nervous system.

FOUND: In all foods of animal origin, especially liver, kidney, fish, milk, cheese, eggs, breakfast cereals.

LOST: By adding bicarbonate of soda to cooking water, which completely destroys it. It is stable in most cooking processes but dissolves in water.

Vitamin B: Folate

Also known as folic acid. There is inconclusive evidence that folic acid gives some protection against cancers of the cervix and lungs. Other recent research suggests a link with other birth defects including Fragile-X syndrome, which is second only to

Down's syndrome as an identified cause of mental retardation.
NEEDED: For red blood cell production. It works closely with
vitamin B12 (see above). Too little can affect the synthesis of
DNA. A very high intake of folate given to mothers of one
child with spina bifida reduces the likelihood that a second child
will also have the condition, according to a recent study.
FOUND: In potatoes and vegetables (mainly the green leafy ones),
wholemeal bread, breakfast cereals, malt and yeast extracts,
nuts, pulses, citrus fruits and liver.
LOST: By heat and air and long or poor storage. It is also leached
out into cooking liquids. Because it is so easily destroyed it is
not easy to get enough and the Government is now advising
women to take folic acid supplement during the first 12 weeks
of pregnancy, which means that ideally they should start before
conceiving.

Vitamin B: Biotin
Biotin was originally known as vitamin H.
NEEDED: For energy production from fat, carbohydrates and
proteins and involved in the production of hormones.
FOUND: In meat, milk, egg yolks, oatflakes, wheatbran, wheat-
germ, wholegrains, wholemeal bread and brown rice. Hardly
anyone gets too little.
LOST: As for vitamin B1.

Vitamin C: Ascorbic acid
It was the absence of vitamin C from the diets of long-distance
seafarers that, for centuries, made them vulnerable to scurvy, a
disease typified by haemorrhaging under the skin, swollen and
bleeding gums (which caused the teeth to loosen and fall out),
listlessness and poor healing ability. Less extreme deficiency
causes bleeding gums, a tendency to bruise easily, swollen
joints, lowered resistance to infection, nose bleeds, anaemia
and lack of energy.
    The first controlled clinical experiment in the medical history
books was in the 1750s when a British doctor added limes to
the rations of one group of sailors and compared how they fared
with another group who had, otherwise, the same diet. The
sailors given the vitamin C-rich limes did not get scurvy. The

other group did. Thereafter, British sailors carried limes or other citrus fruits on all long sea voyages – earning the nickname 'limeys' as well as protection from the dreaded scurvy.

We used to think that scurvy was a thing of the past, especially in the developed Western world, but we now know that heavy drinkers are particularly susceptible because alcohol inhibits the uptake of the vitamin. And studies have found high rates of deficiency – though not severe enough to cause scurvy – among the elderly and institutionalised, some cancer patients and some people undergoing kidney dialysis.

Vitamin C is a fragile vitamin vulnerable to light, heat and air and cannot be stored in the body, so we need a steady supply in our diets. Foods containing it also need care in the kitchen to maximise the amount we obtain for them. It helps to buy and use fruit and vegetables as fresh as possible, store them in a cool dark place – the salad drawer of the refrigerator is ideal – and prepare them with a sharp knife to minimise loss from bruising. Shredding or chopping coarsely rather than finely keeps exposed surfaces to a minimum, further reducing vitamin C loss. (You'll find further hints on how best to store fruit and vegetables in **Chapter 3** and how best to cook them in **Chapter 4**.)

Although the current UK official guideline is that about 40mg a day is enough vitamin C for a healthy, non-pregnant, non-smoking adult, other countries put it higher. In the US, the recommendation is 60mg and some researchers would like to see the figure raised to as much as 100mg. If you follow the WHO advice about getting five portions of fruit and vegetables a day (outlined in the previous chapter) you will be getting around 100mg anyway.

One thing worth knowing when you are reading food labels is that vitamin C is often added during processing. If it is listed on the label as vitamin C, then it has probably been added for its nutritional value to enhance the natural vitamin C content of the food or to replace the vitamin C lost during processing. But if it is referred to as L-ascorbic acid or E300, then it has been used as an antioxidant or as a flour improver. And when it is used as a flour improver, the vitamin C itself is destroyed in baking so it doesn't add any nutritional value.

The Nobel prize-winning chemist Dr Linus Pauling promoted the use of megadoses of vitamin C as a cure for the common cold. Current research findings suggest that vitamin C will not prevent or cure colds but high doses may relieve symptoms. Since Pauling, similarly large doses of vitamin C (1–2g a day) have been used to treat or prevent conditions such as cancer, schizophrenia, arthritis and some allergies. So far, such use is controversial. The results of studies are difficult to interpret and the amounts of vitamin C needed to have an effect are still not clear.

NEEDED: To make collagen, the substance that binds the cells of our tissues; to help wounds heal quickly; to help us absorb the iron from plant sources that our bodies find more difficult to use; to protect against infection; to help relieve stress; to act as a natural anti-histamine; to control blood cholesterol levels and as an antioxidant (see above).

FOUND: Mainly in fruit and vegetables, particularly kiwi-fruits, citrus and soft fruits (especially blackcurrants) and green leafy vegetables. Liver and fish roe provide some. Other foods contain little unless it is added during manufacture. Potatoes are the most important single source.

LOST: Easily, to light, air, time; by bruising, or leaving to soak after preparation or stand after cooking. Also lost by cooking with bicarbonate of soda or in copper pots or in water.

Vitamin D

Vitamin D deficiency is probably the most common vitamin deficiency in the northern hemisphere. It is the cause of rickets, which gives babies and children bow-legs because it impairs the process of depositing the minerals that give rigidity in the bone. It is also a danger for the elderly, who may have inadequate exposure to sunlight, take drugs which interfere with the uptake or metabolism of the vitamin, and eat less food containing it. The incidence of rickets in Britain has been reduced since the introduction of smokeless zones, which cleaned up the air and allowed greater exposure to sunlight, one of the major sources of vitamin D, in UK cities. Most at risk now are children of Indian-Asian-African origin whose bodies make less vitamin D than do those with fairer skins. But as the use of sunscreens to protect against skin cancer increases, so could our need for vitamin D in all our diets. In the elderly, deficiency causes osteomalacia or softening of and pain in the bone.

Evidence is also beginning to accumulate for claims that vitamin D offers some protection against cancers of the rectum, colon and breast.

NEEDED: To help the body absorb calcium and for the growth and repair of body tissue, for healthy gums and bones.

FOUND: Mainly from exposure of the skin to sunlight but also in oily fish, eggs, butter and added to some margarines and breakfast cereals.

LOST: Little. Vitamin D is remarkably stable and there is little loss through processing, cooking or storage.

Vitamin E

This is another of the antioxidant vitamins thought to help decrease the incidence of heart disease and some cancers. It has a role, too, in protecting against neurological disorders, and the possibility that it may be useful in the management of epilepsy is currently under investigation. It has been claimed that it can delay ageing and improve sexual performance, but there is little evidence for this. It is also used as an antioxidant in the food industry to prevent fat becoming rancid.

There is no recommended daily intake for vitamin E in the UK. The US recommendation is 7–9mg.

NEEDED: To protect against harmful substances in the blood.

FOUND: In vegetable oils (especially cold-pressed), nuts, egg yolks, butter, wholegrain cereals, wheatgerm.

LOST: When oils are heated, and in refining and processing. Even during storing in a refrigerator or freezer vitamin E is lost at quite a rate.

Vitamin K

Vitamin K has several forms, the most important of which are the naturally occurring K1 and K2 and the synthetic K3. It is sometimes called nature's Band-Aid because of its role in preventing bleeding – in fact, the K comes from the German *Koagulation*. Vitamin K deficiency is rare because it is widespread in the food chain and because bacteria in the gut synthesises much of what we need anyway. But deficiency can happen, particularly in those with malabsorption problems, people who need to be fed through their veins, those on prolonged antibiotic treatment and very low-calorie diets and people taking certain drugs. Symptoms that give a clue to deficiency include bruising easily.

There is test-tube evidence that vitamin K may have a role in the treatment of some tumour-type cancers and human trials are currently under way. There is also preliminary evidence that vitamin K may help protect against osteoporosis.

NEEDED: To synthesise several factors involved in blood clotting and in the maintenance of normal bone, and for fracture-healing.

FOUND: Widely, especially in vegetables and dairy produce.

LOST: Not easily.

Minerals and trace elements

The carbohydrates, proteins and fats in our diet are all organic substances, which means that they are all compounds of the element carbon. But we need, as well, some minerals in their inorganic forms, not bound to carbon. We conventionally divide them into two groups. Those we need in amounts of more than 100 milligrams a day – for example calcium, magnesium, sodium and potassium – we call minerals. Those, such as iron, iodine, zinc and selenium, of which we need less, we call trace elements. People on low-calorie diets, old, pregnant, vegetarian, taking certain drugs (such as diuretics), or living where soil is poor in certain minerals, are more likely to be deficient in minerals or trace elements than in vitamins.

Essential minerals make up about one per cent of our diet and we need them for water balance, for development of the skeleton and for the production of blood. Equally essential is to ensure that we do not get too much sodium and chloride. (See under **Salt**, which is sodium chloride, above.)

Calcium

Calcium is of enormous importance: too little in early life and through to the thirties contributes to osteoporosis in later life,

Changes in bone mass

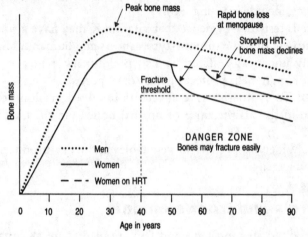

The curves represent an average, but individual bone mass varies a lot. Nobody has traced bone mass for a lifetime using modern bone measurement techniques, but the curves give a general picture of the changes thought to take place.

especially in menopausal and post-menopausal women. Bone is made up of collagen, which gives it flexibility, and calcium, which provides its strength. Osteoporosis is a honeycombing of the bone as it loses both collagen and calcium, which reduces its mass, so bone breaks more easily, especially at the hips, wrists and spine. It leads, as well, to curvature of the spine. Because recovery from major fractures tends to be poorer later in life, osteoporosis fractures can start a cycle which leads to permanent loss of mobility and independence.

Women tend to suffer from osteoporosis earlier than men, but the condition is now beginning to be recognised in older men as well. In theory, everyone would get it if they lived long enough.

Calcium intake is not the only way to delay the onset of osteoporosis. Taking regular exercise and not smoking also help to maintain bone mass, and hormone replacement therapy (HRT) provides women with the bone-protecting hormone oestrogen that the body stops making for itself at the menopause. When women on HRT for five or ten years finally stop taking it, bone density decline sets in. However, not only does this occur later but it seems to be less severe than in women who have not taken HRT, so reaching the fracture threshold comes even later.

Vegans who have no milk or milk products in their diet may have a problem with calcium deficiency unless they take care to ensure they get enough from other sources. If they bake their own bread they could add calcium carbonate (chalk) to it to help make up their needs. Some soya milks are also richer in calcium than others. Most at risk are teenagers who need more calcium during adolescence, when bone is growing more rapidly than at any other time. Not only teenagers who avoid dairy foods but those who are constantly dieting and those who live mostly on junk foods, which tend to contain little calcium, are also particularly at risk.

NEEDED: For healthy teeth and bones. Also for the transmission of nerve impulses, to help the blood clot, to ensure normal heart function, to help control cholesterol levels and to assist the body absorb vitamin B12.

FOUND: In all types of milk, cheese, sardines and whitebait, yogurt, tofu, watercress, parsley, dried figs, nuts (especially almonds), soya flour, dried apricots, cabbage, oatmeal and sesame seeds. Bought white bread has some calcium carbonate (chalk) added and, as a result, is higher in calcium than wholemeal bread. Choosing muesli or a cereal with plenty of nuts and dried fruit is one way of increasing calcium intake. Another is adding dried skimmed milk to milk puddings, soups or stews. London tap water contains a lot. There are calcium-enriched milks such as Calcia, Vital and own-brand equivalents on the market. Women, especially if they are post-menopausal, might also like to have a milky drink at bedtime – they lose more calcium at night.

LOST: In refining. Not taken up in the absence of sufficient vitamin D. Bran content in foods interferes with uptake.

Iron

Iron comes in two forms. Haem, from animal sources, is very efficiently absorbed. Non-haem iron, from vegetable and grain foods, is not well absorbed, though absorption is enhanced by the presence of haem iron and of vitamin C. So a bran breakfast cereal or a bacon sandwich is better for your iron intake if you have a glass of orange juice with it.

NEEDED: To prevent anaemia, which causes tiredness, pallor, lack of stamina, breathlessness and even reduced brain function. Iron makes haemoglobin, which gives red blood cells their colour and transports oxygen round the body. Haemoglobin is also indirectly involved in the removal of waste carbon dioxide.

FOUND: In red meat, kidney and liver, poultry, seafood (including cockles, mussels and prawns), fish (including herring and canned tuna), cereals, chocolate, nuts and wholemeal bread.

LOST: Non-haem iron is lost in refining and processing. Absorption of iron is inhibited by phytic acid, found in cereals and pulses, and oxalic acid found in spinach. There is also some evidence that tea and coffee decrease absorption.

Zinc

Zinc is needed for growth and repair. The body contains a gram or two but most of it is in the bones and is not available for use when the body's supply runs low. Zinc is lost every day through sweat and urine.

Zinc has a role in healing. It is essential for taste and flavour perception, is used in protein manufacture for body growth and repair, in cell division and multiplication and in the metabolism of vitamin A. It is also essential for more than 50 enzymes.

There has been some success in treating anorexia with zinc though the nature of the relationship is, as yet, poorly understood. Long-term shortages are known to disturb growth and sexual maturation and to cause diarrhoea, skin inflammation and hair loss. Even less serious deficiency can restrict growth, leading to poor healing, and impair sperm production. The highest incidence of malformations of the central nervous system at birth are found in countries where zinc deficiency is also common. This suggests a relationship between birth defects and low zinc levels in mothers but zinc supplements do not seem to provide a solution, so there may be another factor that has not yet been teased out by research. Malnutrition, alcoholism, diabetes, stress from burns or surgery and treatment on kidney machines can all run down the body's zinc levels.

Women on the contraceptive pill have lower zinc levels than other women.

NEEDED: To help cells divide and grow.

FOUND: In meat and poultry, fish and seafood, milk, yogurt, cottage cheese, beans, pulses, wholegrain foods.

LOST: By refining – though what is left may be more easily absorbed because of the reduction in phytase in fibre which hinders absorption. Absorption can be slowed down by old age. Eating soya meat replacement products also impairs take-up, which could put vegans and vegetarians at risk, but there is evidence that, in the long-term, they adapt and start to absorb a higher proportion of zinc from the food they eat.

Selenium

Selenium, as mentioned under **Antioxidants** above, has come in for a lot of recent attention for the role it is thought to play in helping protect against certain cancers and heart disease. There have also been claims that it helps protect against arthritis, rheumatism, infectious diseases and even ageing. However, it is one of the most recently discovered of the essential nutrients and we still know relatively little about its role beyond the fact that our bodies do need it, though in small amounts.

Exactly how small is difficult to quantify. There are no British guidelines yet, though nutritionists believe that most people need between 25µg (millionths of a gram) and 70µg a day. There is no evidence of deficiency at these levels and they correspond with the US recommendations which start at between 10µg and 15µg a day for babies and go up to 70 for men and 75 for breastfeeding mothers. We do know that too much can be harmful. People on supplements of more than 1000µg a day have reported problems including breath and skin that smell like garlic, hair loss, diseased nails, stomach upsets and skin complaints. More serious effects of selenium poisoning – or selenosis – are thought to include joint, skin and liver and kidney problems.

How much we get is difficult to calculate, too, because the selenium content of the same type of food grown or raised in different places can vary considerably, so we have to work from rough estimates. They are also changeable. For example, ten years ago half of all British bread was made from Canadian wheat. Now only about a tenth is. European flour, which has largely replaced it, contains less selenium. Some researchers believe that, partly because of this flour change, we now get only about 30µg a day on average, although the Ministry of Agriculture, Fisheries and Food estimates it at around 60µg a day. These figures suggest that we are getting more selenium from milk and dairy produce, making up for the lower amounts now in our bread.

NEEDED: As an antioxidant for possible protection against cancers, heart disease and so on, as described above.

FOUND: In meat, especially kidney, brazil nuts, oily fish, bread, rice.

LOST: In food processing and refining.

Magnesium

The body is very efficient at regulating its own magnesium content. When there is less in our diet, we use a higher percentage of what is there, and our kidneys become more efficient at conserving it. So magnesium deficiency is rare and seems to occur only in exceptional circumstances like starvation, inflammation of the pancreas, alcoholism, or prolonged diarrhoea and vomiting.

When magnesium deficiency does occur, it shows up as nervous problems like twitching, anxiety, hyperactivity and convulsions, and as progressive muscle weakness, tiredness, muscle cramps, tremor, depression and palpitations. People who have had a heart attack have been found to be low in magnesium but it now looks as if the deficiency is a result of the heart attack rather than the cause. Research on the practice of giving magnesium supplements to people suffering from myalgic encephalomyelitis (ME, or chronic or post-viral fatigue syndrome) and using magnesium plus B6 to treat post-menstrual syndrome are so far inconclusive.

NEEDED: Essential for life – it is involved in many of the chemical processes that keep our body's cells working. Also helps break down food for energy. Calcium absorption would be poor without it and take-up of vitamin B6 from foods even worse. Magnesium, like calcium, is needed to build bones and it works with calcium to ensure a smooth, steady flow of nerve impulses.

FOUND: In a wide variety of foods: sources with the highest concentrations include spinach and Chinese leaves, cereals, nuts, pulses (especially soya beans), grains, plain chocolate, wholemeal bread, oats, sardines, sweetcorn, bananas and milk. Most people probably get about 10 per cent of their daily magnesium requirement from their tap water, and that can go as high as 15 per cent in hard water areas.

Vitamin and mineral supplements

A deficiency of vitamins in our diet can cause a number of illnesses including beriberi, rickets and anaemia, although vitamin deficiency diseases are rare in the developed world. Most people who follow the guidelines in this book and eat a diet that includes starchy foods, dairy products, vegetables and fruit, and meat, poultry, fish or vegetarian protein sources (see under **Protein**, page 42) as recommended generally, get all the vitamins and minerals they need from their food.

And getting the vitamins we need through our diet is always preferable to taking a diet supplement where it is practicable. At best, an unneeded supplement is a waste of money. At worst, it can actually be damaging to good health.

Although we do need a small amount of each of the vitamins and minerals, it does not follow that more is better. Overdosing on the water-soluble vitamins can cause unpleasant side effects such as nausea and even vomiting but, with the exception of vitamin B6, the excess can be excreted in urine and so does not accumulate in the body. More serious is too high an intake of the fat-soluble vitamins which do accumulate. There have actually been deaths in people who have taken too much vitamin A. Megadoses of vitamin C can destroy precious vitamin B12 to produce a toxic substance caused oxalic acid. With minerals it is a similar story. Iron and zinc are poisonous if taken in excess quantities and anyone who has to take an iron supplement should be particularly careful to keep it out of the reach of young children.

People who feel rundown may decide to try a vitamin

supplement. Parents of children with serious eating problems may also want to consider giving a vitamin supplement at least as a temporary measure to take off some of the nutritional and emotional pressure while they find longer-term behavioural solutions, such as those discussed further in Chapter 8.

Generally, if you do decide to supplement your diet or that of your child by taking extra vitamins and minerals, it is advisable to take a multi-vitamin and mineral supplement which contains nutrients in approximately the recommended daily amounts.

But some people may be at more risk of vitamin shortage than average. Smokers, for example, have lower levels of antioxidants in their blood than non-smokers and may benefit from a higher intake of the ACE vitamins plus selenium. Vegetarians and especially vegans need to take care that they get enough vitamins D and B12 and calcium. Elderly people and people on long-term drug treatment may not absorb vitamins as well as they used to do and may run short of some of the B vitamins and vitamin C. Pregnant and breastfeeding women need extra vitamin C. Illness also depletes vitamin C more readily, and it needs constant replenishing as it cannot be stored in the body.

Iron deficiency is a danger, particularly for young children, for adolescent boys going through the growth spurt and for women of child-bearing age who lose iron in menstrual blood. And osteoporosis – bone loss that can lead to fractures – results from too low a calcium intake from birth to about the age of 35. Pregnant and nursing mothers may need extra nutrients, especially iron and calcium, and also folic acid. In fact, women need extra folic acid even before they conceive. Women on the contraceptive pill may also need extra vitamins.

There are other special cases such as elderly people living alone or with poor appetites, reluctant to prepare nutritious meals for themselves. One survey found that adolescent vegetarians were low on iron, zinc, calcium and folic acid in their diets. According to a Department of Health survey, 90 per cent of all adolescent girls were deficient in iron, 50 per cent in calcium, and 100 per cent in vitamin D, which is needed to absorb calcium.

People who cannot meet their calcium needs in their diet –
those who do not eat milk or dairy foods, for example – might
want to consider taking a calcium supplement. If they do, they
will find that it pays to shop around. *Which? way to Health*
magazine (December 1991) published a survey of the supplements then on the market and found the price of 500mg of pure
calcium ranged from 4p to 43p. You would probably want to
look for a dose of around 500mg a day. Chewy or effervescent
preparations are better absorbed because they dissolve more
easily in the stomach. But beware – although too much calcium
is not toxic, it can interfere with the absorption of iron.

There are some special cases where extra caution is needed:

- If you have a peptic ulcer, liver disease, gout or a disturbed
  heart rhythm, take niacin (vitamin B3) only under the supervision of your doctor.
- If you are on a drug for Parkinson's disease, check with your
  doctor before you take vitamin B6.
- If you think you are anaemic, don't just treat yourself with
  an iron supplement. There can be other causes besides iron
  deficiency, so you should see your doctor. Besides, high iron
  intake can inhibit the uptake of other minerals.
- Don't take vitamin C with aspirin, as it may increase intestinal irritation and even bleeding. Stop taking it if you develop
  kidney stones or gout. If you do take large doses over a long
  period, don't stop abruptly but taper off over some days.
- High doses of vitamin D (more than 1,000mg daily) may
  cause hypercalcaemia (symptoms: anorexia, nausea, vomiting, constipation, tiredness leading to confusion, high blood
  pressure, kidney failure and coma).
- Don't take vitamin E at the same time as you take inorganic
  iron or the contraceptive pill, both of which interfere with
  uptake. Take the vitamin several hours before c. after the pill
  or iron.
- Don't take vitamin E if you are on anti-coagulant drugs, such
  as warfarin, or have a blood–clotting deficiency, unless under
  the supervision of your doctor.
- Don't continue taking vitamin E if you develop fatigue,
  nausea, muscle weakness, stomach upset or unexplained

bleeding, or find cuts or burns taking longer than usual to heal.

- Don't take a calcium supplement (unless under medical supervision) if you have cancer or an overactive parathyroid gland or form kidney stones, or while taking high doses of vitamin D.

CHAPTER 3

THE HEALTHY
SHOPPING BASKET

HEALTHY eating at home begins for most of us in the super-market trolley. That is where our habits, our tastes, our knowledge and our beliefs about food meet head-on other factors such as availability, cost, time and hidden persuaders. The supermarket trolley is where most of the real decisions are made, and how healthy those choices are depends, in part, on how informed we are.

Eating patterns are changing. We eat alone more. We snack more. Grazing has replaced some of the 'square meals' that used to be considered best for us – though the evidence is that most people still like to sit down with others from time to time and eat a 'proper' meal with a protein source (such as meat or fish) and a couple of vegetables. That protein source can, of course, be a convenience dish.

Home cooking is on the decline – between 1980 and 1987 it decreased by a third. While the over-65s still have at least one item of food cooked at home in 75 per cent of their meals, the figure for people aged between 17 and 24 is just 17 per cent of meals.

With 44 per cent of women out at work all day, it becomes increasingly difficult for parents to organise healthy eating for the whole family when time and possibly budget are stretched. For the jobless, budgetary constraints may often be the over-whelming ones. A study quoted by Suzi Leather, author of a chapter on poverty and diet in *Your Food: Whose Choice?* (edited by the National Consumer Council, November 1992), found that women in poor families tend to give the most nutritious food to their families and to live on tea and toast themselves for up to two days at a time. In one study more than a quarter of women on low incomes were deficient in eight essential nutrients.

The myth that these women are victims of ignorance rather than poverty is firmly nailed by the results of a survey done by the National Children's Home. Low-income mothers were asked what they would buy if they had another £10 a week to spend. Sixty per cent said more fruit, half said more lean fresh meat, and 38 per cent more vegetables. Fewer than one in ten mentioned items like cakes, biscuits, ice-cream and snack foods. And when low-income parents do buy sweet biscuits rather than fruit, it does not necessarily mean that they don't know any better – rather the reverse. As Leather points out, one custard cream biscuit costs 3p. Three small apples, which would provide the same 100 calories of energy, could cost 29p. When it comes to trying to find foods to fill up on as cheaply as possible, the attraction of the packet of biscuits hardly needs to be spelt out.

Unfortunately, being knowledgeable is not a magic wand, but it can help you to be sure that you make your time and money go as far as they possibly can. A good place to start is understanding the real meaning of what's on the label.

What's on a label?

Food products must display an ingredients list and a date mark, and manufacturers are increasingly responding to consumer pressure by volunteering additional nutritional information. Even if there is nothing more than an ingredients list, this can be revealing. The order in which ingredients are listed must reflect the quantity of each one used by weight – the more of something there is in a product the earlier it gets a mention. So even though manufacturers may not want to draw your attention to, say, how much sugar is added to a particular product, they are forced by law to give you a strong clue. If sugar features high up the ingredients list, you may not know exactly how much there is of it, but you do know there is a lot. More details will have to be shown when new EC regulations come in, but with 12 countries having a say in the new rules, it will take time and compromises before these are finalised.

One improvement has already come into force. Since June 1992 **frozen food**, which used not to have to carry a 'best before' date, now does, so we no longer have to guess how long something has been sitting in a shop's freezer before being bought. **Canned food** now carries a 'best before' date as well.

Another move in the right direction are various proposals for more explicit labelling for **bottled beers**, **lager** and **wine and spirits**. If agreed, these could list ingredients, enabling consumers to compare value for money and helping them to judge more accurately which will have a flavour that appeals to them.

More crucially for some, including the five to ten per cent of asthma sufferers who experience mild to severe attacks if they drink sulphites in beer, lager or wine, additives could be identified, too. Sulphites (E220) are used to help stop the drink from going off. Lagers and ciders can contain yellow tartrazine (E102) colouring, to which some people have adverse reactions. Others contain caramel colouring (E150), which is not the same thing as burnt sugar and which people who drink a lot of dark beer can find they are consuming in unacceptably high doses. Some makers add propane-1,2-diol alginate (E405) to prevent the head on a beer collapsing.

The new labels will also tell you if, for example, wheat or maize has been used as well as barley either to contribute to the flavour or to compensate for the poor quality of barley in a bad year. They will reveal, too, whether hop pellets and extracts have replaced whole hops as a means of reducing the cost, and whether artificial sweeteners have been used.

Consumers may be less happy to discover that the EC is extending the list of about 350 **additives** permitted in the UK – there could be around 100 new E numbers on labels. Better news is that lists of approved, permitted **flavourings** are being drawn up for the first time and limits are to be set on the amount of **colourings** allowed in food. At the moment, most food additives have to be included on the ingredients list by name, or UK number (with an E, if it has also been approved by the EC), or both. Before each name the label has to state the type of additive, for example 'preservative'. As for flavourings, labels must state whether they have been used but not which ones.

The EC has under discussion the possibility of new regulations on labelling fruit and vegetables with details of **pesticides** applied during growing and of post-harvest pesticides used to prolong storage life. Residues left behind by post-picking treatments tend to be higher than those remaining after application of pesticides to growing crops. Pregnant women eating too much food treated with pesticides like thiabendazole, which is used on some citrus fruit and potatoes, could be putting at risk developing foetuses. Some animal tests have shown damage to embryos and the nervous system, liver and other organs at very high doses of pesticides.

The implications of these findings for people are still under debate. But without labelling it is impossible for them to know what to avoid. The EC has to decide whether to make universal regulations like those in Germany where a typical citrus fruit label might read: 'Treated with diphenyl, orthophenyl phenol and thiabendazole. Skin not suitable for eating.' Producers are against the proposal.

Eventually, if Consumers' Association has its way, EC labelling rules will cover nutritional data, the percentages of most ingredients, and exactly how terms like 'meat' in ingredients lists may be used. There will also be rules defining claims on labels.

One initiative already under way is a bid to sort out the **QUID** – Quantitative Unit Ingredient Information – rules on foods which put special emphasis on an ingredient. At present, if a food manufacturer gives particular emphasis to an ingredient, it must be quantified, by giving the percentage of that ingredient in the product. The problem comes when different countries interpret what constitutes 'special emphasis'. For example, in the UK a chicken and mushroom pie with 'extra chicken' would give the percentage of chicken. But in France 'special emphasis' is interpreted as any mention of an ingredient, so there the percentages of both chicken and mushroom would be given.

At the moment, the EC is redrafting the regulations and it should mean that whenever an ingredient is mentioned in the name or packet description of a food, it will also be quantified. Meanwhile, some foods, such as those sold by Marks and Spencer, which sell in both the UK and France, have more QUID in the French language ingredient list than in the English.

Some **irradiation** of food is allowed in the UK and food that has been irradiated should be labelled either 'irradiated' or 'treated with ionising irradiation'. But you could have been buying irradiated food without knowing it because of two loopholes in the law, described in **Chapter 4**.

Meanwhile, here are some of the things you will still see on food labels and how much – or how little – they actually mean:

'Use by' This is used on food such as meat pies or chilled ready-made meals that can go off within days. They must be cooked and eaten or frozen by that day – or you should throw them out. It is dangerous to eat and illegal to sell food after its 'use by' date.

'Best before' Used on food that will last longer than a few days. Food past its 'best before' is not necessarily dangerous – it may be just past its best in terms of taste, texture or nutritional value.

'Low fat' There's no law to say how low 'low' has to be. A low-fat spread may contain less fat than butter or margarine, but not necessarily a great deal less – you still have to read the small print. 'Low-fat' means different things in different contexts: a low-fat butter substitute might have 40 per cent fat while a 'low-fat' flash on a yogurt pot label might indicate about 0.5 per cent. (See also under **Fats** below.)

'Low cholesterol' To make this claim, foods must have no more than 0.005 per cent of food cholesterol in them and must also carry a statement revealing how much polyunsaturated fat they contain. The actual cholesterol content matters less, for most people, than the overall amount of fat in their diets.

'Can help reduce cholesterol' Maybe. Some foods high in soluble fibre can help to reduce cholesterol levels. You need to eat, for example, a bowl of porridge a day to make a noticeable difference in your cholesterol levels.

'No artificial additives' In fact, natural ones are not necessarily any more healthy. Natural colour annatto, for example, causes an allergic reaction in a small number of people, just as artificial colours such as tartrazine do.

'Low-calorie' Can only be used at present if there are no more than 40 kilocalories (Kcal) in both a serving and 100g or 100ml.

'Reduced-calorie' Can be used if there are less than three-quarters of the calories of comparable products.

'Light' or **'Lite'** Can mean anything. For example, Kerrygold Light bread spread (one spread with the word Light in its name) has 39 per cent fat while another butter substitute, Stork Light, has 60. 'Light' or 'Lite' can refer to calories, colour, taste or alcoholic strength. You have to read the small print.

'Diet' Don't assume that calorie content is more or less the same as that of other similar 'diet' products. It is back to the small print.

'No added sugar' Usually means no added sucrose, but there are other sugars in fruit juice, honey and malt extract that are no lower in calories and can be equally bad for the teeth. Look out for the words 'sucrose', 'glucose', 'dextrose', 'fructose' and 'maltose' in ingredients lists: they are all types of sugar. Other names that indicate sugar include 'honey', 'syrup', 'raw sugar', 'cane sugar', 'muscovado' and 'concentrated fruit juice'.

But it is not only labels that can be a minefield for the shopper.

Fats

The role and the risks of fats in our diet has been outlined in the previous two chapters. Now we cover how best to put that theory into shopping practice.

Below are suggestions of some easy ways to reduce your fat intake to a healthier level. Pick out from them the ones that suit you best to help you reduce fat in your daily diet with the minimum of suffering.

♥ Shop with an eye out for reduced-fat versions of standard products, such as low-fat crisps, low-fat sausages, low-fat yogurt, reduced-fat cheese.

♥ But bear in mind that a whole new generation of fat substitutes have yet to build up a reliable track record. You may want to use them only in moderation for that reason.

♥ Read the small print – there are still big variations in fat content from brand to brand.

♥ Better still, try all the fat-free products you can find. Some of them taste surprisingly good.

♥ Almost fat-free mayonnaise works well instead of butter in sandwiches.

♥ Keep asking at your supermarket for more fat-free foods and write to the head office. (Fat-free sour cream that is useful for cooking has yet to cross the Atlantic.)

♥ Another great pair of ideas from the US for health-conscious gourmets that are still not available in the UK but worth nagging for are defatted butter and sour cream powders which can be stirred into sauces and risotto, dotted on vegetables and so on to give the flavour of the real thing but none of the fat.

♥ If you or your family must have chips, oven chips are better than thick-cut, deep-fried ones, and very much better than thin-cut.

♥ There's not much to choose between beef and lamb on the fat front. Pork varies widely from cut to cut and depends on the pig's diet – it can be better or worse than beef and lamb.

♥ Bacon is pork at its worst.

♥ When you do buy meat, buy less and put more vegetables on the plate. That gives a double health bonus.

♥ Meat products such as sausages are worse for fat than meat you cook healthily yourself; combined with pastry in pies, sausage rolls and so on, they tend to be worse still.

♥ If you do buy pies, look for them with pastry on top only rather than top and bottom.

♥ Go for chicken or fish in preference to red meat as your main source of protein.

♥ Or try turkey – the leanest poultry of all.

♥ When you do buy red meat, buy the leanest-looking.

♥ Venison is not cheap but it has less than a third of the fat of beef.

♥ Beans, pulses, pasta and grains are all fat-free – unless you put butter or high-fat sauces or oils with them. If you aren't a full-time vegetarian, consider having meals without meat on some days.

♥ Have a tin or two of evaporated skimmed milk in the storecupboard ready for substituting for cream.

♥ If you use double cream in sauces and so on, freeze a tub of it in ice-cube trays. That way you can thaw only as much as you need.

♥ In many situations you can use buttermilk or low-fat yogurt instead of cream.

♥ Experiment with low-fat or almost fat-free fromage frais. It has a lovely creamy texture and happily takes up both sweet and savoury flavours for a wide range of uses. (For further suggestions, see the next chapter.)

♥ Cottage cheese is lower in fat than other cheeses.

♥ There are reduced-fat versions of other cheeses such as Cheddar, too. Would you or your children notice the difference in a cheese and salad sandwich?

♥ If you are using Cheddar to flavour sauces or other cooked cheese dishes go for the strongest flavour you can find. It will then take less cheese (and therefore less fat) to achieve the same depth of flavour than if you use a milder one.

♥ But lower-fat doesn't equal no fat. You may decide you would rather have less than lower, and just go for a little of the real (full-fat) cheese.

♥ 'Low-fat' ready-made meals from the freezer can be a trap. If 'low-fat' really only means 'low-volume', beware! A low-fat meal with negligible meat is likely to leave you hungry – vulnerable to the temptation to fill up with a quick fix of something fatty.

What's better than butter?

Supermarket shelves are bowed down under the weight of butters and margarines and substitute bread spreads. By law, all margarines must contain 80 per cent of fat, so margarines contain about the same amount of both fat and calories as butter. The other 20 per cent of both is water. Butter is also restricted in that all the fat in it must be milk fat, hence the high level of saturates. The only permitted addition is salt. By tradition, English butters are made by churning cream and are salted, while continental butters are made from cream with the addition of lactic acid, which gives a sharper, tangier flavour, and are either slightly salted or unsalted. Spreadable butters are simply butters churned or whipped to improve the 'spreadability' of their consistency. Calorie and fat content are unaffected.

Sunflower and soya margarines are healthier than butter because they are lower in saturates and higher in polyunsaturates. However, not all margarines made from vegetable oils are polyunsaturates. The oils may have been hydrogenated (see page 37) and hydrogenating produces trans-fatty acids which behave in much the same way as saturates in our bodies. Check, if you can, on the label. Unfortunately, though they must declare the total fat content, no manufacturer is legally obliged to list nutritional information on the label. Most now choose to do so but some don't, while some producers list total fat content without saying what proportion is made up of saturates. You are unlikely to find the term 'trans-fatty acids' on the label – the clue to watch for is 'hydrogenated vegetable oil' in the ingredients list.

There is no legally binding definition of a low-fat spread. Expect (but check) something with around 40–50 per cent of the fat of butter if the label says 'low-fat' and perhaps 20–25 if it calls itself 'very low fat'. One fat spread made by Tesco, Lowest Ever Fat Spread, has a fat substitute made from milk protein called Simplesse which has only about 5 per cent fat. Government guidelines recommend the use of 'low-fat' only for foods with less than 5g of fat per 100g or 5 per cent. By that criterion, the 'low-fat' spreads are not low-fat at all. 'Relatively low-fat' or 'comparatively low-fat' would be nearer the mark. The non-fat portion of the lower-fat spreads is made up of water and emulsifiers and stabilisers.

Changing the fat content of what we spread on our bread (and/or spreading less) can make a significant contribution to a healthier diet. It can help cut the total of both the saturates and unsaturates. But if you go for a lower-fat spread, you cannot assume that saturates and polyunsaturates have been cut in the same proportions. Some spreads low in fat are still relatively high in saturates. Again, there is no substitute for label-reading.

The lower the fat content, the greater the need for stabilisers to thicken the spread, preservatives to stop mould growing, and colouring to add a yellow, buttery look. If you like to buy in bulk and freeze spreads or keep an emergency supply in the freezer you will need to check the label, too. Some very low-fat products are not suitable for freezing.

For years, Anchor butter and Flora margarine have dominated the market but they get more competition every year. And when *Which?* did a taste test (report published September 1992) the results suggested that things could be changing. The trend now seems to be towards spreads with a lighter texture not just on health grounds but because people prefer their taste.

The *Which?* test involved asking 300 people who usually use butter, margarine or spreads on bread to taste 29 different products, including Anchor and Flora, 25 spreads with half or less than half the fat of Anchor and Flora, and two other spreads, I Can't Believe It's Not Butter and Olivio, which have been widely promoted and which have more than half the fat of butter. Tasting was done blind – tasters did not know what they were tasting – and they were asked to rate each sample for a range of qualities including how buttery, light and cloying it was. The biggest surprise was that the best-liked for taste was Sainsbury's County Light with only half the fat of butter. It beat both Anchor and Flora as well as all the other options lower in fat than them.

Manufacturers change products from time to time, so it is important to keep checking labels for fat content and whatever other details of nutritional content they do give.

Although we can make a significant improvement in the healthiness of our diets by switching to lower-fat butter substitutes, the lower-fat spreads can't do everything butter and margarine can. Generally, butter and margarines are suitable not only for spreading but for all cooking processes including grilling, shallow- and stir-frying, baking, and making sauces and pastry. Spreads with 65–80 per cent fat (including I Can't Believe It's Not Butter, Krona, Clover and Golden Crown) can be used for most cooking purposes. Once you get down to about 60 per cent fat (e.g. Stork, Vitalite, Olivio), you have a spread that can be used for some cooking but the extra water means that they may spit if you try to use them for frying. At half the fat of butter or margarine, there are spreads such as Flora Light, Delight Low Fat, Gold Low Fat, and Half-Fat Anchor, not intended to be used for pastry or frying. Below that (e.g. Delight Extra Low, Gold Lowest, Outline) you have such high proportions of water that the spreads are not suitable for use in cooking at all. You will usually find some guidance from the manufacturer on the packaging, but it is not always consistent. There is more information about fats that are suitable for cooking immediately below.

Oil's well

There has been almost as great a proliferation of oils on the UK market as there has been of butter substitutes. The range of flavours as well as prices available is enormous.

The first thing to be aware of when buying oils is that they are virtually 100 per cent fat and all have the same calorie content – around 135 calories in a tablespoon. What varies, besides taste and cost, is the proportion of saturates to polyunsaturates and monounsaturates and consequently the oil's contribution to healthy (or otherwise) eating. Olive oil, for example, is very high in monounsaturates and low in polyunsaturates. The proportions in sunflower and safflower oils are reversed.

There is a further complicating factor: not enough is yet known about the relative health benefits of the two types of unsaturated fats – polyunsaturated and monounsaturated. The guidelines outlined in **Chapter 1** recommend that we reduce our overall fat intake, and particularly of saturates, on the strength of evidence that polyunsaturates reduce levels of LDLs and so cut the risk of heart disease. (See also **Cholesterol** in the previous chapter.) But researchers are attempting to improve further our understanding.

More recent experiments have suggested that a very high intake of polyunsaturates could have adverse side effects. Then again, some researchers now think that as well as reducing the harmful LDL levels a high polyunsaturate intake may also reduce the beneficial HDL levels, though others believe that such an effect would need amounts of polyunsaturates unlikely to be found in any normal diet.

Confirmation of the possibly superior contribution of mono-unsaturates to a healthy diet comes from studies of people living on a Mediterranean-type diet rich in monounsaturates, who may be assumed to consume a fair amount of olive oil. These people have been found to have much lower levels of blood cholesterol and heart disease than people in other countries with similar total fat intakes. Some experiments have also shown that replacing highly saturated fats with highly monounsaturated fats has reduced levels of LDLs and therefore of cholesterol in the blood as effectively as switching to a diet high in polyunsaturates, but, at the same time, maintaining or improving the levels of the beneficial HDLs.

Perhaps the most sensible line until there is greater agreement among researchers and nutritionists is to follow the universally accepted advice about cutting intake of total fat, and to cut intake of saturates by replacing them with a mixture of polyunsaturates and monounsaturates.

Meanwhile, some things are clear:

♥ All the cooking oils (except coconut) are much lower in saturates than the traditional solid fats like butter and lard, and are therefore better for us.

♥ Solid hydrogenated vegetable oils sold in block form are less saturated than traditional solid fats such as butter, and so are a better choice for pastry-making for which oils and low-fat spreads are unsuitable.

♥ Coconut oil, despite its tempting flavour, is very high in saturates – 90 per cent of the total – and gets a thumbs-down on health grounds. If you cannot resist it, try to limit the amount you use.

♥ Next worst is palm oil.

♥ We need to be particularly vigilant about how much coconut and palm oil we are eating by default. Reading the small print of ingredients lists on the packets of ready-made foods and snacks can be revealing.

♥ The more we cut down on the amount of any cooking fat, the better for our health.

All culinary oils come from the crushed seeds of fruits of plants, including nuts, beans and grains. The flavour depends on which plant it has come from and, to some extent, the extraction method. Cold-pressing, in which the nut, seed or fruit is not subjected to heat to extract oil but pressed by a screw or press, produces highly coloured and richly flavoured oils ideal for dressing salads. Some oils, especially extra virgin olive oil and hazelnut, walnut and almond oils, add a distinctive flavour of their own to a salad dressing or cooked dish. Others are neutral, allowing the flavour of the food with which they are being used to come through. These blander oils are better, from a taste point of view, for frying.

Olive oil grades depend on the quality of the olives used and on the way the oil was extracted and treated. The better the grade the stronger the taste, the deeper the colour and the higher the cost. Again, the most appropriate to use depends on both price and purpose. Extra virgin olive oil comes from top-quality barely ripe olives and must have perfect flavour, perfect aroma, perfect (light yellow to green) colour and a maximum acidity of 1 per cent. If the maximum acidity is 3 per cent, and it reaches acceptable flavour, aroma and colour, it is virgin olive oil.

An oil currently being hyped in the United States as a healthy rival to olive oil is on sale in Britain as rapeseed or canola oil. It has the lowest saturated fat of all the oils and a lot of monounsaturated fat. It looks good on paper, though there is no comparable data (unlike olive oil with its excellent track record) on how it affects people who eat it over long periods.

There is another consideration besides health, price and flavour in choice of oil. Different oils with their different fatty acids are differently affected by heat. For frying, the temperature at which the oil starts to foam or smoke is critical. Olive oil is the finest cooking oil, excellent for shallow-frying, but its low smoking temperature makes it unsuitable for deep-frying. For that you need oils which can get to a high temperature before they reach smoking point. Blended vegetable, corn, grape seed, groundnut, rapeseed, safflower and sunflower are best. Amber-coloured sesame oil adds its distinctive and delicious nutty flavour to stir-fries but it is costly; you may prefer to stir-fry in as little as possible of a neutral-tasting oil and add a dash of sesame for flavour at the end of cooking.

Fears have been expressed in recent years about re-using fat for frying. The worry is that when oxygen comes into contact with oil at high temperatures it can produce oxidised fats which are thought to damage body cells, which may lead to an increased risk of coronary heart disease, cancer and premature ageing. The level at which oxidised fat becomes toxic has not yet been established, although one school of thought is that it does not become toxic until after it has gone rancid, so oil would have been discarded on taste grounds before it became a danger to health anyway. If you want to be really cautious, you could use oil for frying only once. But the best advice at the moment is probably to limit the amount of frying you do to an absolute minimum.

Of course, the fats we cook with or add to our diet are only part of the story. Hidden fats abound. Even when the visible fat has been cut off meat, for example, there is still fat lurking in what looks to the naked eye like completely lean meat. Cakes, chocolate and biscuits add not only sugar but fats, too. And bought biscuits, crisps and pastry all add invisible fat to our total intake. In the average British diet, visible fats such as butter, margarine and cooking oils and fats account for only about a third of total fat intake. A quarter comes from meat and meat products, a fifth from milk, cheese and cream and the rest – along with a lot of sugar – from biscuits, pastries, cakes and other products.

Sugar

Sugar is a recurring theme throughout this chapter and indeed throughout the whole healthy eating story. Here are a few extra hints.

☺ If you buy made-up puddings and so on, look for low-sugar varieties.

☺ Cut down on the amounts of cakes, biscuits and sweet pastries on your shopping list. If you usually buy a lot, it's probably better to reduce gradually rather than trying to cut them out overnight – and abandoning your healthy eating drive a week later.

☺ Currant buns without icing, scones or tea-breads are better for you than Danish pastries or iced buns or cakes.

☺ Do the same gradual cut-back on the amount of jam, marmalade, syrup, treacle or honey in your shopping basket (and, of course, of sugar itself).

☹ Don't buy sweets, especially chocolates.

☺ If you have been in the habit of using sweets as snacks, put extra fresh fruit, dried fruit, raw vegetables, plain popcorn, small quantities of unsalted nuts, bread and bread sticks, crispbreads or rice cakes into your basket as the basis for healthier snacks.

☺ If you buy soft drinks, look for low-calorie ones or switch to unsweetened fruit juices diluted with water or soda water.

☺ Canned fruit should be in fruit juice rather than syrup.

Eggs

Eggs are naturally covered by a waxy substance which the packer does not wash off because it protects the porous shell. The outside may be contaminated if the egg comes from an infected bird or environment. Bacteria will stay on the outside while the shell is unbroken but can come in contact with the egg when the shell is cracked. Check eggs before you buy and reject any that look dirty or have damaged shells. (Raw eggs can still be a health hazard. Thorough cooking kills the bacteria. See further details in **Chapter 6** on food hazards.)

Also check the packing date now given on the box by law. Some retailers also add a 'Best before' or 'Display until' date, and some are now starting to mark them 'Use by'.

Fruit and vegetables

Fruit and vegetables are low in fat and high in fibre, especially if the skin is eaten, and should be generous providers of vitamins and minerals. One kiwi fruit, for example, contains all the vitamin C an adult needs for a day. All fruit is very low in sodium and high in potassium – a good nutritional balance. It is also a source of calcium, magnesium and iron. Fruit has sugar, but fructose (fruit sugar) doesn't do much harm to teeth or insulin levels because of the extent to which it is diluted by fibre and fluid. And it is fairly low in calories (though bananas and grapes are higher than the rest).

Fruit's trump card is that there is now evidence that eating lots of it offers added protection against heart disease and some forms of cancer. Although eating too much of it can be acidic, the healthy eating message is that most of us need to eat more. But how good is fruit's nutrient status when it reaches us, not direct from our own gardens, but from the other end of the country or even the other side of the world?

Fresh *vs.* frozen

Which? way to Health magazine tested vitamin C content in samples of fresh, frozen and canned fruit and vegetables in 1992. Vitamin C was chosen because it is the most sensitive of the vitamins, easily destroyed by heat, light, air and poor storage. If a food can retain a good proportion of its vitamin C, we can assume that other nutrients have survived as well or better. And the survey results suggested that more retained vitamins are likely to be found in the freezer section of the supermarket than in the fruit and vegetable department.

It is perhaps not really surprising. 'Fresh' doesn't necessarily mean fresh: it could be days, weeks or even months old. Main crop potatoes, for example, are harvested in September and October and stored for sale right through the winter and spring. Even with careful temperature and humidity control potatoes harvested in October can have lost a third of their vitamin C by early spring. Apples picked in August could be going on sale the following July. Some produce is not only transported halfway round the world but also spends time in the store when it arrives at its destination.

Frozen food, on the other hand, is likely to have had its ripening arrested by freezing very quickly after it was picked. 'Quick frozen' on labels is meaningless: all commercially frozen food is frozen quickly. Canned produce, too, is normally processed no more than a few hours after picking. In both cases, nutrients have had little time to deteriorate.

Among the *Which? way to Health* investigation findings were:

- All the frozen varieties tested had about the same amount of vitamin C as the fresh, except for spinach which had twice as much in the frozen.
- Canned fruit did just as well as fresh for vitamin C content but canned vegetables did less well than fresh and frozen.
- Green beans in a can were particularly low in vitamin C, probably because the canning process is not geared to vitamin preservation. Blanching the vegetables before canning destroys some vitamins and heating in the can at high temperatures to make the contents sterile destroys still more.
- Canned fruit and vegetables probably both lose some vitamins into the canning liquid. With fruit, the liquid is likely to be used, too, so the vitamins are not so much lost as transferred. The canning liquid for vegetables is more likely to be thrown away.
- Even when canned fruit in the survey had lost vitamin C, as had, for example, canned strawberries compared with fresh, it still had enough to make a valuable contribution to healthy eating.
- But canned food can have added salt or sugar.
- There was little to choose between the vitamin C content of fresh produce from different sources. Fruit and vegetables from supermarkets, greengrocers, market stalls and farm shops all produced similar results.
- But greengrocers were slightly ahead of supermarkets, probably because they are more likely to buy from wholesalers themselves, whereas supermarket deliveries go via distribution centres, increasing handling and possibly delivery time.
- Farm shops, which might have been expected to have the freshest produce, didn't always do as well as greengrocers or supermarkets. The ready-picked produce on 'Pick your own' farms had obviously not always been rushed straight in from the fields that morning. It may also have been kept in an unrefrigerated environment.
- Most expensive of the fruit and vegetables was fresh produce

from supermarkets. The cheapest was canned food. The price and availability of fresh produce varies throughout the year, of course.

Choosing fruit

The best guide to the freshness of fruit is how it looks and smells, but that still tells you little about flavour or texture – in fact, it may be exactly the reverse. There has been a tendency in recent years to grow for uniformity and attractiveness of appearance at the expense of taste. One example is the Cox's Orange Pippin, a naturally small apple manipulated into becoming much bigger. The small ones, when you can find them, still have more of the traditional crispness and taste.

Varieties

More varieties of fruit are now being made available. Supermarkets have responded to demand from consumers and now give more information about varieties, though more still would be welcome. A typical fruit contains at least 200 identifiable flavouring components. Not only have dozens of new fruits been imported into the UK in the last few years but there has also been a movement to revive and reinstate older 'lost'

Vitamin C in apples

Variety	Vitamin C (mg/120g)	
	Unpeeled	Peeled
Cox's Orange Pippin	6.0	3.6
Granny Smith	9.6	2.4
Golden Delicious	12.0	3.6
Laxton Superb	12.0	3.6
Newton Wonder	12.0	3.6
Worcester Pearmain	19.0	12.0
Sturmer Pippin	36.0	24.0

Source: McCance and Widdowson

varieties of familiar fruit, some only available for a brief season each year. If they interest you, look for them not only in the supermarket but at farm gate shops.

Varying your variety can also increase the spread of nutrients – and the nutritional value can vary surprisingly too. For example, a Sturmer Pippin apple has six times the vitamin C as the same weight of Cox's Orange Pippin.

Grades

Fruit for sale in Britain should be labelled with its quality class, its place of origin, and, in some cases, its variety. Here is what the labels mean:

- **Extra class** means 'excellent quality and usually only very specially selected product'. It is rarely seen, except in luxury hampers.
- **Class I** means 'good quality product with no important defects'. It covers most of the fruit sold in Britain.
- **Class II** means 'reasonably good quality but deficient in one or two requirements such as shape, colour, small blemishes and marks'. It is not often seen.

Labelling tends not to be enforced in shops and it is not of immense use anyway since, for example, fruit that is Class I when it is put on display may become Class II if it remains unsold long enough.

Here are some more hints for choosing fruit:

- **Apples** should be firm with no bruises or wrinkles and should smell sweet. A flexible green stalk is a sign of freshness.
- **Bananas** are picked green and ripen yellow. The yellower they are the sweeter. How ripe you eat yours is a matter of personal taste. Some people enjoy them most when they are yellow, others not until they have begun to develop plenty of brown patches. When they are quite brown, they still have a good flavour for sandwiches and make the best-tasting fools and mousses. Shops will often sell them off cheaply at this stage.
- Eat **grapes** within a few days and avoid bunches with bruised or discoloured fruits.

- **Mangoes** are best bought firm and unblemished and ripened at home in a warm place.
- **Melons** smell fragrant when they are ripe. Galia and cantaloupe melons also give slightly when pressed gently at the stalk end and honeydew melons at the other end. Watermelons should be firm and sound hollow when tapped.
- **Oranges** should be unblemished, unbruised and unwrinkled. They should feel heavy – indicating a high juice'content – and look bright. Green patches will ripen to orange, given time.
- **Passion-fruit** is the exception to the usual rule. It is not at its tastiest until its skin has become really wrinkled.
- **Pears** are easily damaged once they are ripe so are best bought firm and ripened at home.
- **Pineapples** should smell ripe – much more reliable than pulling a leaf out of the top. Avoid bruises or soft patches. You can buy pineapples green and let them ripen.
- **Soft fruit** should have bright, rich colours and the stalks, if still attached, should be fresh-looking.
- **Stone fruit** should be plump and firm to touch with a bloom on the skin. Peaches and nectarines should give to the touch, be full, unblemished and feel heavy for their size. Avoid damaged, bruised or wrinkled skin.

Organic vs. non-organic

In 1992 *Which?* found that a basket of organic fruit and vegetables cost on average a little over a third more than non-organic – though the premium varied from twice the price for tomatoes to 11 per cent or about four pence a pound more for white cabbage.

The magazine also found that one in three people in its survey was already buying organic and nine out of ten said they would if it didn't cost more. One person in four was buying organic on grounds of taste and 42 per cent believed it was free from chemical or pesticide residues – both big increases since a similar survey by the magazine two years earlier.

So why is organic dearer? Does it taste better? And how does it compare nutritionally with non-organic produce?

Organic's biggest cost drawback is that it relies on more

traditional farming methods and tends to be done on too small a scale to compete with the economies available to larger non-organic farmers. Organic farmers do not use man-made fertilisers, pesticides, growth regulators or feed additives but rely on crop rotation and animal and plant manures, hand weeding and biological pest control. Weeding and hoeing by hand is not only more expensive but often needs wider crop spacing to make it possible – further contributing to lower yields. Then there is less scope for large harvesting and packing machinery on smaller, organic farms, and organic farmers don't use post-harvest treatments. Cold storage is more expensive than using storage chemicals and can also allow greater nutritional loss. Finally, transporting smaller crops, usually via central stations where they are packed by hand, is also more expensive than larger-scale transport. Farming on a larger scale would help to reduce the cost of organic produce.

When it comes to taste, it is more difficult to give a straight answer. *Which?*'s blind tasting of little gem lettuce, galia melons and bananas was inconclusive.

The panel included such well-known foodies as Alistair Little, chef of his restaurant of the same name in London; cookery writer Jocelyn Dimbleby; Antonio Carluccio, chef/proprietor of the Neal Street Restaurant in London; and the editors of both *Which? way to Health* and *Which?*. Tasters described organic little gem lettuce as 'beautifully grown', 'fresh-tasting and pleasant' and 'better than average'. But 'oozing with flavour' and 'deliciously chewy' were to be found among the tasters' notes describing non-organic. One described an organic melon as 'attractive if rather artificially so' while some non-organic melons scored badly on appearance with comments like 'grotty', 'off-putting' and 'awful'. And if appearance did not always follow expectations, taste did not always follow appearance, either. One 'tired and unappealing' organic banana had 'a fine and delicate taste' while a 'perfect-looking' non-organic melon was downgraded to 'nasty' on the taste test.

So if organic does not win outright on taste or appearance, how about health? Beside the 42 per cent of the survey group who thought that organic produce was free of chemical or pesticide residues, another 12 per cent considered organic better for health and half that number also thought that it was higher in vitamins and minerals. But there is no conclusive evidence that they are right.

When the Ministry of Agriculture, Fisheries and Food tested non-organic food in 1989–90, they found detectable pesticide residues in 31 per cent of non-organic food. But there is no guarantee that organic is always residue-free. Pesticides can linger in the soil for years. Lindane, for example, can be detected 20 years later and pesticide sprays can be blown across from neighbouring farms. Organic vegetables have been found to contain some nitrates but slightly fewer than non-organic produce. This is because although organic crops escape the nitrates in artificial fertiliser some also occur naturally in the soil.

Several studies have shown higher levels of protein, vitamin C, calcium, iron and potassium in organic vegetables. But there is little evidence of major nutritional advantages. If you don't keep all the juice or cooking water from your fruit and vegetables, you could be throwing away all the slight extra benefit anyway.

Environmental concern is also a motivation for some supporters of organic produce. One of organic farming's avowed aims is sustainable agriculture – methods that protect the environment and wildlife and its habitat from pollution – hence the ban on pesticides which kill not only unwanted pests but beneficial insects and on artificial fertilisers and pesticides which contribute to water pollution; and the avoidance of man-made chemicals and the use of crop rotation and hand-weeding, all of which minimise erosion, for the sake of the environment and wildlife.

On balance, the evidence so far suggests that organic is a question that consumers have to decide on grounds of aesthetics, cost and conscience – rather then nutrition.

Five organisations are registered with the United Kingdom Register of Organic Food Standards, whose regulations cover all organic food except animal products (which are to have regulations of their own, probably from about the end of 1993). The UKROF rules cover the use of manures, fertilisers and mineral additives, list the permitted pest and disease control methods and substances, require crop rotation and production methods that are sensitive to the environment and wildlife habitats, specify what packaging is acceptable and require detailed record-keeping on and regular inspection of farms.

The five conforming organisations are the Soil Association, Bio-Dynamic Agricultural Association, Organic Farmers and Growers, Organic Food Manufacturers Federation, and Scottish Organic Producers Association. Look for their symbols when you buy organic food.

Here are a few more things you should know when you shop for fruit and vegetables:

- When you do buy canned, avoid dented cans. If air has got into the can food will have started to deteriorate. If the lacquer coating inside the can is broken, the food will also have been exposed to metal. The risk is slight – but it does exist.
- Avoid bruised or wilting fruit and vegetables when you shop. Their nutritional value will already have been reduced.
- Always get frozen food home and in the freezer as quickly as you can. Use an insulated bag, and visit the frozen food section towards the end of your shopping trip rather than at the beginning.

Best-dressed salad

Salad dressings are a bit of a healthy eater's minefield. A generous sprinkling is enough to turn a healthy, nutritious meal into one that is high in both calories and fat. Even reduced-calorie or reduced-fat dressings may not be all they seem.

Salad dressings tend to be one of three types – salad cream, mayonnaise, and vinaigrette or French dressing. Although different versions of each may differ greatly in calorie content and taste, the same basic ingredients are common to most: oil, vinegar, water, sugar, salt, lemon juice, herbs and spices. Salad cream and mayonnaise contain egg yolks as well.

Salad creams contain no cream but usually have malt vinegar, starch and gums. On average, these are the lowest in fats and calories of the ready-made salad dressings. They tend to be both low in saturated fat and the cheapest of the salad dressings, too. There is not much to choose between major brands on health grounds.

Mayonnaise is traditionally home-made with olive oil but ready-made ones now rarely contain any. Most are made with sunflower or vegetable oil and some have soya oil. On average, they have the highest calorie and fat content of all the salad dressings. Reduced-calorie versions usually have about half the fat content, but a reduced-calorie version of one brand can be almost as high as the standard version of another. The saturated fat content of most is relatively low but higher, on average, than that of other salad dressings.

Vinaigrette or French dressing is usually a mixture of oil, vinegar and seasoning and is often home-made. But there are a variety of ready-prepared ones on the market made usually with sunflower or vegetable oil although some, including Newman's Own Italian and Sainsbury's French and Italian vinaigrettes, use olive. Bought vinaigrettes vary most widely in fat and calorie content, so it really does pay to look before you buy. The highest in fat are about on a par with mayonnaise while the lowest are as low as an average salad cream. There are ultra-reduced-calorie versions, such as Kraft Free Choice 97 per cent Fat-Free, which contain very little fat at all. A home-made vinaigrette using equal quantities of oil and vinegar should have slightly less fat and fewer calories than an average shop-bought version, although you may find it too vinegary for your taste. If so, you might prefer it diluted with water. Foodies usually recommend a ratio of about four times the oil to vinegar.

Blue cheese dressings are usually made of vegetable or sunflower oil and egg yolk as well as cheese and have, on average, calorie and fat contents similar to those of vinaigrette. There is not a lot of variation between brands. (The Ministry of Agriculture, Fisheries and Food says the danger of listeria from the blue cheese in blue cheese dressings is slight. Pasteurisation and heat treatment before bottling should kill off any bacteria present. However, once the dressing is opened, bacteria can be introduced from kitchen utensils and so on and could spread if the dressing is stored for long periods after opening. See more about the danger of listeria for pregnant women on pages 185–6.)

Thousand island dressings contain vinegar, egg, tomato puree and other vegetables, herbs and spices, as well as oil. They are generally lower in fat and calories than blue cheese dressings and there is not much difference between brands – except for the low-fat one from Kraft. They also do a fat-free version.

Yogurt, sour cream and garlic dressings vary widely in content. One of the advantages of bought over home-made dressings containing egg yolk is that bought ones are either pasteurised, which should kill any salmonella in the eggs used, or made of dried egg, which has usually been pasteurised before drying or processed in a way similar to pasteurisation. (See the box on the danger of raw eggs for pregnant women, the very young, the very old, and anyone with a weak immune system on page 186.)

Labelling

Obviously, if you are looking for the healthy choices, it pays to study the nutritional information given on the label before you buy – if it is given. Unfortunately, it is not compulsory and, though many manufacturers choose to show it, not all do. Those who do are not obliged to follow a standard format, which makes quick on-the-spot comparisons more difficult. The next best bet is to read the ingredients list which must be provided: take note of the order of listing, which will be by weight order. If one has water listed first and another oil, the one with water first is going to be lower in overall oil content and probably also in calories, though you need to look at the position or absence of sugar in the list, too, to be sure.

You might like to know that:

☹ A generous sprinkling of vinaigrette can contain almost as much fat as four chocolate biscuits.

☹ A dollop of mayonnaise can have more fat than a bag of crisps.

☺ Lower-fat needn't mean lesser flavour. When *Which?* magazine did a tasting test of salad dressings in 1992, one of the three best-liked was Hellmann's Light Calorie Reduced with less than half the calories and just over a third the fat of the standard Hellmann's Real. The 112 tasters did not detect that it was a reduced-fat dressing.

☺ There are lower-fat ways to make salad dressings at home. See **Chapter 4** for suggestions.

Fish

The nutritional virtues of fish have been extolled in the previous two chapters. Fish is a good source of protein and of many minerals and vitamins. White fish is low in fat and the fat in oily fish is mostly polyunsaturated and includes the highly valued omega-3 fatty acids now believed to give some protection against coronary heart disease and some cancers, and under investigation for a whole host of further claims.

Here are some fish facts you will find helpful when shopping for it.

Family favourites

Cod and haddock are Europe's top-selling white species – so popular that they are now endangered. Some estimates say that both could disappear from the North Sea in five years unless strict conservationist measures are introduced. The winter of 1992/3 saw a slight improvement in haddock stocks but cod is giving even more cause for concern than before. There are moves to limit fishing to attempt to conserve and replenish stocks, but consumers are also being urged to try other options including coley, huss, pollock and hoki.

Cod   Available fresh and smoked. Best wet cod between June and February.

Haddock   Second to cod in quantity caught and bought. Sold fresh or smoked and best between May and February. The Scots (who eat most white fish per head in the UK) are particularly partial to it, and it is the most popular choice in fish-and-chip shops in the north of England too.

Plaice   Plaice is the UK's best-selling flat fish. It is caught in shallow water from the North Sea to Spain and is best between May and February.

Coley   Caught off the south coast of England and the north of Iceland and Norway and available fresh between August and February.

Finding the freshest

Here are some tips for choosing the freshest fish:

- Buy only from a supplier with a quick turnover.
- Look for a display where fresh fish is on plenty of ice, where the display unit looks clean and is protected by a glass front, for instance, from dirt and contamination.
- Avoid buying where the fish is piled in a heap on a warm, messy, open counter.
- Cooked or smoked fish should be on a tray or in a refrigerator rather than directly on ice.
- Cooked and raw products need to be displayed separately to avoid contamination.
- There should be a fly killer such as an ultraviolet light machine.
- Water from melting ice should drain into a drainage system, not on to the floor.
- Lights should be placed so they don't warm the fish up.
- The staff should look clean and be wearing clean overalls and disposable gloves.
- The areas where fish is prepared and utensils used should be easy to keep clean – plastic and metal rather than wood, for example.
- Fish from the sea should smell of sea rather than fish. Avoid a shop with strong, sour fish odours hanging about.

And when it comes to choosing the fish itself:

- The eyes should be bright, clear and prominent, not sunken or cloudy.
- The gills should be red, with no discoloured slime or unpleasant smell coming from them.

- Natural markings (like the orange dot on plaice) should be bright and clear.
- Avoid fish that looks stale or dry, with grey or yellow slime, with dull skin or a strong fishy smell. Fresh fish will have bright skin with a good sheen and scales still firmly attached.
- If you are buying steaks or cutlets, look for plump, firm flesh. There should be no discoloration such as redness along the backbone, no bruising and no blood clots.

Buying chilled and pre-packed

Fish sold is this way usually comes in modified-atmosphere packaging (a type of packaging in sealed containers) or is vacuum-packed to stay fresh longer and be cleaner and easier to handle.

When buying:

☹ Avoid fish in damaged packaging.
☹ Avoid fish that looks old or as if it has been handled badly.

Buying frozen

Wet fish is often three to five days old by the time you buy it. If it has been carefully handled it should still be in an acceptable condition, but its average age may be one reason that taste tests favour frozen (see **Fresh fish** *vs.* **frozen** below).

When you buy frozen:

- Make sure packaging is tightly sealed and undamaged.
- The package should feel hard, never mushy.
- If there are dull white patches on the fish or small white ice crystals, don't buy.

Best-buy oily fish

Owing to its health benefits, oily fish has become increasingly popular over the past few years.

Types of oily fish include:

Tuna Britain's canned favourite. But if it is omega-3 fatty acids you are looking for, you are backing a loser. Tuna starts out with it, but omega-3 does not survive the process when it is canned in oil. When it is canned in brine, a little omega-3 survives and the tuna has a lower overall fat content but is higher in salt than when canned in oil.

Sardines and pilchards   Sardines are young pilchards. Both are best in their fresh state between February and July. Most people eat them canned, often in a sauce.

Herrings   Herring, caught from the sea around Britain and Norway, is a good source of omega-3 fatty acids. The quality is best in those sold between July and February.

Kippers   Kippers are herrings split open, cleaned and soaked in brine (cured), which increases the salt content, before being smoked in a kiln. Some kippers are dyed before the smoking stage.

Mackerel   Mackerel belongs to the same family as tuna and is exceedingly rich in omega-3. In Britain, mackerel is mostly eaten smoked. Best-quality fresh is available between August and April. Canned mackerel remains a good source of omega-3 – it is processed differently from tuna.

Salmon   Wild salmon is rarer than it used to be. Most fresh salmon now comes from fish farms either in Scotland or from Norway, which has brought the price down considerably during the 1980s and 1990s. Canned salmon also remains a good source of omega-3.

Trout   Most of the trout available in the shops is rainbow trout and, like salmon, it is now usually farmed.

Fresh fish *vs.* frozen – the taste test

In 1991/2 *Which?* conducted a series of taste tests in which the magazine asked first professional fish tasters and then non-experts to compare 'blind' fresh, chilled, pre-packed and frozen cod fillets, all of which had been steamed. Both panels reached the same conclusion – frozen tasted fresher than fresh.

The professionals described the taste of the frozen cod as 'sweet and fishy' and the wet as 'neutral'. The pre-packed chilled fish they found 'insipid' and the least fresh-tasting of the three. So surprised were the *Which?* researchers that they decided to ask 60 people not in the fish industry to compare samples of the same three types of cod. Frozen fish won once again, with its flavour preferred to either of the other two. Wet fish was thought to have too little flavour, while pre-packed came out part-way between the other two. It was only when fish was presented with parsley sauce that the panel switched its preference to the less strong flavour of fresh fish.

Shellfish

Most shellfish – from the luxurious lobster and oyster to the humbler cockle and mussel – are also good low-fat sources of protein and nutrients but (with the exception of cockles, oysters and scallops) contain higher levels of cholesterol. There are two groups of shellfish – crustaceans have jointed shells and molluscs hinged or single. Crabs, lobsters, crawfish and crayfish, Dublin Bay prawns (also called Norway lobster, scampi and langoustine), prawns and shrimps are crustaceans. Oysters, clams, cockles, mussels, whelks and winkles are molluscs.

Finding the freshest
The freshest of most types of shellfish are those actually sold live and killed by cooking. If you are going to buy uncooked mussels, clams or oysters they must be live, with their shells undamaged and closed tight. Oysters are usually eaten live. Whether you are buying live or freshly cooked shellfish, make sure you use only sources with a good, quick turnover.

Probably the shellfish most people buy most often are frozen prawns. Each prawn is sealed into its own pocket of ice to keep it in the best possible condition until you are ready to use it. But this does mean that you are buying water as well as the prawns. It takes no more than 15 per cent of pack weight to ice-glaze satisfactorily, yet some brands have been found to put nearer 50 per cent of water in their packs. Regulations requiring manufacturers to declare water weight are non-existent but overdue.

Meanwhile, look for weight given as 'net of ice-glaze' or 'deglazed weight' or 'after defrosting' and make your price comparisons on the basis of those weights.

Fish products

Most of the fish sold in the UK is as frozen fish products – fingers, bites, goujons, burgers, breaded scampi and so on. Much is coated - overcoated, in fact. Of eight such products tested in 1991 by *Which? way to Health* six had more coating than fish. Fish content varied from 39 to 55 per cent. Not one had its fish content marked on its packaging and nor did 12 out of the 13 brands of fish fingers examined by the magazine at the same time. Under current labelling regulations, it is hard to know what you are getting.

Fish products grew, in part, out of conservation issues of the 1970s. Fears that fish stocks would run out prompted technologists to look at ways to use the large amounts of fish flesh then not being used as food. Leftovers from filleting and fish that were too small to fillet contained good flesh, but it was hard to use until a process to remove it was developed. This mechanically recovered fish flesh has become known as minced fish and is widely used in fish products.

So, too, are fish blocks – fish fillets packed in a large block-shaped mould and frozen with or without minced fish and with or without water and polyphosphate. (If the label states that the product contains *only* fillet there will be no added water.) The blocks that manufacturers produce can be 100 per cent fillet to 100 per cent minced fish and water, and variations in between.

Frozen breaded scampi may be whole tails or small scampi tails with bits stuck on to them and the whole thing frozen together into a tail shape. The UK Association of Frozen Food Producers now has a voluntary code which recommends that manufacturers say on the label whether the package contains whole or 'reformed' tails. As members supply between them about 90 per cent of the breaded scampi sold in the country, supermarket scampi is usually labelled, though you still have no way of knowing what you are getting if you order it in a restaurant or pub. And if UKAFFP members say whether the scampi is whole or 'reformed', they rarely label it with the percentage of fish. Their code of conduct recommends that the 'core' content – scampi *plus* water – should be, on average, 50 per cent. UKAFFP members favour content labelling, but not until other European manufacturers have to come into line and do likewise.

There is often as much as ten per cent of water, in the form of polyphosphate solution, in scampi and about the same in fish blocks. There are good reasons for the polyphosphate – it reduces drip loss when products thaw, makes them a more regular shape (so easier to transport and process) and helps bind scampi together. But only if added water makes up more than five per cent of the final food weight – that's fish plus coating – need its presence be declared on the ingredients list at all and even then the manufacturer will not tell you how much there is. If polyphosphate solution is added you should see polyphosphates on the list. But that won't tell you how much water you are paying for, and, as the water makes the finished product heavier, you won't know how much fish you are actually getting for your money. The only clue is to notice the position of water on the ingredients list. The higher up it comes, the more water, and therefore the less fish, you get.

Poultry

Chicken, turkey, duckling, goose and guinea-fowl are now all farmed. Most birds are raised under conditions designed to fatten them up in the shortest possible time and get them on to the market young and tender. However, some are now reared free-range.

As with organic fruit and vegetables, the choice of farmed or free-range has to be made by individual consumers according to conscience and/or cost and flavour preference. Nutritionally, there is nothing to choose between them.

When you are buying poultry:

- Look out for a bird with a plump breast, pliable breastbone tip, and smooth unbroken skin if it is unwrapped.
- If it is wrapped, make sure the plastic covering is unbroken.

- When you select a frozen chicken, again look for an undamaged bag without much visible frozen liquid inside it.
- The amount of water added to frozen chicken is limited by law to 7.4 per cent of the weight of the frozen bird. There is no regulation for other poultry.
- Turkeys have been found with as much as a pint and a half of extra water. Besides the unappetising sogginess, more water means you are getting less bird for your money. Look for descriptions like 'dry-chilled' on the bag to indicate less added water.
- A frozen bird may have a bag of giblets inside it. If it has, take out the bag as soon as the bird has thawed enough to make this possible.

Meat

For years, health educators have been telling us about the drawbacks of red meat and advocating that we eat less of it. One adult in ten now claims that he or she no longer eats it at all on grounds of health, conscience and/or cost. But we still eat almost as much in Britain in total as we did in the 1970s. On average, meat-eaters get through 2kg of meat or meat products each week.

Meat is a concentrated source of high-quality protein, though in the developed world only people on too low-calorie a diet are likely to have any protein shortages. Meat is a good source of the B vitamins and especially of B12, which is found only in foods of animal origin. It is an important source of iron, too. Liver provides a number of other vitamins and minerals. (But see the **warning to pregnant women** to avoid liver in the previous chapter.) And all meat contains some fat, no matter how lean it looks. All the nutritional value in meat is in the lean muscle tissue. The fat has no nutritional value – only some taste and a lot of calories.

The fat in meat comes in two types. Structural fat is part of the animal's cell membranes and is invisible to the naked eye. Storage fat is visible and includes the fat laid down under the skin between muscles or inside the muscles themselves. Although it is obviously all animal fat, not all of it is saturated. Most meats contain a small percentage of polyunsaturates and about 40 per cent each of saturates and monounsaturates.

The fat in meat plays a role in releasing flavour-enhancing compounds during cooking and improving the meat's juiciness but that function requires only the tiny amount of fat that is present in even the leanest. More fat in the meat brings only the smallest improvement in flavour. The condition of the animal at slaughter has far more effect on tenderness than fat does. Meat from old or stressed animals or from carcasses chilled too rapidly after slaughter will be tougher. The flavour of meat is also improved by hanging for up to a month after slaughter, depending on the animal. The trend in the industry now is to breed leaner and slaughter younger. Some UK butchers are also switching to a continental style of cutting up a carcass which gets rid of fat deposits between muscles and gives leaner, boneless joints.

Meat can contribute to a healthy diet but the best advice is to eat little, lean and not every day. Besides reducing frequency and portion size, serving more vegetables with it and removing all the visible fat, the cut or product you choose also helps to determine how healthy or otherwise a meat meal is.

♥ Meat products are the real baddies. Salami is around 45 per cent fat, for example, and traditional pork sausages nearly 25, compared with ham at about 5 per cent and well-trimmed steak at under 10.

♥ The leanest cuts of beef are sirloin, rump, topside, fore ribs, back ribs and top ribs.

♥ Fillet and leg are the leanest lamb cuts. Next best are chump chops and loin.

♥ Leg, loin and tenderloin or fillet are the lowest-fat pork cuts, as long as they have been trimmed well.

♥ Offal is lower in fat, and higher in protein and vitamins and minerals, than carcass meats (the meats such as leg, shoulder and so on that are attached to the skeletal frame).

♥ There is no numerical fat content labelling on unminced meat. Most supermarkets use descriptive labels, such as 'extra lean' or 'lean', but they are only relative. The only other guide is your eye.

- Grow-faster hormones have been banned in Britain since 1986 and in the EC since 1988. However, they are still used in some countries but not, the experts assure us, in meat imported into the UK.
- Some farmers give their pigs and calves antibiotics to reduce the risk of disease and to promote growth. There is a limit on the minimum interval between administering them and sending an animal for slaughter. And because of the concern about bacteria becoming antibiotic-resistant, the antibiotics used in food should now be different from those used in human medicine.
- Cattle tissues such as brain, spleen and intestines likely to carry the BSE agent in cattle with BSE (mad cow disease) have been banned from use by food manufacturers since November 1989. However, scientists say they think the chance of BSE passing to humans is remote.

Mincing matters

The amount of fat in mince depends on the quality of the meat used and how well it has been trimmed. When there's a fat content of more than 20 per cent, the meat is unlikely to have been trimmed of excess fat before mincing.

When *Which? way to Health* investigated mince in 1990, 18 out of 60 samples had 20 per cent of fat or more. Five of them had fat over 25 per cent, the level at which trading standards officers would consider prosecuting. Lean meat trimmed of visible fat should have a fat content of between 4 and 8.5 per cent, depending on the cut. For example, mince from lean meat should have well below 10 per cent fat. Yet the magazine found that 21 out of 48 'lean' minces had more than 10 per cent fat, including some actually described as 'less than 10 per cent fat' on the label.

Seven of the minces bought also had levels of connective tissue too high to have come solely from the tissue in the meat itself, indicating the addition of sinews and tendons. Until improved labelling is introduced, the only way to be absolutely certain of what you are getting would seem to be to buy meat and make your own mince.

SOIL ASSOCIATION

Based on Soil Association Standards for Organic Food and Farming. Livestock must be reared humanely with access to organic pastureland and no prolonged confinement. Food should come principally from organic sources (crops grown without chemical pesticides or fertilisers). No routine drug medication or growth promoters may be used in animal feed. Routine or prophylactic use of veterinary treatments are restricted and alternative treatments such as homoeopathy are recommended where applicable. For more details write to: The Soil Association, 86 Colston Street, Bristol BS1 5BB.

REAL MEAT COMPANY

Producers must comply with the company's specific welfare/diet codes. Livestock is reared without the use of any form of growth promoters, antibiotics or hormones during the animal's entire life. Among other things, codes cover method and length of transport of animals. Codes are publicly available. For more details contact: Real Meat Company Ltd, Warminster BA12 7DZ (tel: 0985 40436).

Alternative meat

The anti-cruelty meat-eating lobby, incensed by reports of the way some farm animals are treated, has created a demand for alternatively reared meat. Supermarkets are now beginning to come up with labels like 'Waitrose Traditional English Pork', 'Sainsbury's Naturally Produced Traditional Beef', 'Tesco Traditionally Reared Prime Beef', and so on. Along with the names come descriptions, such as: 'less intensive methods of feeding and husbandry are used'; 'cattle graze on natural pastures free from artificial fertilisers'; and 'all animals graze freely in open fields on a diet of grass'.

Unfortunately, none of the supermarkets has revealed its exact specifications beyond vague descriptions like the meaningless 'time-honoured' and terms like 'traditional' and 'naturally produced' that have no legally defined or binding meanings.

Two organisations – the Soil Association and the Real Meat Company – have developed their own symbols and specifications. You may see their symbols on meat in high street butchers and supermarkets. They inspect and monitor farms using their symbols and give details of their specifications on request.

If you decide you want what you feel is 'kinder' meat you will certainly have to be prepared to pay for it – it can cost up to twice the price. Where taste is concerned, attempts to compare conventionally and more kindly reared products have so far been inconsistent and inconclusive. And there may be a trade-off between taste and texture. Alternative rearing systems may allow animals to mature more slowly so they will be older by the time they are slaughtered and thus less tender, if more full of flavour.

There is no real nutritional evidence that less intensively farmed meats can offer any advantage. It could be the reverse – animals reared out of doors may need more fat to withstand the cold. That goes against the trend to respond to the demand for healthier meat by breeding leaner animals.

So, as with fruit and vegetables, which you buy will be determined by your own personal equation of cost, conscience and aesthetic judgement rather than on grounds of what constitutes healthy eating.

Alternatives to meat

Infrequent or non-meat-eaters have turned increasingly to bridging the gap with beans and other pulses, vegetable burgers and pasta, and textured vegetable protein used as a replacement for meat in, for example, soya mince and vegetable burgers. Sales of previously minority foods such as tofu have also increased. And the food industry is attempting to woo this market with new products such as the tiny fungus-based Quorn. So how do these rising meat alternatives compare with meat for taste, cost and healthiness?

Tofu

Tofu (bean curd) is soya milk curd made when soya beans are curdled with calcium sulphate (gypsum), much the way cheese is made from cows' milk. The curds are pressed and drained and the firm curd left is tofu. Unlike most cheeses, it is not left to mature but eaten fresh.

Tofu is sold in cartons, as tofu burgers, and in ready-made meals from stir-fry and sweet-and-sour to biriani and salami-style slices. There are tofu grills and tofu desserts and ice-cream. Silken tofu is like a soya version of fromage frais. Unlike meat replacement foods designed to look and taste like meat – sometimes called meat-copy products – soya has a texture, appearance and neutrality of taste quite unlike that of meat. Tofu has little taste of its own, but absorbs other flavours wonderfully and has long had its place, not merely as a meat substitute but in its own right, in the traditional cuisines of a number of Asian countries. And both vegetarian and non-vegetarian cooks in the West have increasingly been discovering its virtues. (See **Chapter 4** for hints on using it in recipes.)

TVP

Textured vegetable protein is a meat-copy product made of flour from soya beans with the oil removed. The flour is mixed to a dough with water and forced through a small hole under pressure at a high temperature. Extruding actually cooks the dough, opens up its texture and creates long air bubbles which give it its finished fibrous meat-like texture.

TVP is made into vegetable burgers and burger mixes, vegetable sausages, grills and ravioli and is sold in dry meal mixes like vegetable stroganoff.

Quorn

This is a myco-protein, a type of food made from a fungus grown suspended in a glucose solution in a 50-metre fermenting tower. It grows fast: it doubles its weight every six hours. After a few days it is heat-treated to stop it growing further and then harvested in sheets. Vegetable-based flavourings and sometimes colourings are added, with egg white to bind the fungus together. The sheets are rolled and pressed for texture, and set by steaming. The Quorn is then sliced, minced, diced or chopped into chunks. Although it is a distant relative of mushrooms and truffles, Quorn has a texture similar to that of chicken but little flavour of its own. It is used with other ingredients in ready-made meals such as curries, casseroles, sweet-and-sour, potato-topped pies, crispbakes, escalopes and pastry pies.

How do they compare?

All three are almost as nutritious as meat, on the whole, and in some ways more so. Tofu, TVP and Quorn are lower in fat and calories than meat – though for ready-made dishes you still have to check the label, especially if they include pastry. All three are good sources of protein. Tofu is a particularly good source of calcium and TVP is quite a good one, too.

Tofu contains almost no fibre, but meat doesn't either. TVP and Quorn *are* good sources of fibre, which means that they are filling and satisfying as well as being low in calories – an ideal combination for people concerned about their weight. The three have different levels of vitamins and minerals from meat but if you decide to change from meat to meat replacements and ring the changes you won't be at much risk of developing deficiencies.

Tofu is roughly a quarter of the price of lean rump steak per serving, and two-thirds of the cost of mince. TVP soya mince is only about two-thirds of the price of tofu, so giving even more of a saving. Quorn is dearer – about halfway in cost between mince and chicken breast.

When *Which? way to Health* investigated meat replacements in 1991 most tasters did not much like the ready-made tofu meals and most could tell it was not meat. However, nearly half did like the home-made tofu stir-fry.

On the whole, testers preferred real meat burgers to the TVP burgers they tried. But TVP mince in bolognaise sauce went down well – more than a third of testers thought it was meat and even those who didn't said they preferred it to a similar real meat dish. Best-liked of the ready-made dishes, though, were

Quorn curries, even though most people could tell they were not made of meat. (See **Chapter 4** for more on how to use both TVP and Quorn at home.)

Pulses

This is the term used for around 20 different varieties of dried beans, peas and lentils. They range widely in colour, shape and taste, and can be used for healthy soups, stews, pâtés, casseroles, curries, burgers, moussakas, lasagnes, salads and pancake fillings. They are cheap and a good source of nutrition – though only soya beans provide 'complete' proteins, such as those found in meat, with all eight essential amino acids in the proportions the body needs. Mixing pulses with grains, nuts and seeds makes up the difference for the rest. Pulses could also be considered ecologically sound: land planted with soya beans can support more than 30 times as many people as the same piece of land dedicated to beef cattle production.

If pulses are a must for the healthy shopper, there is still one question to be resolved – home-cooked *versus* factory-cooked and canned. If you do buy uncooked, make sure you buy from an established supplier where stock is turned over fast enough to ensure they are fresh. Buy small quantities regularly, rather than keeping them for too long.

- Canned beans need only be heated through.
- Canned beans are often heavy in sugar and salt. If you do use them, drain off the liquid and rinse the beans thoroughly.
- Most uncooked pulses have to be soaked for at least eight hours and cooked for half an hour to an hour or more after that. Some (see the next chapter) have to be boiled hard for between ten minutes and the whole of their cooking time or they are dangerous to your health.
- The cooking time can be reduced by using a pressure cooker.
- Being organised helps. If you cook extra each time you can freeze the balance, turning it into a real convenience food.
- There is also a 'soak and boil' method that can be used to save time for most pulses. (See the next chapter.)
- Besides cooking, you can sprout pulses to make your salads more interesting – and nutritious.

- If you find pulses rather indigestible, you can lengthen the soaking and cooking time at home.

Bread

We eat less bread than we used to do, less than our neighbours in Europe, and less than we should for the sake of our health. The Italians and Germans top the bread-eating Euroleague, munching their way through almost twice as much as we do. On average, men in the UK eat seven slices of bread a day and women four. To meet the World Health Organization recommendation that we should get half our daily calories from complex carbohydrates, we need to double our intake.

Complex carbohydrates make up 43 per cent of a loaf of bread by weight. Bread is also an important source of protein – protein makes up about another 9 per cent. All bread also contains dietary fibre though there is much more in wholemeal than in white. Bread is low in fat and also has useful amounts of most B vitamins and a wide variety of minerals, including calcium and iron.

Wholemeal bread has some nutritional advantage over white because it is made from whole grain and so is richer in fibre. But eating plenty of any kind of bread is good for you. Since 1953 brown and white flours have, by law, had thiamine, niacin, iron and calcium added, so white and brown loaves do as well as wholemeal on all these nutrients except calcium, where they score almost twice as well.

Bread need not be boring. There are around 70 varieties on sale in the UK, with such favourites as the baguette and pitta and nan now joined by more trendy newcomers such as ciabatta (which is Italian for old slipper). Around a thousand in-store bakeries in supermarkets offer a range of breads, some of which are made on the premises and many finished from half-baked frozen dough delivered to the store. Bread made from frozen dough is generally good, though the crust may be a little tougher than on a bread baked from a fresh dough.

Fresh bread has the advantage that it doesn't really need butter or other spread. Or, if you do use it, you can spread it more thinly. Warming bread for just a few seconds in the microwave makes it seem fresher, but don't overdo it or the bread will become too warm – and as soon as it cools will be much staler than before because it will have dried out even more. You can also freshen bread by giving it a few minutes in a hot oven.

Wholemeal bread costs about 12p a loaf more than white. It needs more expensive higher-gluten flour to rise and less is sold, so there are fewer economies of scale. Retailers can negotiate very low prices for wrapped sliced white bread because it is an over-supplied market and they use it as a 'loss leader' anyway, accepting lower profit margins.

Cereals

The inhabitants of the UK are among the world's biggest cereal-eaters. On average, we chomp our way through 17 boxes a year – which is good news . . . and bad.

Some of us are doing more than our share on the breakfast statistics front, since more than one person in four in the UK still leaves home without having had breakfast in the morning. It's a poor strategy. A number of studies have found performance of students and schoolchildren better if they have had breakfast than if they have not. And skipping the first meal of the day often leads to mid-morning temptation to sticky buns, cakes and pastries.

A bowl of cereal, low-fat milk, and a glass of fruit juice in the mornings can make a real contribution to healthy eating – but only if the cereal is chosen with care, a choice made harder by the constantly proliferating number on the market. It is worth it. A cereal breakfast can be a meal rich in fibre, vitamins and minerals and low in fat. But a bowl of some cereals can start the day with as much fat as a couple of fried eggs and more sugar than a tube of fruit gums, for example. Some have as much sugar and less fibre than you would get from eating three gingernut biscuits. Some also score badly on salt. And the added sugar and salt figures on the packet don't include sugar or salt in ingredients like dried fruit or nuts, so you have to make a mental adjustment for that. It would be far more helpful if they did.

One more word of caution. Even where the manufacturer has

provided all the nutritional information you need, don't trust the suggested serving size. *Which? way to Health* looked at the serving sizes suggested on the packets for four breakfasts, including cornflakes and muesli, and compared them with the sizes measured by the Ministry of Agriculture, Fisheries and Food and with what W?wtH staff actually ate themselves, and found the Ministry figures were always higher than the manufacturers' and the staff breakfasts mostly higher still. While that might be good news if you are totting up, say, the percentage of your daily requirement of a particular vitamin that your breakfast is supplying, it can further mislead the unwary about how much fat, sugar or salt they are getting in a day.

Cereals are basically a grain – wheat, maize (corn), rice or oats – processed to turn it into flakes or puffs or whatever. That processing makes little difference to the nutritional content of the final product. Whether the cereal was made with whole or refined grains does make a difference. So do the proportions of other ingredients such as fruit, nuts, salt and sugar, and some manufacturers also add vitamins and minerals to their products.

There are more than 200 cereals on the shelves and the range keeps changing. In addition, the manufacturers can and do change the composition of existing lines without changing the name, so you should check each time before you buy.

What you need to look for are:

- A good fibre intake of at least 2g a serving. Generally, cornflakes, puffed rice and a lot of cereals aimed at children have less than 1g in fibre, while bran flakes, sultana flakes and 'fruit and fibre' type cereals have more than 3g. Muesli usually has more.
- It's much better to eat a high-fibre breakfast cereal than to add raw wheat bran to boost fibre intake. Neat bran is high in phytates, compounds which interfere with the absorption of iron, zinc and calcium. Phytates are destroyed by heating during the manufacture of cereals.
- Oat bran does not contain phytates and experts now agree that soluble oat bran can help people with high blood cholesterol to lower it.
- Less than 5g (one teaspoonful) of sugar, or 10g if the cereal

includes dried fruit. The sugar in dried fruit is less of a problem. Good, old-fashioned porridge has no sugar, unless you add it after cooking, or salt.

- At the other end of the scale, a pair of Kellogg's popular and child-friendly Pop-tarts for breakfast would start your day with a massive 34g of sugar, more than half of all you should have in a day. They are also high on salt (400g of sodium) and fat (12g).
- Most wheatflakes are low in sugar and salt and provide more than a sixth of a healthy daily fibre intake, but check because you can find wheatflakes with three times as much sugar and twice as much salt as the rest.
- Less than 500mg of sodium per 100g. Shredded bran-type cereals such as All Bran are the saltiest, providing at least a sixth of the daily average healthy salt limit in a single serving. Shredded wheat and mini wheats do exceptionally well on salt as well as fibre and sugar. Weetabix scores equally well for sugar but has more than seven times as much salt as them.
- Low-fat. Fat tends to be a problem, especially with some mueslis, granolas and crunchy oat cereals made by roasting rolled oats in a mixture of sugar and oil. Muesli fat comes mostly from nuts and is mainly polyunsaturated. In some crunchy oat cereals most of the fat is saturated. One has coconut oil (see caution under oils above) as its second biggest ingredient. The best mueslis are very high in fibre (with as much as 9g in a 70g serving) and very low in salt (as little as 20g of sodium), and with fat between about 4 and 5g a serving.
- Swiss-style mueslis are made with dried skimmed milk or whey powder so tend to be more powdery. They also tend to be lower in fibre and sweeter than other mueslis. The healthiest versions have no added sugar or salt.
- Read critically the information on cereals aimed at slimmers. For example, plain puffed wheat comes in with a low calorie content per serving because it's so light and you can't fit much (by weight) in a bowl.

Milk

Milk and milk products are a major source of calcium. Until the early 1980s they had had a very good press. Then, growing awareness of the hazards of too much fat forced nutritionists to have second thoughts and gave the industry something of a headache. The milk men fought back by attacking the fat and coming up with the generally healthier skimmed and semi-skimmed. Today, 98 per cent of families in the UK buy milk. Milk is good but not essential for healthy eating. People who don't like it or are allergic to or intolerant of it can devise perfectly healthy diets without it.

Nevertheless, nutrient-dense milk is useful for children, especially for babies and at times of rapid growth, and for teenagers whose bones grow rapidly. Women can use it to ensure that they have enough calcium for themselves and their babies during pregnancy and while they are breast-feeding, and again during and after the menopause when calcium may help delay the onset of osteoporosis. Milk is also particularly useful for the elderly, especially if they are finding that they are eating less, and vegetarians, who must ensure that they make up for the vitamin B12 they don't get in meat.

There has never been so much choice in the range of milks. So what is the difference between them and who should drink which?

Pasteurised   Milk that has been heated to 72°C for at least 15 seconds to kill harmful bacteria.

Sterilised   Heated much further – to 130°C for 10–30 minutes, which destroys most bacteria and other micro-organisms, so it can be kept unopened for several months. The appearance and flavour are changed and some of the thiamin, vitamin C, folic acid and B12 are destroyed. (Its slightly caramelised taste makes it good for rice and other milk puddings.)

UHT   A better taste option if you want a long-life milk that seems more like fresh. It is heated to 132°C for a short time and packed in sterile conditions. (Sterilised and UHT milks are both available in whole, semi-skimmed and skimmed versions.)

Whole milk   Has a fat content of 23g a pint. Drinking it can add a lot of fat and saturated fats to your diet, but it is good for children under two, and for children between two and five who don't eat a good balanced diet, for very active people such as athletes and anyone who is eating very little.

Semi-skimmed milk   Has 10g of fat a pint, but similar amounts of other nutrients. Good for children of two and over, teenagers and adults.

Skimmed milk   Has only 0.6g of fat a pint. It tastes thinner, and if you change to it straight from whole milk it takes time to get used to it. The difference is less noticeable in soups, hot drinks and sauces than on cereals or when drunk neat. It has more calcium than whole milk but is low on vitamins A and D. Good for adults who drink a lot of milk and anyone worried about his or her weight.

Channel Islands milk   Produced by Jersey and Guernsey cows; has an even higher fat content than whole or full-fat milk – 30g a pint. Good for people recovering from illness.

Homogenised milk   The fat globules (cream) are dispersed through the milk so it is easier to digest.

Breakfast milk   Homogenised Channel Islands milk. Good for everyone who, like some elderly people, find ordinary milk hard to digest.

Calcium-enriched milk   Can be skimmed or semi-skimmed and has extra calcium and skimmed milk powder which gives it extra body. Good for teenagers and elderly people who don't drink much milk.

Vitamin-enriched milks   Are produced when vitamins A and D are added back to skimmed and semi-skimmed milk to replace the fat-soluble vitamins A and D removed with the fat. Good for anyone bedridden who may go short on vitamin D (of which sunshine is the main source).

Green top or raw milk   Untreated milk. How safe it is depends on whether the cows from which it is taken are infected with food poisoning bacteria and how good hygiene is in the dairy. (Milk and milk products were found guilty of 136 outbreaks of food poisoning, affecting 4,313 people and killing 14, in England and Wales in the 1980s. About two-thirds of the outbreaks were Salmonellas and most of the rest Campylobacters – explained further in **Chapter 6**. Untreated milk was involved in 80 per cent of the outbreaks.)

Standardised milk   Introduced in 1993. Instead of a fat content that varies in the UK between 3.9 and 4 per cent, according to the season, it is standardised, like most of Europe's, at 3.5 per cent all year.

Bio-milk   Also new. Live bacterial cultures like Acidophilus and Bifidus found in live yogurt are added. They are claimed to aid digestion, but if the milk is heated or added to hot drinks, the live cultures are destroyed.

Fibre milk   Semi-skimmed milk with added fibre, which other milk lacks.

Organic milk   Comes from cows that graze freely on land subjected to no chemical treatments.

Dried skimmed milk   The dry residue when milk first has its fat skimmed off and then its water evaporated. It may have vegetable fat added for drying which increases both fat and calorie content. Vitamins A and D are usually added to make up for processing losses and there may be sugar and other additives as well.

Evaporated milk   Is concentrated to about half its original volume and then sterilised in the can. Some of the thiamin and vitamin C are lost but the milk is fortified with vitamin D. A 'light' version has half the fat. (See the next chapter for fatbusting uses of evaporated milk.)

Condensed milk   Similar to evaporated but with added sugar. It is lower in fat than cream, but the added sugar makes it higher in calories. Available made from whole or skimmed milk.

Flavoured milk drinks   Usually made from semi-skimmed milk and flavourings and sugar. Can be a useful lunchbox option.

Canned milk   Sterilised semi-skimmed milk in a can. Good as an alternative to sugary soft drinks.

Baby milk powders   Based on cow's milk but modified to be closer in composition to breast milk. The only milk suitable for babies up to six months old.

Soya milk   One of various milk substitutes for people who are allergic to cow's milk or react adversely to lactose, the sugar in cow's milk. It is made from soya beans, differs in composition from cow's milk and is less nutritious. There is less calcium, and little vitamin D or vitamin B12, though soya milk is sometimes fortified with these nutrients. Available sweetened and unsweetened, plain and flavoured, but people allergic to cow's milk may also be allergic to soya milk.

Goat's milk   Similar in fat content to whole cow's milk. Some people find it more digestible than cow's milk, though, because it is naturally homogenised.

Sheep's milk   Higher in fat than cow's milk and used mainly for making yogurt and cheese.

Dairy produce

Dairy produce, being made from milk, can provide a similar range of nutrients, but the fat levels vary enormously. The options are:

Hard cheeses   Usually made from whole milk and therefore high in fat. Reduced- and half-fat cheeses are made from skimmed milk and contain up to half the fat. Hard cheeses are good for calcium, vitamin A and B12 and may protect against dental caries (tooth decay) when eaten at the end of a meal.

Soft cheeses Vary widely, depending on the type of milk or cream from which they are made. Lower-fat options include cottage cheese at 1.5 to 4 per cent fat.

Medium-fat soft cheeses Those such as Philadelphia Light have about 15 per cent fat; a 4-oz portion will give you about a fifth of the calcium that most people need in a day.

Fromage frais Made from fermented skimmed milk so it is low in fat. Unflavoured fromage frais is a great low-fat cream substitute. You can cook with it or serve it with fruit or puddings. It is a reasonable source of calcium, vitamin A and riboflavin and a very good one for the elusive B12.

Quark Also made from skimmed milk, though cream is sometimes added to improve flavour and texture, so fat varies from 5 to 10 or 12 per cent. Usually used in savoury dishes. Just two tablespoonsful of it will give you about a quarter of your riboflavin and folate needs for a day and almost half the B12 and almost a fifth of the calcium you need.

Yogurt Made by adding a bacteria culture to boiled milk and keeping it warm for several hours while the bacteria multiply and turn the lactose to lactic acid, which partially curdles the milk, preserving and thickening it. People with poor lactose tolerance may find yogurt suits them better, probably because the thicker curd is held longer in the stomach. Yogurt can be made from whole or lower-fat milk and the luxury yogurts usually have added cream, so the fat content range is wide – from about 1 to 10 per cent. All are reasonably good sources of calcium and riboflavin. The consistency can be anywhere from the liquid of drinking yogurts to quite firm 'set' yogurts.

Smatana Made from cultured milk. At 10 per cent fat it is a good substitute for sour cream, which has twice as much.

Buttermilk Used to be the liquid left after butter-making. Today's buttermilk is a similar culture-soured skimmed milk product. It has virtually no fat, as much calcium as milk, and can replace milk or yogurt in recipes for scones, muffins and soda bread.

Cream   The part of milk that's rich in fat. It can be from 13 per cent fat (half fat) up to 64 (clotted). If you use cream, buy single or half rather than double or whipping. Extra thick creams can also have a role in reducing fat in our diets. Double and single creams are available in extra thick versions, made by homogenising to break up the fat globules and give a thicker, more even texture. Thickening makes single cream seem like double and double acquire a spreadable texture similar to clotted. Both single and double are suitable for spooning, cooking and pouring but not for whipping. You can cut fat further without calcium loss by substituting fromage frais, quark, yogurt or smatana. But read the labels on **synthetic creams** like Elmlea. They can be almost as high in fat and calories as real cream but provide less calcium.

Storing food

Storing food carefully is just as important for a healthy diet as choosing it well. It affects its nutritional value by the time you cook and serve it. It can even determine whether it is still safe to eat, or has been turned into a danger to you and your family. In **Chapter 6** you will find information on storage hazards and best practice that starts right from the moment you begin to unpack your shopping bags.

ONE LAST WORD

If you are dissatisfied with or concerned about any product you buy, first take it up with the shop where you bought it, who is responsible to you. But you should also find on the food label the name and address of the maker, packer or seller.

Your local Trading Standards Department is responsible for enforcing food labelling laws.

CHAPTER 4

HEALTHY COOKING

ONCE you have begun to change the way you shop, the next step on the road to healthy eating is to look again at the way you cook.

This is the crunch point. Any ingredient, no matter how healthy in itself, can be transmuted into negative health equity if it is mishandled in the kitchen. Any food, no matter how good for you, can be nutritionally neutered if it is subjected to the wrong treatment.

Conversely, small changes can have big benefits. The key to the assault on unhealthy cooking that this chapter outlines is simply this: there are many ways most of us can change our cooking that will make it healthier. If we know what they are we are then free to weigh up our preferences, priorities, fears and family histories, to measure what we do now against the healthy eating guidelines (see **Chapter 1**) – and to decide which of the changes are the most useful and least painful ones for us. And we will know how to make sure we don't unwittingly squander any of the nutritional value of the foods we buy. We will be able to decide how we want to stack the odds in favour of good health for ourselves and our families in the way that best suits us.

The suggestions in this chapter are based on ways to cut the fat (especially saturates) in our diet, get our energy increasingly from complex carbohydrates, and ensure that we eat lots of fruit and vegetables and extract the maximum benefit from them – all in line with what the guidelines recommend. They are also designed to help keep our salt and sugar intakes down.

But do keep in mind that these suggestions about healthier methods of cooking and about how to use ingredients and to modify recipes in healthier ways are not meant to be an all-or-nothing prescription. They are intended to offer choices of different ways that different people might meet the guidelines, not to take options away. And they are by no means exhaustive – they are meant to help stimulate ideas of your own.

Be realistic

There are several further important considerations. First, the guidelines don't mean that we need to get every dish or every meal or every single day's eating exactly in line with the recommendations. You are doing fine if your average over several days gets it about right. Don't feel you have to live with a fork in one hand and a calculator in the other.

Secondly, don't feel pressured into making too many changes too quickly. It may well be counterproductive if you do. If it's all too much trouble or too restrictive or too 'anti-pleasure' you will probably give up and go back to your old ways before the week is over – or find yourself with a counter-revolution on your hands. You are more likely to make life-saving changes to last a lifetime if you feel your way gently into your new regime, giving yourself time to experiment and find what you can change easily and what you really don't want to give up. Another advantage of altering slowly is that you will give your tastes time to adapt. Make changes gradually and you will probably find that you will come to like high-fat, salty or over-sweet foods less and less.

And thirdly, it is probably a bad move to swear right off the foods you really like most, no matter how unhealthy they are. A strategy in which you permit them occasionally, and perhaps in smaller quantities than before, is more likely to succeed long-term.

Cooking methods

Grilling vs. frying

The conventional wisdom has been for years that healthy cooks grill, and when *Which? way to Health* magazine put it to the test in 1990 it proved to be true. But not all the results were exactly what you might have predicted.

In the trial middle-cut **bacon** rashers were grilled, fried and microwaved. When the bacon (minus its rind and the fat attached to it) was grilled under a hot grill on a rack which let fat drain away, more than a third of the fat dripped out. Predictably, it was the best way by far.

But, surprisingly, bacon fried in a quarter-inch of oil which was heated before the meat was added came second, with 20 per cent of fat lost. Shallow-frying that way was actually better than dry-frying in a non-stick pan with no fat (15 per cent lost) or with only a teaspoonful of hot oil (just 5 per cent). Putting bacon into a quarter-inch of cold oil got rid of 15 per cent, the same as no fat at all. It seems that putting the bacon in enough hot fat had the effect of making the bacon hotter, which in turn coaxed it to shed more of its own fat. But a little fat wasn't enough to make the same difference to the temperature at which the bacon cooked.

However, a rasher specially cut three-quarters of an inch thick for the test managed to lose 12 per cent of its own fat when it was cooked in a teaspoonful of oil because, being thicker, it was cooking for longer. So, the thicker the meat, the more fat it can shed dry-fried with just a little lubrication.

The experiment also established that microwaving bacon gave the most disappointing result of all. It lost only 1 per cent of its fat because it cooked too quickly to have time to shed more.

Which? way to Health tested methods of cooking **steak** and **mince** at the same time. Lean steak, grilled, fried in a little oil and stir-fried, all had about the same fat levels after as before cooking. But cooking eight different samples of supermarket minces by browning them in a pan without extra fat for five minutes and draining removed around 40 per cent of the original fat. So if you brown and then drain mince, you will end up with 40 per cent less fat than you started with.

If you are worried that grilling indoors or on the barbecue will leave **meat**, **poultry** or **fish** dry and boring, you can marinate it in advance for tenderness and added flavour with ingredients such as yogurt, fruit juice, wine, vinegar, soy sauce or the more elegant naturally fermented Japanese 'soy' (called shoyu or tamari), with or without a little honey, garlic and ginger. Oil, though often used in marinades, is not essential. And you can baste during grilling with more of the marinade to counteract moisture loss.

To sum up:

♥ Healthy fat savings can be made by the way you cook.
♥ Grilling bacon on a grill rack was a winner.
♥ If you shallow-fry, having the oil hot matters more than how much fat or oil you put in the pan.
♥ Reducing the fat in bacon is not one of the things a microwave does well.

BETTER BURGERS

Use 500g/1lb of the leanest mince you can find and mix in about 125g/4oz each of fresh wholemeal breadcrumbs or cooked bulgar (buckwheat) and scrubbed or peeled and grated carrots, a small grated onion, a beaten egg, and a handful of chopped parsley or a teaspoonful of the herb or spice of your choice. You might like to add a little finely chopped chilli or a pinch of chilli powder, a dash of Tabasco, a little cumin, or a touch of curry powder.

You can either flavour only what you are using immediately and freeze the rest to ring the changes later, or you can season it all and, when you have shaped it into patties, freeze for later those you don't want to use immediately. (Or you can leave out the breadcrumbs, and use soya meat mince substitute instead of some or all of the meat.)

To cook, grill on a rack for about eight minutes a side. Absorb as much surface fat as you can on kitchen paper before you serve.

Serve on wholemeal buns or bagels with lettuce, tomato and onion rings and mustard or perhaps a dollop of almost fat-free mayonnaise.

♥ Use kitchen paper to remove fat surface grease after cooking.
♥ There's nothing to choose between grilling, frying and stir-frying lean steak – and little fat to lose either.
♥ Mince is a different story. Brown in a dry pan for five minutes and drain, using the lid as a strainer before you carry on as usual – you will save a useful 40 per cent of fat.
♥ Marinate food for grilling for 1–24 hours in a glass or unchipped enamel bowl for extra flavour and tenderness.

Dry-frying

If dry-frying has limitations for cooking meat like bacon, where the healthy aim is to coax it to shed its own fat, dry-frying can come into its own for ingredients like breasts of chicken and turkey which have little fat of their own. Try removing the skin, dredging in flour, and browning on a heavy pre-heated dry pan.

Deep-frying

Deep-frying doesn't win a lot of prizes in the healthy eating stakes, but there are ways to make it less unhealthy.

Putting the food into the fat at the right temperature is important. Too hot and it can burn on the outside while it is still raw inside. Not hot enough, and it will absorb more oil than it needs and become soggy. At the right temperature the food will seal quickly on the outside and then steam in its own moisture, so taking up the minimum of fat.

Getting the temperature right depends on both the equipment you use and the oil. Ideal is an electric, thermostatically controlled deep-fryer, but you can use a deep saucepan with a frying basket. If you have no thermostat, a thermometer is useful to check the temperature. Failing that, you can test the temperature of the oil by seeing how long it takes to make a one-inch cube of bread brown and crisp. At 180°C (350°F) it will take 60 seconds, at 190°C (375°F) 40 seconds, and at 200°C (400°F) 20 seconds.

The temperature to aim for varies with the food being cooked but it is usually at least 200°C (400°F), which means you need an oil with a smoking temperature of at least that. Both sunflower and corn oils have high smoking temperatures. Groundnut is good, too. And they are all low in saturated fats, for damage limitation.

Polyunsaturated oils deteriorate with prolonged heating to produce oxidised fats. In large enough quantities, they are thought to cause the damage to the cells of the body which may be the start of coronary heart disease, cancer and premature ageing. As yet, no one knows the level at which oxidised fat becomes toxic and most authorities think over-used fat would become rancid and be thrown out because of its unpleasant taste before it became dangerous. But, if you want to be ultra-cautious, you might want to avoid re-using oil for frying. Or you might see it as yet one more reason to limit the amount of fried food in your diet.

Many families would happily renounce deep-frying forever except for one thing – chips. Lowest in fat are oven chips, but if you do deep-fry ordinary chips then chunky ones with straight sides are healthier than the slimline and crinkly types because there is less surface area to soak up fat. However you make chips, they probably retain more vitamin C than boiled potato does.

CHUNKY CHIPS

Cut potatoes into slices about ¾-inch wide and then cut the slices lengthways into ½-inch strips. Soak in cold water to get rid of excess starch, drain and dry well. Heat oil to 180°C (350°F) and lower a layer of chips into the basket. Cook for 4–5 minutes until they are cooked and look pale golden. Take them out and drain well. Cook more batches as required. Just before serving, heat the oil again to 200°C (400°F) and put all the chips back to fry again for another 1–2 minutes, until they are crisp and golden brown. Drain well again in the basket and then on absorbent kitchen paper. If you like, try sprinkling with herbs and pepper instead of salt.

Here are some more tips to make deep-frying less unhealthy than it would otherwise be:

♥ Deep-fry a little at a time – adding too much too quickly brings the temperature down.
♥ Let oil heat up again between batches.
♥ Avoid blended vegetable oils – they often contain some coconut or palm oil, which are particularly high in saturates.
♥ Never more than half-fill the pan with oil.
♥ Cook food in even-sized pieces so that they are ready at the same time.
♥ Drain well in a basket or a slotted spoon and then again on kitchen paper.
♥ Discard oil if it looks dark or thick or smells unpleasant.
♥ To re-use oil, strain it through a metal sieve into a clean saucepan and leave it to cool before you pour it back in the bottle.
♥ A slight blue haze rising from the surface of hot oil is a warning that it is getting very hot. First, it will break down to form acrolein (which is indigestible and has an unpleasantly acrid smell), then it will catch fire.
♥ Never leave food that is being deep-fried unattended.

Stir-frying

Stir-frying is suitable for poultry, seafood, meat, vegetables and tofu. It is done by using a very small amount of fat, heating it to a high temperature, and sealing the food quickly in it. Food stir-fried correctly absorbs little fat because the outside is sealed at the start, and the food is then partly steamed in its own moisture. The speed of cooking minimises the loss of vitamins and minerals.

The basic rules are:

♥ A wok is a good shape for stir-frying but not essential – any large pan can be used.
♥ Prepare all the ingredients before you start, cutting each into reasonably uniform shapes and sizes.
♥ Make sure the fat is really hot before you start frying.

♥ Add ingredients one at a time, starting with whatever needs the longest cooking time and ending with the one that needs the least.

♥ Keep it all moving in the wok until it is cooked, and serve quickly.

♥ Vegetables should be still al dente.

♥ A meal in a wok, prepared in just minutes, can meet the healthy eating guidelines if you use very little fat, a small amount of protein (such as chicken or tofu) and lots of vegetables, and add some cooked noodles right at the end to provide carbohydrate.

♥ To give the tofu a real taste lift, try marinating it in ginger, garlic, wine and a little soy or shoyu before you cook (or use ready-smoked tofu).

♥ Go easy with the soy, or you will overdo the salt.

Baking and roasting

Roasting can be a healthy way to cook if **meat** or **poultry** is put on a rack over water so the fat can drain off and if you don't baste to put the fat back. Unfortunately, this method works best for quick-roasting at high temperatures, suitable only for the best and most expensive cuts.

Slower roasting at lower heat is more suitable for less tender cuts but does tend to encourage the meat to dry out more if it is done without basting. One solution is to make a foil cover for the roasting pan so the natural water content of the meat is kept inside it and helps keep the meat moist (a bit like pot-roasting). If you do it this way, uncover towards the end of cooking to allow the meat to brown. (The tent will also keep the inside of the cooker cleaner than if you let fat spatter.)

Wrapping meat or poultry in a foil parcel or using a roasting bag is equally helpful for keeping the oven clean but less good for encouraging the fat that does come out to stay out.

On the other hand, making a foil parcel, perhaps with some onion and lemon juice or a splash of wine, can keep **fish**, which has no fat, or skinned chicken, which has little, from becoming dry. Fish can be baked whole and fish steaks, cutlets and so on can be cooked in stock or wine and herbs in a baking dish, with a lid or covered with foil to minimise the time it takes.

Skinned chicken breasts or other chicken pieces can be dredged in seasoned flour and baked in a single layer in a baking tin in the oven.

As well, it helps to know:

♥ Meat and especially poultry should be thawed completely if it has been in the freezer before going in the oven.
♥ Meat and poultry should be left out of the fridge for about an hour to come to room temperature before you start to cook them.
♥ Pricking thoroughly the skin of ducks and geese persuades them to shed so much fat that they can be cooked at high temperatures with no basting or covering at all, and with no drying out.
♥ Pricking turkey skin also reduces the fat in the final dish. Put some water in the tin under the turkey and cover it with foil to prevent it drying out too much.
♥ Leaving the skin on chicken during roasting keeps it moist, but you can reduce the fat if you discard the skin before serving.
♥ If your oven has a spit use it as a healthy way to roast. It allows fat to run off while basting the revolving meat in its own juices.
♥ Pork will be less fatty if you trim all the visible fat off before you start and replace it with a coating of herbs and bread-crumbs seasoned with mustard.
♥ It pays to remove as much fat as possible from the roasting tin before you make gravy in it with (defatted) stock, vegetable cooking water and/or wine.
♥ A jug or gravy boat with two spouts opposite one another helps. One spout starts deeper down into the liquid than the other. Serve the gravy through the deeper one for minimum fat – this settles at the top and can be poured off through the other.

Casseroling and stewing

The cheaper, tougher cuts of meat are better put into casseroles or stews to make them tender and allow their flavours to develop.

123

To make them healthier:

- ♥ Use less meat but double the quantity of vegetables.
- ♥ Or replace some of the meat with pulses.
- ♥ Trim all visible fat from the meat before you start and take skin off chicken.
- ♥ A lot of recipes work just as well if you don't brown the ingredients in fat before you start. Just put everything in the pot together, in layers, from cold.
- ♥ You can soften onion in a little stock or wine or even water, rather than frying it.
- ♥ If you do brown the meat first, make sure your fat is hot before you put anything in it so that it seals the surfaces.
- ♥ Brown a little at a time. Too much will bring down the temperature of the fat too much.
- ♥ When you finish browning, either lift the ingredients out and start again with a clean pot or drain off as much fat as you can before you add the cooking liquid.
- ♥ If you are using home-made stock, make sure you have got rid of as much fat as possible by putting it in the fridge until the fat sets on top and then discarding it. (Keep stock in the fridge for up to three days, or a week if you strain and degrease it, and boil for two minutes every second day. Or freeze stock for up to two months.)
- ♥ Make casseroles or stews at least hours, even a day, ahead and cool them right down, so that you can get rid of the fat that will set on the surface. It will also give flavours time to develop and blend.

Steaming

Vegetables, fish and grains can be steamed in a specially designed double boiler, or a metal vegetable steamer, or an improvised arrangement of a trivet in a saucepan, or a metal basket or plate over a pan of boiling water, or a bamboo Chinese steamer. Whichever way, you need a tight-fitting lid to stop steam escaping – if you are improvising, aluminium foil can be a help.

An excellent way to steam **fish** is on a plate resting on a bamboo rack or trivet in a wok with a little water in it. Before you put the lid on, make sure the water is not deep enough to splash on to the plate when it bubbles, or you will be boiling rather than steaming. The fresher the fish for this, the more delicious the result.

Steaming **vegetables** preserves their flavour and colour beautifully. Put only an inch of water in the pan – a tight lid and a close eye are needed to make sure it does not boil dry. Take them off the heat while they are still crunchy. They not only taste better but are more filling and lose less of their nutritional value that way.

You can steam **rice** to retain more B vitamins than boiling does in either a tiered bamboo steamer, or a rice ball suspended from the saucepan's handle to float in boiling water. **Bulgar wheat** (processed cracked wheat) needs to be soaked before steaming and **couscous**, a semolina-type grain used in North African cooking, is traditionally steamed over, and flavoured by, the stew with which it is to be eaten.

Wine or stock can be used or added to water to give steamed food extra taste. Or try herbs or a little ginger in the water under vegetables to give them a subtle hint of additional interest.

Poaching

Poaching is one way of cooking poultry, fish and fruit without adding fat and without drying them out. A bonus is that when the poaching liquid is part of the final dish none of the nutrients are lost.

Large fish like whole salmon are usually poached in an oblong fish kettle with a lid, in either a stock made with fish trimmings or a court-bouillon of wine, vinegar, cider or lemon juice flavoured with finely chopped vegetables, herbs and peppercorns. Pieces of fish can be poached similarly in a frying-pan. Smoked haddock poaches deliciously with just water in the pan. (Serve topped with an egg poached in the same water after it.)

Chicken poached in water with added vegetables, herbs and peppercorns gives lovely moist flesh, particularly good for serving cold. Unlike roast chicken, the skin is unappetising enough not to be much of a temptation. The broth in which the chicken has been cooked makes good stock or soup and can be quite low in fat as long as you cool it right down and take off the fat that settles on the top before using it.

A **poached egg** for breakfast given you much less fat than a fried one.

Boiling

Boiling vegetables leaches out some of the vitamins, particularly the B and C vitamins, and transfers them to the cooking water. The shorter the cooking time, the less the loss – so crunchy beats soggy for nutritional value. Don't add salt to the cooking water – vegetables take longer to cook if you do.

Frozen vegetables should go straight into boiling water from the freezer. Cooking times are still shorter than for fresh. The instructions on the packet give an indication – some manufacturers now give a choice of times for crunchy or well done. Crunchy is healthier. If two times are not suggested, try giving the vegetables less time than the packet says.

You will also minimise vitamin loss if you:

- Keep vegetables chilled until you are going to prepare – the enzymes that attack the vitamins in fruit and vegetables thrive at room temperature.
- Don't cut or shred until the last minute and work quickly to minimise exposure to light and air.
- Don't cut or shred vegetables any smaller than you have to.
- Don't pre-soak vegetables.
- Always bring water to the boil before adding vegetables: the heat destroys the enzymes which otherwise destroy the vitamins.
- Don't put bicarbonate of soda in the cooking water: it helps destroy vitamin C and several B vitamins.
- For a big batch of vegetables, add them to the water a little at a time so it barely goes off the boil.
- Use less water – a heavy-based saucepan with a well-fitting lid means you can cook by half-boiling, half-steaming in a very little water without risking burning.

- Recycle rather than waste nutrients by using vegetable cooking water in soup, sauces or gravy.
- Use a tight-fitting lid to speed up cooking time.
- Serve as soon as you can: keeping food warm destroys vitamins – after several hours three-quarters would be lost.

Pulses

The easy way to prepare pulses (dried beans, peas and lentils) is to open a can. If you cook them yourself, a pressure cooker (see below) makes it much quicker. Otherwise, most pulses need lengthy boiling and some need lengthy soaking beforehand as well. A few respond to soaking in boiling water for 30 minutes instead of cold water for eight hours or so, and then cooking for 20–30 minutes instead of up to two hours. The chart shows which works for what.

The chart also draws attention to a **serious hazard** in cooking some pulses. Beans in the **kidney bean** family contain a toxin called haemagglutonin which causes gastroenteritis and even death if it is not destroyed in cooking. So these beans must be boiled rapidly for 10–15 minutes first to get rid of the toxins. **Soya beans** contain trypsin-inhibitor, which must also be destroyed in cooking, this time by keeping a rapid boil going for the first hour, or it will prevent the body from absorbing protein.

Some nutritionists recommend rapid boiling for all beans and peas because there is a slight suspicion that other pulses may contain toxins, too. This is probably not necessary, but you may wish to do so to be on the safe side.

After the rapid boiling, reduce the heat and leave the pan to simmer, partly covered, for another 30–50 minutes, or another hour or more for soya beans.

When you are cooking pulses:

- Never add salt to the cooking liquid because it increases the cooking time and makes the skins tough.
- They are done when they retain their shape but have a floury consistency inside.
- Lentils, which don't need soaking, are cooked when they become soft and mushy.

Pulses – cooking times

The chart shows suggested cooking times. These will vary depending on how old the pulses are, and how soft you want them.

	Soaking [1]	Cooking time (mins)	Rapid boil? [1]
Aduki beans	yes	1 hr	yes
Black-eyed beans	yes	40–50	
Broad beans	12 hrs	1 hr	
Butter beans	yes	50–60	
Flageolet beans	yes	40–50	yes
Haricot beans	yes	50–60	yes
Mung beans	no	30–40	
Pinto beans	yes	50–60	
Kidney beans	yes	50–60	yes
Soya beans	12 hrs	2 hrs	yes
Chick peas	yes	40–50	
Split peas	no [2]	35–40	no
Green lentils	no	30–40	no
Brown lentils	no	40	no
Red split lentils	no [3]	40	no

[1] the table shows where 8-hour soaking or 10–15 minutes' rapid boiling is advisable, and when it is not necessary; where no entry is given, rapid boiling is optional
[2] alternatively, soak in boiling hot water for 30 minutes and reduce cooking time to 30 minutes
[3] alternatively, soak in boiling hot water for 30 minutes and reduce cooking time to 20–30 minutes

- If you are finding pulses indigestible, increase the soaking and cooking time. Or try canned ones.
- Microwaves and slow-cookers are suitable only if the beans have had their first 10–15 minutes' conventional cooking.
- It is always worth cooking more pulses than you want for immediate use. Drained and cooked pulses keep in the freezer for 3–4 months or in airtight containers in the fridge for up to three days.

- Using a pressure cooker speeds up the process and does away with the need for rapid boiling at the start, because it cooks the pulses at a higher temperature.

Pressure cooking

Pressure cookers have rather gone out of fashion as family labour-savers. With the advent of freezers, the pressure cooker's ability to turn storecupboard ingredients into quick meals is less valued than it used to be, just as the microwave has usurped it as champion of speed. But pressure cookers do still have a contribution to make to healthy – and convenient – cooking.

The temperature at which liquids boil is determined by the atmospheric pressure. Pressure cooker lids have a seal which keeps in the steam when liquid boils in them. The build-up of steam increases the pressure inside the cooker and so raises the boiling point of the liquid. It is the resulting higher temperature that speeds up cooking.

The health plus points of pressure cookers are:

- Shorter cooking time can mean that fewer nutrients are lost – though because pressure cookers accelerate cooking it is easy to overcook and destroy nutrients, too.
- The reduced cooking time can make it more practicable to cook (and freeze) your own healthy alternatives to meat such as pulses.
- Pressure cookers make home-made soup, which can be low-fat and highly nutritious, fast.
- They reduce the cooking time for stock from hours to less than an hour.
- They cook with less liquid and without added fat.
- Pressure cookers are also good for cooking dried fruits after a minimum of soaking, fresh fruits in their own juices, and milk puddings.

Microwaving

The microwave really comes into its own for fish, which it cooks without fat, and vegetables, which it cooks with a minimum of water, but with maximum flavour and nutritional value. Fish can stay beautiful moist if it is cooked correctly. Vegetables can be tender yet crisp and keep a bright, appetising colour. Fruit also keeps a better flavour, shape and colour when it is cooked by microwave.

Microwaves are under-used. Many families use them only to thaw and reheat, either because they don't realise what a healthy aid to delicious cooking the microwave can be or because they have tried, been disappointed and given up. Because some food is cooked so fast in them, it is easy to overcook and give microwaving an unfair assessment. A piece of fish overdone by just a couple of minutes, for example, can be tough, dry and tasteless enough to persuade you that the microwave will never be for you. But if you are prepared to read the makers' manual, weigh, watch and time you may be won over.

Microwaving is widely misunderstood. Many people still believe it is 'cooking from the inside out'. It isn't. The waves penetrate only a short way in from the surface of food and raise the temperature by agitating the water molecules in it until they 'boil'. So, in a sense, microwaved food is steamed food. Vegetables are cooked in a small amount (usually a few table-spoonsful) of water, which also produces steam. Beyond the point where the microwaves stop penetrating, the temperature can be raised only by conduction of heat. So, the more you give the process a helping hand by stirring and turning, the more even the result will be.

Dr Tom Saunders and Peter Bazalgette, authors of *The Food Revolution* (published by Bantam Press) compared samples of broccoli and potato raw and cooked them in six different ways to see how much vitamin C survived each method. The idea behind choosing vitamin C was that it is water-soluble, and therefore easily lost in cooking water. Its loss may reflect the loss of other water-soluble vitamins as well. The authors found that microwaving and steaming were the best methods and boiling the worst.

Microwaving also comes into its own for making delicious soup with a minimum of time and nutritional loss and a maximum of flavour. Like poaching, it has a way with cold chicken. It can produce chicken pieces with moist and succulent flesh, good for serving hot as well as in chicken salads and sandwiches. And, as with poached birds, the skin is less tempting than when it has been roasted, which is all to the good. But check carefully with a skewer through the thickest part to ensure they are cooked. And because of the risk of Salmonella *do not microwave whole birds.*

Cooking utensils

If you boil vegetables, it's best to use stainless steel or enamel pots (with the enamel surface undamaged). Copper and iron can help to destroy vitamin C.

Don't cook anything acidic – which usually means fruit or vinegar in the recipe – in copper. If you do, they will react with the copper to form salts that are poisonous. Acidic foods in aluminium will take up a little aluminium and those in iron will increase the iron content of whatever is cooking. Acidic food is best cooked in Pyrex, anodised aluminium, enamel, non-stick coated or stainless steel.

There is some link between aluminium and Alzheimer's disease, a form of dementia, but the relationship is not a straightforward one and there is no evidence that it is caused or exacerbated by aluminium in our diets. Nevertheless, some people are anxious to steer clear of it in food and use filters to avoid it in water.

Never use anything metallic in a microwave.

When raw scores

Fresh fruit and vegetables are best eaten raw because they have been exposed to a minimum of vitamin-thieving heat, light, oxygen and liquid. Adding fresh sprouted seeds (bought or home-sprouted) to salads, sandwiches and so on also increases your vitamin intake.

Sea vegetables like nori, wakame or dulse are also extremely rich sources of vitamins and can be added to salads, soups and so on. Health food shops sell them and they need only be soaked before using, though you can cook them if you prefer.

Ideally:

- Prepare fruit for serving or making a fruit salad at the last minute. Toss it in a little lemon juice to prevent oxidation of cut surfaces and eat at once if you can. If that isn't possible, keep the fruit covered in the fridge.
- A salad is best eaten as soon as it is made. If it has to wait, cover the bowl with a non-PVC clingfilm and store it in the fridge.

Cheerful changes

It is not only how and what you cook that determines how healthy a dish is. Even when you have chosen what dish you will prepare and what cooking method you will use, there is still plenty of scope for making your version healthier – often without sacrificing anything in taste or texture.

To get you thinking healthily, here are some ideas for substitutions that will usually make little or no difference to the flavour of the finished product, but will make a useful contribution to how healthy the dish is:

☺ Instead of cream, use low-fat yogurt, smatana, fromage frais, evaporated milk.

☺ Instead of sour cream, use low-fat yogurt, smatana or buttermilk.

☺ Instead of cream cheese, use lower-fat cream cheese or yogurt cheese. (See how to make this under **Nibbles and snacks** below.)

☺ Instead of butter in baking, use polyunsaturated (soft) margarine.

☺ Instead of butter on vegetables, use fresh herbs and/or a splash of lemon juice.

☺ Instead of fat in casseroles, use tomato puree, herbs and spices for added flavour.

☺ Instead of some of the flour and fat in pastry for savoury dishes, use mashed potato.

☺ Instead of at least some of the salt in dishes, use herbs.

☺ Instead of whole eggs in many recipes, you can use the same number of whites but fewer yolks (or fewer eggs).

☺ Instead of pork in recipes, use chicken.

☺ Instead of veal cutlets, use turkey.

☺ Instead of chicken stock, use fat-free vegetable stock made from assorted vegetables, including carrot and onion and a little bit of onion skin, herbs, pepper and (optional) garlic.

☺ Instead of whole milk in sauces, use semi-skimmed or skimmed milk or low-fat yogurt.

☺ Instead of the usual amount of sugar in home-made jams, use less (but you will need to store the jam in the fridge).

☺ Instead of some of the sugar in home-made chutney, use a minimum of cane or raw sugar and top up the sweetness with apple juice and dried fruit like dates, sultanas and raisins. (It will be ready to use after a couple of weeks rather than a couple of months, too.)

☺ Instead of water or wine in gravy, use the vegetable cooking water.

☺ Instead of automatically adding salt to your food, use your tastebuds to see if you really need it. Make it a habit to try first.

☺ Instead of accepting the high salt content of ham, bacon and salty fish, use cold water to soak it for 12 hours. Drain, put in a pan of cold water, bring to the boil and drain again.

Better breakfasts

If you have toast, wholemeal is better than brown and brown is better than white and thicker better than thinner. Spread with a thin scrape of a low-fat, high polyunsaturated spread rather than butter. If you have marmalade, don't be over-generous.

• Porridge made with skimmed or semi-skimmed milk is also a healthy breakfast choice and so are some cereals. There is more detailed information about their relative merits in **Chapter 3**. Or make porridge with water and reduce the fat even more.

• A glass of orange juice or a piece of fruit with cereal or a slice of toast is a good way to start the day.

• Another healthy option is fresh fruit with plain or flavoured low-fat fromage frais or yogurt on top.

- For a change try kedgeree or kippers for breakfast once in a while, or scrambled eggs, or mushrooms on toast.
- Reduce or cut out sugar from your tea and coffee.

Best-dressed salads

Home-made salad dressings often add an unhealthy dollop of fat to an otherwise extremely healthy eating choice. Here are some ways to make sure your dressings don't turn salad into a fat trap.

♥ When you do use an oil to make a dressing, avoid the ones that are high in saturates. Olive oil, high in monounsaturates, is a good choice for both health and taste. Walnut is high in polyunsaturates and hazelnut in monounsaturates and both add interesting and distinctive flavours to dressings. Or you can go for a high-polyunsaturated option like sunflower if you are looking for a neutral taste. (But if you are worried about your weight, don't forget that all oils contain the same calories.)

♥ Mayonnaise can be mixed with yogurt to make it a better choice.

♥ Low-fat salad dressings can be made by starting with low-fat

---

SALAD DRESSING FLAVOURINGS

● mustard ● herbs ● curry powder or paste ● minced onion ● crushed garlic ● a little soy or shoyu ● grated ginger ● a few chopped olives ● capers ● a little tahini (sesame paste) ● lemon juice (not recommended for yogurt alone – the taste's too acidic ● a little honey (especially if you find yogurt too acidic for your taste) ● an interesting vinegar – like a fruit- or herb-flavoured one, sherry or balsamic ● pepper ● horseradish ● a dash of Tabasco ● Worcestershire sauce ● a little chilli powder ● a pinch of cayenne ● turmeric ● celery seeds ● mustard seeds ● Marmite or Bovril yogurt, reduced fat or almost fat-free mayonnaise, or a mixture of mayonnaise and yogurt or fromage frais.

♥ Flavour with one or more of the ingredients suggested in the box.

♥ Low-fat or virtually no-fat fromage frais is also a good starting point for a healthy salad dressing. Give it bite with yogurt and vinegar or lemon juice, bulk with yogurt cheese (see below), seasoning with pepper and perhaps a pinch of salt, colour with tomato paste, and oomph from the list of flavourings in the box.

♥ Low-fat yogurt thinned with a little water and livened up with a vinegar (try sherry or balsamic) and a generous quantity of chopped herbs is a very healthy option.

♥ Any mayonnaise will coat a leafy salad better as well as being healthier if you thin it with tomato juice, skimmed milk, water or yogurt.

♥ Try the Thai way with a salad of uncooked or barely cooked crunchy vegetables. Start with a mixture of equal quantities of vinegar or lemon juice and Thai fish sauce (from oriental stores) to about twice the total quantity of water. Simmer together gently and briefly and then add finely chopped chilli and/or garlic to taste. (Discard the chilli seeds unless you like your flavours really fiery.)

♥ You can reduce the fat in vinaigrette by diluting it with a finely chopped tomato and giving it a quick whisk in a liquidiser, with or without an added pinch of cayenne.

♥ Or you can start with tomato juice, sharpen it with lemon or vinegar, give it an optional dash of oil for body, and flavour with herbs (basil and tomato have an affinity) or the flavourings of your choice from the list in the box. You might want a pinch of sugar with this one, too.

♥ Tofu liquidised with a little water and vinegar is a good mayonnaise-substitute base on which to build flavours. Turn to the box for ideas.

Be imaginative in what you put in your salads. Besides your usual items a wide range of raw or lightly cooked vegetables, such as broccoli, mushrooms and mange-tout as well as cold cooked pulses and sprouted seeds, can help make salads a more substantial part of a healthy eater's diet. Serve with (or include) bread, rice, bulgar wheat, lentils or mixed beans to increase your intake of complex carbohydrates and vitamins.

Healthy lunchboxes

Here are some useful items you might want to include in a healthy packed lunch.

- Sandwiches or filled rolls. Thick bread is better than thin. Or use bagels, pitta bread, pumpernickel, chapatis, crispbreads. Spread thinly with a low-fat spread or almost fat-free mayonnaise. Fill with chicken, cottage cheese, salad, half-fat hard cheese, tuna, sardines, raw vegetables, beansprouts, marinated or smoked tofu or tofu flavoured with curry (powder or paste) and mashed with onion, cucumber and shredded lettuce, mashed banana or peanut butter and jam or banana.
- Buns without icing, scones, tea-breads.
- Raw vegetables such as carrot or celery sticks or a vegetable salad.
- Rice or pasta salads.
- Pulse salads, for example kidney bean.
- Soup in a flask.
- Fresh fruit.
- Low-fat fruit yogurt or fromage frais.
- Fruit canned in juice.
- A small carton of unsweetened fruit juice.
- A flask of fruit juice diluted with water or mineral water.
- A flask of semi-skimmed milk, with or without flavouring.

Home-made muesli, date bars (and similar items) can also be excellent lunchbox additions if you go for recipes with mainly monounsaturated or polyunsaturated fat, and not too much of it, with other ingredients such as seeds (sunflower, sesame, pumpkin), porridge oats, dried fruit.

Health food shops can also be a source of delicious and nutritious snack bars but read the small print on the packets – they can be high in saturates and sugars.

Don't put nuts in lunchboxes. Owing to the number of

children who have choked on them, some schools have banned them.

Lots of the snacks below are also suitable for lunchboxes.

Nibbles and snacks

Some of the lunchbox suggestions above also have nibble and snack potential.

Bread is a good filler, especially for hungry children just home from school and scavenging for biscuits or cakes. Turn it into salad sandwiches with low-fat mayonnaise instead of butter; or cover a slice with a thin scraping of butter or polyunsaturated margarine or low-fat spread and Vegemite or Marmite; or smear bread with peanut butter or fruit turned into instant 'jam' in the blender; or toast it and top with baked beans or sardines or reduced-fat cheese.

Yogurt cream cheese or labna is delicious, is lower in fat than cream cheese and has a multitude of uses from child-friendly snacks to cocktail nibbles. It can be made by putting low-fat natural yogurt in a colander lined with damp muslin and letting it drain over a bowl somewhere cool for about six hours. The whey will drain off, leaving a soft, creamy cheese. Use it, seasoned or unseasoned, in sandwiches, soups, or as a simple snack or hors d'oeuvre rolled into small balls and coated with chopped fresh herbs (try dill, parsley, chives, tarragon or mint), perhaps with a pinch of paprika or cumin, a few olives and some pitta bread.

Use it (or half-fat cream cheese) spread on fresh or toasted bagel halves with mild (Spanish) raw onion, capers, smoked salmon pieces and a dash of lemon juice for a luxurious yet substantial snack. Cut each half into smaller pieces for a sophisticated hors d'oeuvre. A more workaday snack variation on the bagel and labna theme is to replace the smoked salmon and trimmings with lean ham, with or without mustard.

Yogurt cream cheese can also be flavoured with herbs or a spice or spices and served as a dip with raw vegetables or toasted pitta bread squares or melba toast or Scooples. These whole-meal crisps are a good base for snacks and nibbles because they are shaped like scoops with curved sides to hold a dip or filling.

They are also low in fat and high in flavour. Try them, too, with low-fat cottage cheese mixed with chopped raw onion and pineapple, or cottage cheese livened up with a little curry or chilli and a few prawns.

Fromage frais and tofu can also be flavoured as for salad dressings and used as dips. Just keep the consistency a little thicker.

BAGEL CHIPS

This recipe for bagel chips that contain no saturated fat is adapted from the excellent *Eater's Choice – a Food Lover's Guide to Lower Cholesterol* by Dr Ron Goor and Nancy Goor, published in the United States by Houghton Mifflin (for more information, see the **Sources and recommended reading** list at the back of the book).

Bagels (plain, onion, garlic etc.)

Flavour options
1 clove garlic
chilli powder
cinnamon and sugar
Cajun spice mix (combine: 1 teaspoon each of thyme and basil,
    ½ teaspoon onion powder, ¼ teaspoon salt [optional], ½ teaspoon
    cayenne pepper, ¼ teaspoon paprika, ½ teaspoon white pepper,
    ¼ teaspoon freshly ground black pepper)

Preheat the oven to 225°F (110°C, Gas Mark ¼).

Cut the bagels into ¼ to ⅜ inch thick slices. They will look like very thin bagels. (Halve or quarter slices if you want smaller bagel chips.) Place the pieces in a single layer on a baking sheet or tray.

Crush the garlic and spread it over the bagel slices, sprinkle chilli powder or spice mix over them or leave them plain. Or, for a sweet treat, sprinkle a mix of cinnamon and sugar on to plain or sweet (such as cinnamon and currant) bagels.

Bake for 1–2 hours.

You can turn **pitta bread strips or bagel slices** into 'crisps' for nibbles or dips by baking them in the oven.

Here are some more healthy suggestions for snacks and nibbles:

- Popcorn (as long as it is air-dried, not buttered or toffee'd).
- Pretzels for adults and children (but check the small print on the pack: the fat content varies, and they can be very salty, so you might want to brush some of the salt off the surface).
- Fruit is always a good choice if you feel empty between meals. So is dried fruit.
- Raw vegetables are good when you feel peckish. Keep some prepared in a plastic box in the refrigerator to make it more likely when you pick on impulse you will go for them, especially if you are a boredom nibbler with a weight problem.
- Roast chick peas.
- Apple Crackles, crunchy commercially dried apple slices packaged like bags of crisps.
- Bread sticks, wholegrain crackers, crispbreads, matzos, pumpernickel, or rice cakes dipped in or topped with low-fat options.
- Breakfast cereals with skimmed milk, chosen from the recommendations in the previous chapter.

Smarter starters

Soups, especially vegetable soups, can be delicious, nutritious and low-fat. They can be everything from openers for a dinner party to a good way to take the edge off ravenous family appetites at the start of a meal. You can base them on a degreased chicken stock or, for an even lower-fat version, on a home-made vegetable stock. Bought stock cubes tend to be high in salt. If you don't make your own stock, try using fewer cubes and compensating with extra herbs and spices.

To turn any soup into a healthy cream version, add silken tofu at the end, or serve it with yogurt or fromage frais stirred in the middle, or a blob of yogurt cheese (see above). Adding beans or serving with bread increases complex carbohydrates and fibre content.

Cold soups can be refreshing in hot weather, and a pleasantly light start to a dinner party. A dollop of yogurt swirled gently in the centre adds elegance.

Blinis (buckwheat flour pancakes) can be filled with low-fat yogurt or seasoned fromage frais or yogurt cheese (see above) and smoked salmon pieces or lumpfish roe.

Dips can also double as starters. There are suggestions for several under **Nibbles and snacks** above.

Melon with ginger, a splash of port or filled with other fresh fruits is an appetising way to get a meal under way.

Composing light salads for starters can exercise a cook's imagination – and delight family and guests. You can buy a wide variety of leaves but don't stop at those. Shredded smoked chicken (warmed in the microwave) adds sophistication. Lentils can absorb an interesting salad dressing brilliantly. A little well-grilled and drained chopped bacon adds interest. (Lentils and bacon go well together.) The possibilities are as limitless as your imagination. And don't forget the suggestions for healthier salad dressings earlier in the chapter.

Mainly main courses

The healthy eating guidelines urge us to rely more on complex carbohydrates and less on protein, so rice, pasta, bread and pulses should figure heavily in main courses.

- White rice, pasta and bread are good, but for fibre, vitamins and minerals brown is even better.
- Fun shapes can make pasta more attractive to young children.
- Pasta is healthiest served with tomato or other vegetable sauces. Olive oil is a good choice for making them but don't use much. Most recipes suggest more than is either necessary for a good flavour or healthy. You'll probably find that the older the recipe book, the more you can cut back on the quantities of oil it suggests.
- It is not only pasta sauce recipes that usually suggest far more oil than is really needed. Cut it down in curry recipes, too. You can cook the spices in much less oil than most recipes tell you – and get rid of any fat left on top of the finished dish.

- When you want to make a creamy pasta sauce without fat, use low-fat or virtually no-fat fromage frais. For example, add softened or browned chopped onion and chopped ham or bacon grilled to reduce its fat to cooked pasta, then stir in fromage frais (seasoned with pepper and a little salt if you think it needs it). Or invent your own variations.
- A tin of tuna can be turned into a quick, easy and nourishing storecupboard pasta sauce with onions, canned tomato and mashed anchovy, with or without a few capers. For a richer version, you can stir in fromage frais or smatana when the pan is off the heat at the end.
- Or add plain pasta as a side dish to a highly flavoured main course.
- Pulses can be used to make casseroles and stews, bakes and pies or added to meat casseroles, stews and so on to replace some of the meat.
- A lentil loaf can be a delicious main course, much lower in fat than a meat loaf. Pulses can also be a side dish with roast and grilled meats.
- Pulses can help turn a salad from a light side dish into a lunch or supper main course. So can Quorn, which is best marinated or mixed or dressed with some spicy flavours.
- Pulses such as lentils or haricot beans can help turn a soup into a lunch or supper main course, too.
- Some pulses can be bland themselves but take up other flavours well. Experiment with your favourites from the following suggestions: garlic, onion, chillis, tomato, ground cumin, ground coriander seeds, herbs (especially chopped coriander), curry powders and pastes, mustards, soy or shoyu, Worcestershire sauce, Tabasco sauce.
- Rice steamed or cooked in stock on the top of the oven or in the microwave can be turned into a main course by the addition of herbs or spices, vegetables and chicken, turkey, chopped ham, bacon grilled to shed most of its fat and diced, prawns and/or fish pieces. You can flavour and colour it with saffron for serious elegance, or turmeric for an everyday treat. A little wine in the cooking liquid makes it livelier.
- Don't think of rice and pulses as either/ors. A bed of rice topped with a pulse dish (for example, chick peas flavoured

with onions, tomato, thyme and oregano) is delicious and nutritious.

- Explore some of the rice mixes now on the market; for example, you can buy rice with a percentage of wild rice mixed in. They can make an interesting change, especially for dishes like rice with a pulse on top.

- Blinis (see under **Smarter starters** above) or plain pancakes can be made larger and frozen for convenience and served with more substantial fish or seafood (try prawns or strips of smoked mackerel fillet) or lean ham for a lunch or supper main course.

- A savoury version of bread-and-butter pudding is great comfort food for children and adults alike. Make a savoury egg custard with skimmed or semi-skimmed milk, flavoured with mustard, Worcestershire sauce, a dash of Tabasco if you like it hotter, herbs, salt and pepper and a little extra-matured (or a little more low-fat) cheese. This dish works best if the liquid is poured over cubes of unsliced bread and left overnight. Good additions include chopped onion, peppers, a little diced bacon or ham, corn, plus some chopped chilli for the more adventurous. It needs about an hour in a moderate oven.

- Textured vegetable protein (TVP) comes plain or with a savoury 'meat' flavour as dried granules, mince pieces or in chunks. Rehydrate it by cooking in water for 15–20 minutes and then use it in recipes.

- Plain TVP has a slight soya flavour and works best in recipes with strong added flavours such as chilli. Burger mixes or TVP mince could be brightened up with onions and herbs or spices of your choice.

- Quorn has a light savoury taste and takes up other flavours as easily as chicken does. Quorn is also similar in texture and colour to chicken, so substitutes well in many chicken recipes. It only needs heating so it can be added to dishes in the last 10–15 minutes of cooking time.

- Tofu has a slightly beany flavour on its own, but it can absorb other flavours beautifully. You can buy it ready-smoked or marinated, or marinate it yourself (try ginger, soy, garlic, chilli) and grill, stir-fry or barbecue it. Or use it in recipes for quick-cooking delicate fish or meats.

- When you serve meat or fish, gradually reduce the portion size and double the quantity of vegetables with it.
- The same goes for the proportions in stews and casseroles, too. Don't overlook the potato as a vegetable to add to casseroles and stews.
- Serve meat or fish with something starchy such as bread or dumplings.
- Potatoes served with meat can help meet the healthy eating guidelines and cut the amount of meat we eat. And they don't need to be boring: potatoes sliced thinly and microwaved in stock or skimmed milk can be flavoured a dozen different ways. Try onion (softened in the microwave first), garlic, herbs, spices, mustard, a well-drained and pounded anchovy fillet or two – or invent your own version.
- Instead of ordinary roast potatoes, which soak up fat like blotting paper, try cutting them into large chunks and brushing the cut surfaces lightly with oil. Baked on a lightly oiled baking sheet for about 45 minutes, they come out golden brown and crisp.
- Another alternative to roast potatoes is to parboil them, brush lightly with vegetable oil or yogurt, and then crisp in the oven.
- Ring the changes with low-fat polenta or Italian maize meal. If your supermarket doesn't have it, your nearest Italian delicatessen will. There is an instant variety.
- A jacket potato can be a light main course on its own or can be served as part of one. Lace it with butter or sour cream and it is no longer the healthy option. Go instead for yogurt, cottage cheese, fromage frais or smatana, which you can season or flavour in dozens of different ways, including adding chutney.
- A jacket potato becomes a main course when you fill it with baked beans.
- You can substitute tofu towards the end of the cooking time for some of the meat or fish in casseroles and stews. It will hold together better if you give it a bit of a light fry first.
- Finish off casseroles, goulashes and so on with yogurt, smatana or fromage frais rather than cream. Stir in at the end and heat gently, without boiling, to prevent curdling.

143

- For a healthier version of shepherd's pie or spaghetti bolog-naise, follow the guidelines for getting the fat out of mince outlined in the burger recipe on page 118, and increase the ratio of potato or spaghetti to meat.
- Soften the mashed potato for the shepherd's pie or for serving with other meat with skimmed milk or yogurt. Better to skip butter altogether, but if you want a substitute for it, a little well-flavoured olive oil is a reasonable compromise.
- Top savoury dishes with yogurt with an egg beaten into it instead of a cheese 'custard'.
- Chicken and turkey breasts can be browned without added fat by dredging in seasoned flour and putting on a pre-heated non-stick pan or griddle. Either carry on cooking the same way or add liquid such as defatted chicken stock, vegetable stock or wine.
- You can make a perfectly respectable fish-cake with steamed fish flaked and combined with the same quantity of cooked potatoes and an egg white, some chopped herbs and a dash of mustard. Dry-fry or grill.
- Fish is delicious cooked in yogurt in the oven or microwave. It's better still if you marinate it in yogurt first.
- Any fish or meat that's a bit on the dry side can benefit from a little salsa – chopped tomato, onion, chilli, peppers – on the side, which leaves the plate less in need of a sauce or gravy.
- Turn an omelette into a more substantial and healthier main course by adding lots of cooked vegetables (a good way to use up leftovers).
- You can dilute the egg in scrambled eggs and omelettes (and hence reduce fat and cholesterol) by adding about a quarter of a pint of low-fat yogurt to every four or five eggs, or by adding extra egg whites.
- Replace cream with yogurt in quiches.
- Baked beans on a slice or two of toast, preferably wholemeal, makes a healthy lunch or supper main course.
- Most of us eat too much salt. Look for low-salt labels on food products in the shops and try reducing the amount you put in all the dishes you cook little by little. Your palate will adjust if you give it time.

Sauces

- White sauces can be made healthier by substituting skimmed or semi-skimmed milk for whole milk.
- Thicken with cornflour or arrowroot rather than a flour and butter roux.
- Cooked potato whizzed in a liquidiser will also thicken a savoury sauce.
- A vegetable puree can substitute for a more traditional roux-based or cream sauce.
- If you do make a roux, make it with polyunsaturated margarine rather than butter.
- Cheese sauces will be lower in fat if you also use the most strongly flavoured cheese you can find – for example, extra matured Cheddar – so you can cut back on the quantity without losing depth of flavour. Or go the other route and use half-fat cheese.
- Gravy is healthier if you discard as much fat from the roasting pan as you can before you start.
- Yogurt can be used to make all sorts of excellent sauces. Add it to the pan with onion and chicken breasts bashed flat and browned and 'braise' them in it. Or curry it. Yogurt curdles easily, and although this doesn't spoil the taste, for a better-looking finish you could stabilise it with a tablespoonful of flour stirred in a little water or a beaten egg added to a pint of yogurt before you start.
- Cold yogurt makes sauces that go well with rice and grain dishes and alongside grilled meat and fish. Garlic, salt and dried mint makes a Middle Eastern version of this type of sauce that is widely used with rice and bulgar wheat. Or add diced cucumber and capers to yogurt to go with fish or fish-cakes.
- Smatana can be used instead of cream to enrich sauces. Add towards the end and don't boil.
- Half-cream is not a good replacement for heavier creams in sauces. It will dilute rather than enrich.
- Fruit purees make a healthy sweet sauce.

Alternative afters

Here are some suggestions for healthier ways to end a meal:

☺ Fresh fruit, perhaps the healthiest of all.

☺ Fruit salad is a very healthy option, especially if you don't serve it with cream. Use fruit juice rather than a sugar syrup.

☺ Low-fat fruit yogurt and fromage frais bought ready-made are healthy and convenient. (Or, if you make your own yogurt, add fresh fruit and/or puree at the end.)

☺ Low-fat or virtually fat-free fromage frais can be spooned over bananas with a dribble of honey on top.

☺ Tinned fruit – go for fruit canned in juice rather than syrup.

☺ Apples cook beautifully in the microwave. You can core them

---

KHOCHAF

There's a particularly good version of a dried fruit salad in Suzy Benghiat's *Middle Eastern Cookery*, published by Weidenfeld and Nicolson, made by soaking a mixture of 4oz each of raisins, sultanas and dried peaches, and 8oz each of dried apricots and prunes. You cut up anything bigger than a prune and cover all the fruit by at least two inches of water. Leave the mixture in the fridge for three days, giving it an occasional stir and checking when you do if it needs more water to keep the fruit covered. It swells up more than you might think.

If you have a Middle Eastern food store near you, the addition of about a 4-inch square of amardine (apricot paste) makes it even more delicious.

This makes an excellent breakfast dish or between-meals snack as it is. Topped with yogurt, it becomes a delicious pud. To dress it up fit to grace a dinner party table, add an intriguing note by splashing in a little rose water or orange flower water just before you serve it. And for a real treat, top the yogurt with a little coarse-chopped pistachio, walnut, hazelnut or almond.

---

and fill the gap with dried fruit and a little honey and cinnamon.

☺ Poach fresh fruit, and serve the poaching liquid with it. A mixture of no-soak dried fruit and apple rings can be cooked in water, with orange and lemon rind and some juice added, as well as some spices – maybe cloves, a cinnamon stick – and simmered gently for ten minutes or so.

☺ Make a jelly and stir in fresh or canned fruit when the liquid has cooled but not yet set (not fresh pineapple, or the jelly won't set).

☺ Or make your own jelly of fruit juice and gelatin or agar-agar, with or without fresh fruit.

☺ A dried fruit salad is a healthy and useful addition, especially to your winter menus.

☺ Top puds with low-fat yogurt, evaporated milk (chilled and whipped), or almost fat-free or low-fat fromage frais. For sweeter versions, stir in a little honey, sugar or sugar substitute. Vanilla can be good in fromage frais, too.

☺ If you want to use a pouring cream half-cream is better than single and single is better than double or whipping.

☺ Even the thick and creamy Greek-style yogurt is lower in fat than single cream, though it is too high to be recommended as more than an occasional treat.

☺ If you make custard use skimmed or semi-skimmed milk.

☺ Or make a sauce of yogurt, fruit juice and cornflour instead.

☺ There has been an explosion of low-fat frozen yogurts on to the market. They are surprisingly delicious and lower in fat than ice-creams. Most people who say they don't eat yogurt don't know they aren't eating ice-cream if you serve these and don't say. (But go easy on them if you are overweight – they can have a lot of sugar.)

☺ Home-made ice-creams using yogurt or half-yogurt and half-cream are healthier than those based on all cream. They do tend to set much harder, though, so need to be taken from the freezer much earlier to soften.

☺ Sorbet is not exactly slimming food as it has too much sugar, but it does score over ice-cream, which is like sorbet with cream added.

☺ Meringues with fruit and fruit puree. Although there's quite a bit of sugar in meringues, there's no fat at all. Meringues can be elegant enough for a dinner party and can also dress up frozen yogurt or a scoop of sorbet for guests.

☺ A pavlova shell filled with flavoured fromage frais and fresh fruit or low-fat frozen fruit yogurt scoops is another dinner party possibility.

☺ For children, rice pudding is a nutritious option made with semi-skimmed milk or evaporated milk. Cut down the sugar in your recipe.

☺ When you make cheesecake pick a recipe that uses cottage or ricotta or low- or medium-fat soft cheese rather than cream cheese and top with fresh fruit. If you do use cream cheese, make sure it is the lower-fat version.

☺ If your cheesecake has an uncooked crumb base, you can use a lower-fat butter substitute than you would for a cooked base. In either case, go for as high a proportion of polyunsaturates as you can.

☺ Make bread-and-butter pudding with brown bread sliced thicker and skimmed or semi-skimmed milk, and a minimum of butter or butter substitute high in polyunsaturates. Reduce the sugar, and add some dried fruit instead.

☺ Make pancakes with wholemeal flour (or half wholemeal, half white) and skimmed milk, and fill with fruit and yogurt or fromage frais, or a puree of cooked dried fruit.

☺ Adding dried fruit will often sweeten puddings enough to need no sugar or at least less sugar than they otherwise would.

☺ Cinnamon, cloves, vanilla pods, lemon thyme and angelica all have a sweetening effect on dishes. Grated orange rind and grated fresh ginger add sweetness and flavour, too.

☺ Most recipes will work with less sugar than recipes suggest (exceptions are ice-cream and meringue). Often, they need as little as half. Experiment to find the level that suits your taste.

Baking

The last three tips for **Alternative afters** apply to baking generally, too.

Here are some more ways you can modify your usual recipes to give you healthier versions of old favourites:

- Substitute an egg white or an egg white plus a tablespoonful of a highly polyunsaturated oil for an egg. Or just cut the number of eggs.
- Use ready-made apple sauce or canned prune or apple baby food or apple or prune puree instead of oil to add moisture without fat in cake recipes.
- Recipes with apple or prune puree or mashed banana or cooked pumpkin or pineapple chunks will tend to be healthier anyway because some of their moisture is coming from fruit.
- Soak dried fruit overnight in tea and add as much of the soaking liquid as you need to make a fruit cake without adding any fat at all.
- Substitute wholemeal flour for white in everything but choux pastry. If you find that too heavy for your taste, try half of each.
- Substitute one tablespoonful of corn oil and the same of orange juice for every ounce of butter in a sponge mixture.
- Generally, substitute polyunsaturated margarine for butter.
- Instead of lard, butter or hard margarine in scones and tea-breads use two tablespoonsful of corn or groundnut oil for every 1oz of fat.
- Skimmed or semi-skimmed milk can replace whole milk in most recipes.
- In scones, use buttermilk or low-fat yogurt instead of whole milk soured.
- When you make pies, put pastry on top only rather than top and bottom.
- If you are making a crumble topping, add some oat or wheat flake breakfast cereal for extra fibre.
- When you make pastry, use a margarine high in polyunsaturates rather than butter.
- You can make savoury pastry with sunflower oil instead of butter or margarine. You will find that it handles a little differently: rest wholemeal pastry for ten minutes before rolling, but use white at once, or it will become too dry.
- Make sweet pastry with apple puree instead of half the fat.
- You can make a pastry with flour mixed with an equal quantity of skimmed milk powder and enough water to make a doughy consistency. Knead before you roll.

- Olive oil works well as the fat in a lot of recipes, but use one that is fairly bland in taste. Corn oil also does well in many cakes.
- Dried fruit can both substitute for sugar by adding sweetness to recipes and increase the fibre in them as well.
- Low-fat yogurt or buttermilk often does just as well as sour cream in cake recipes.
- It's a myth that fresh yeast needs sugar to work. Warm water is enough. You do need sugar to get dried yeast to work in 20 minutes, but only a pinch.

CHAPTER 5

HEALTHY DRINKING

Water

Healthy drinking starts with making sure we have plenty of water every day.

About four-fifths of our body weight is water already, but we have an enormous daily need for more. Just breathing rids us of more than a litre a day. When it is hot and dry we shed more through sweat. We need to drink about eight glasses of fluid daily and we get around another litre (not quite two pints) from our food.

One crucial role of water in healthy eating is turning soluble fibre into a gooey mass in the large intestine, which adds bulk to stools, helping to avoid constipation and straining, and such consequent problems as piles and diverticular disease (small pouches in the wall of the large intestine which can become inflamed and infected). As we increase the fibre in our diets in response to the healthy eating guidelines, we need to ensure that we get plenty of water, too.

The water supply

Unfortunately, it is not easy to know how good the tap water in your area is. Your water supplier is obliged to tell you what's in your water when you ask. But when in 1990 *Which? way to Health* investigated by asking 172 members of Consumers' Association to write off for reports on their local water, the magazine reported that it did not feel the information most of the water suppliers provided was adequate.

The magazine felt enquirers should have been given:

- Not only the levels of substances in their water but the maximum permitted levels, so that enquirers would have the information they needed to evaluate what they were told.
- The number of times or the proportion of samples in which substances went over the permitted maximum.
- Data collected over the year (levels of some contaminants in water are higher at certain times of the year).

The survey obtained information from 44 of the 51 suppliers in Britain. It found that 21 of the 44 did not give maximum permitted levels for comparison and 17 gave neither permitted levels nor data about the number of samples that went over them. Nine based their data on three months or less.

The maximum permitted levels are based on estimates of safety over a lifetime's drinking the water. So one-off breaches needn't necessarily be health hazards.

The permitted limits are as follows.

Aluminium   0.2mg per litre

Aluminium is naturally present in water and some suppliers use more to remove suspended organic matter. There has been concern that, at this level, aluminium may cause Alzheimer's disease, but the case is not proven. (See under **Cooking utensils** in the previous chapter.)

Nitrates   50mg per litre

Nitrates leach into water from fertilisers and manure. High levels can lead to a rare condition in bottle-fed babies called methaemoglobinaemia or blue baby syndrome. It reduces the flow of oxygen to the brain and other tissues, which first shows as a blue-grey tinge to the skin. It can, in extreme cases, cause death. The last confirmed case in Britain was in 1972 and recorded cases have usually involved levels above 100 mg/litre.

The body turns nitrates into nitrites, which can cause cancer in animals, though they have not been proved to cause it in people.

If you live in an area with high levels, it is better not to make up a baby's bottles from water that has been boiled repeatedly because the nitrate concentration will be higher.

Pesticides $0.1\mu g$ ($1\mu g$ = one millionth of a gram) of any one pesticide and $0.5\mu g$ total of all pesticides per litre of water.

This figure was based not on toxicity but on the smallest amount that could be measured at the time when levels were set. There are higher levels that the Government regards as safe, but toxicity data needs updating. The tests used at the time when many pesticides were approved are now considered inadequate.

Trihalomethanes (TMHs) $100\mu g$ per litre

Chlorine is added to water to disinfect it by killing the bacteria that cause typhoid, cholera and gastro-enteritis. But it can react with naturally occurring organic substances in the water to form trihalomethanes, such as chloroform. It has been found to cause cancer in animals but only at levels hundreds of times higher than the permitted maximum.

Polycyclic aromatic hydrocarbons (PAHs) $0.2\mu g$ per litre

Some cause cancer in animals and may be dangerous to humans. They can get into the water from old water mains pipes lined with coal tar pitch. (We get most of our PAH intake from food.)

Cryptosporidium   This is a microscopic parasite which seems to get through normal purification methods when accidental pollution puts unusually large numbers of eggs in the water. It can cause serious diarrhoea for several weeks, and would be even more serious in people already ill. Research into its control is under way.

Lead

But if those figures enable you to read between the lines of any report you get from your local water supplier, what the supplier cannot tell you is how much lead there is in your tap water, because most of it comes from lead pipes and tanks in your own home and garden. The lead level in such a report will merely be the average of a small number of random samples from taps in homes in the area.

Exposure to very high levels of lead is rare. It can cause

stomach pain, damage to the nervous system and muscle-wasting. More difficult to pin down, but possibly more pervasive, are the effects of long exposure to lower levels of lead. Some studies have blamed it for behavioural problems and poor ability to learn. One, for example, measured the levels of lead in the teeth of children with learning difficulties and found it was higher than in a group of more able learners. Other studies have failed to measure the same effect. Part of the problem is that high levels tend to be found in areas that are also socially deprived, so it is difficult to separate out the effects of poor housing, poor levels of nutrition and so on from those of any increased levels of lead.

Using lead for new pipes has been banned since 1976, but if you live in an older house you may still have them. If you scrape the pipe by your stopcock and find you can dent it, it is probably lead. Lead-based solder on copper pipes may also contribute some lead to drinking water. It has been banned since 1989.

If you want to check your own water supply, contact your supplier and ask for advice, or go to the local environmental health department and ask for testing. Have it done on a sample taken first thing in the morning after the water has been standing overnight. That way, you will be finding the highest level. If it comes out at more than 50μg a litre, the maximum permitted level, you may be able to get a grant from your council towards the cost of replacing pipes or tank.

People generally like the taste of water better in granite areas where water is soft and slightly acidic. However, taste comes at a price. Lead pipes or tanks will contaminate your water more if you live in a soft water area. Glasgow is one of the worst areas of the country from that point of view. And if hard water, which comes from calcium salts dissolving into water in chalk or limestone areas, does less well in the taste test, it is better on other health grounds. People living in hard water areas might have to suffer more scale in their kettles and other appliances and scum on their drinks but they tend – though no one is sure why – to have lower rates of cardiovascular disease. A cause for concern is whether 50μg a litre is a safe enough lead limit. In 1989, a Government report said that water used for making babies' bottles should not contain more than 10–15µg and for adults to drink should have no more than 30µg on average.

If you have lead pipes or tanks and you are worried about the level of lead in your water, besides having your water tested and considering replacement plumbing you can:

- Run the cold water tap for three minutes first thing in the morning and for a minute every time you turn on after water has been in the pipes for more than a few hours. Or, for speed, leave a kettle with water in it at night to use in the morning.
- Only drink and cook with water from the cold water tap in the kitchen.
- Don't make bottle feeds for babies with tap water – either breastfeed or use low-sodium bottled water that has been boiled once.

Is bottled better?

Bottled water is one of the marketing successes of recent years. We drink four times as much in the first half of the 1990s as we did in the mid-1980s. In 1990, £253,000,000 of our housekeeping bills went on water. The market has proliferated. You can now take your pick from almost 100 different brands. But are we paying all that money for substance – or image?

On visits to developing countries, bottled water might eat into your holiday budget but it can be the price of avoiding a bout of something fairly nasty, as the next chapter discusses. Back home, it is more difficult to argue that bottled is better. It is expensive. It may not be as closely monitored as tap water. (A study of 37 brands in the USA in 1989 found that 24 of them had levels of minerals higher than those permitted in drinking water there.) Some have high levels of sodium, not recommended when most people – particularly those with high blood pressure – need to try to cut down on it.

Fashion, habit and taste have secured bottled water a fairly comfortable niche in the market. Choosing the taste that suits you is a daunting prospect with such a wide range. There are clues on most labels. Waters with very high trace mineral levels tend to have more distinctive flavours that you may like or dislike but probably won't feel neutral about. At the opposite end of the scale are waters which make a virtue of tasting of almost nothing at all. If you like high-flavour (particularly high-sodium) waters, take care that you aren't drinking too much of them, and if you have to watch your salt intake particularly carefully, you might want to avoid altogether the brands which do not publish their composition on their labels as well as the ones that you can see are particularly high in sodium.

The information given on the front of the label can be difficult to read. **Mineral waters** must comply with strict regulations which allow filtration, decanting and oxygenation as long as these processes do not alter the natural composition of the water. **Spring waters** do not meet these regulations in some way. **Effervescent natural mineral water** is mineral water with bubbles just the way it comes out of the ground. **Carbonated natural mineral water** has carbon from another source. **Natural mineral water** has carbonation from the spring and in addition has had its carbonation level raised above the natural level but from the same source. **Naturally carbonated mineral water** has had its carbonation topped up but not so that it exceeds its normal level of carbonation.

Fruit drinks

Fruit juices retain most of their valuable vitamin C if they are packed in cans, cartons or bottles and stored in a cool dark place. Once they are opened, however, the juice loses its vitamin C quickly. Apple juice, for example, loses half its vitamin C after a day or two. Shaking the juice circulates the air in the container, oxidising the juice and accelerating the loss.

Unfortunately, fruit juices are a source not only of vitamins but also of sugar. Even the ones marked 'unsweetened' on the carton still contain the natural sugar of the fruit, so they should be drunk in moderation. A sensible ceiling is probably around a glass a day.

Fruit juice diluted with water is lower in sugar than neat fruit juice.

Fruit drinks have water and sugar added. The sugar may not be a calorie problem for growing children with high energy needs, though it tends to contribute to adult obesity. But if your children have fruit drinks, it is better, in the battle against tooth decay, to restrict them to home rather than away drinking and ensure that they brush their teeth afterwards.

Fizzy drinks

Most fizzy drinks have the same added sugar problem. You can avoid that by going for low-calorie versions, but strictly in moderation to avoid too high an intake of artificial sweeteners. A Ministry of Agriculture report in 1990 found that some people were having more than an acceptable daily intake of **saccharin**. However, the artificial sweetener (actually 200 times sweeter than sugar) has been in use for more than 50 years and has no direct evidence against it. It has caused bladder cancer in rats, but only when fed to them in huge quantities, and there is no evidence of the same effect in people.

The other sweetener you will find in drinks is **aspartame**, also marketed as Nutrasweet, which was first licensed in the USA in 1981, allowed in soft drinks there in 1983 and permitted in Britain soon after. It has been extensively tested, does not have the after-taste that saccharin does, and is used in lower concentrations. However, it must be avoided by people born with the genetic metabolic disorder phenylketonuria (PKT).

The long-term effects of high intakes of artificial sweeteners are unknown. Some experts also regard as a problem the fact that they cater for a taste for sweet things rather than encouraging people to retrain their palates away from sweetness.

Then there is a group of adult fizzy drinks that use fruit juice to flavour sparkling water. Aqua Libra, one of the first into the field, uses passion-fruit, grape and apple. Mostly, these drinks have no added sugar but there is some fruit sugar in them. Aqua Libra, for example, has between a quarter and a half less fruit sugar than commercially packed, unsweetened fruit juices.

Milk and milk drinks

Milk is a healthy drink. It should be full-fat for under-twos. From the age of two onwards, semi-skimmed is fine for children who are not faddy and have a well-balanced diet, if that's what the rest of the family are having. If they are not eating well, they should continue on full cream milk until they are five. Semi-skimmed is best then until the end of adolescence, and the choice is semi-skimmed or skimmed thereafter.

Flavoured milk or yogurt drinks may appeal to children who won't drink milk straight. Unfortunately, commercial flavouring almost invariably means added sugar.

Home-made milkshakes can be a good drink-cum-snack option. Use a liquidiser or processor to combine a fruit yogurt or a piece of fruit with a quarter of a pint of milk. Fruit puree and buttermilk is a healthy combination with a refreshing, if slightly acidic, flavour.

There are dozens of variations on **drinking chocolate** or drinking chocolate-plus – chocolate and orange, chocolate and toffee, and so on – that can be made with skimmed milk or water. Some are low in fat, but that doesn't necessarily mean that they are also low in sugar. If you are looking for both you will just have to read the nutritional information on the label.

Coffee and tea

Caffeine is a drug – one of a family of drugs called the xanthines – which occurs naturally in around 60 species of plant including coffee beans, tea leaves, coco seeds and the cola nut. Biologists don't understand why plants make it. One theory is that it has evolved as a natural herbicide to help growing shrubs beat the competition. Neat, caffeine consists either of odourless white crystals with a silky feel or a white powder with a bitter taste. If that sounds unappetising, most people don't seem to find it so. It has been described as the most widely consumed behaviour-modifying drug in the world.

The way it works is complex. Caffeine stimulates the brain and the nervous system by fitting itself on to brain receptors which are designed to take another chemical called adenosine. Adenosine is a natural sedative that tells the body's cells to slow down. Caffeine overrides adenosine and kicks the body into top gear. The result is increased blood pressure, urine output and central nervous system activity. It accelerates breathing, strengthens muscles and constricts blood vessels in the brain.

Most people have experienced how fast-acting it is. It is easily absorbed in the gut and spreads within minutes via the blood to all the tissues and organs of the body. It can help you to feel less tired and more attentive almost immediately, but part of the effect may be illusory. Studies have been unable to show to date that it improves intellectual or learning performance, and it is a myth that it is helpful with the effects of alcohol either at the time or the morning after. If anything, it aggravates the symptoms because it is a diuretic and increases dehydration. In a hot drink, it can also increase the rate at which alcohol is absorbed into the bloodstream. In other words, black coffee, far from being a sobering influence, can make you drunk faster.

Not just coffee
Many people think of caffeine and coffee as almost synonymous. Weight-for-weight, tea contains more. It is only because less tea than coffee is used to brew an average cup that the caffeine content tends to be higher in coffee, but the length of time that tea is allowed to brew affects the caffeine content, and a strong cup of tea can have more caffeine than a weak cup of coffee. Plant variety and method of production affect caffeine strength, too. Arabica coffee has less caffeine than Robustas. Caffeine is present in chocolate and a number of medicines, too.

Guilty or not guilty?
Coffee has had a bad press in recent years. More than 20 published studies had already concluded that it raised the amount of cholesterol in the blood, so increasing the risk of a heart attack, before a study in Norway came to an even gloomier verdict. That study, reported in the *British Medical Journal* in March 1990, claimed to have found an increased mortality rate from heart disease linked to coffee over and above the effect it had on blood cholesterol. Then the Finns weighed in with a study also published in the *BMJ* the following week, relating coffee-drinking to high rates of diabetes.

A group of diabetes experts from Oxford countered with an

attack published in the *BMJ* the following month, pointing out that the incidence of the problem related just as closely to the distance they lived from the equator as to their coffee consumption. The link, they said, might be between diabetes and hours of daylight.

There have been other criticisms of studies linking caffeine and cholesterol, too. Some studies, for example, failed to take account of whether coffee-drinkers might also have been having more milk or cream than the volunteers who did not drink coffee, and some found an increase in cholesterol only when coffee had been boiled, and not with filtered or instant. Caffeine in tea seems not to have the same effect in studies, leaving open the question of whether the high tannin in tea is in some way protective, or whether cholesterol is raised not by caffeine but possibly by something else in coffee.

Some studies have looked not at an increase in cholesterol as predictive of increased likelihood of heart disease, but at actual incidence of heart attacks among coffee drinkers. One large-scale study found that men who drank ten cups a day were three times more likely to have a heart attack and five-cup men twice as likely as people who did without. Another study found that nine cups of coffee or tea a day seemed to cause irregular heartbeats, which have been associated with increased risk of sudden cardiac death. But other studies have failed to confirm these findings. Similarly, caffeine raises blood pressure slightly and briefly, but high caffeine intake is not a proven risk factor for high blood pressure and the effect may decrease as regular tea and coffee drinkers acclimatise to their effects.

Part of the problem is that heavy coffee drinking cannot be isolated from other aspects of personality and lifestyle. It may be, for example, that heavy coffee consumption is another symptom of whatever it is that is increasing the heart attack risk, not its cause. Studies have not always been designed to tease out these complex effects.

There have also been a series of studies since the early 1980s attempting to see if there is a link between caffeine and cancers of the bowel, breast, ovaries, bladder, pancreas, bones and kidneys. For every one that seems to find there is, another finds the opposite. Four out of seven studies of coffee and bowel cancer actually associated drinking coffee with a reduced risk of developing it.

Caffeine has also been in the dock for causing infertility, but recent studies have contradicted the earlier and smaller ones that suggested a link. Recent research also seems to contradict earlier suggestions that high caffeine intake could be linked with higher rates of miscarriage. Foetal abnormalities such as cleft palate have been found in mice force-fed caffeine during pregnancy, but not when they sipped it in water as we do. No study on humans has established any evidence linking caffeine and birth defects.

The drug is known to cross the placenta in pregnant women and foetuses are slow to eliminate it from their blood, so unborn babies show higher levels than their mothers. Doctors have diagnosed withdrawal symptoms in newborn babies who were irritable, jittery and sick and whose mothers had a lot of caffeine during pregnancy.

The estimated fatal overdose of caffeine for an adult is between three and ten grams. To absorb that amount, you would have to drink between 50 and 160 cups of instant coffee within a half-hour. Or, for a child of around four stone, the equivalent would be about 60 cans of cola in the same time. Overdose deaths are therefore unlikely.

But, if it is unlikely to kill and the jury is still out on possible serious long-term effects of drinking tea and coffee, there are known harmful effects. Too much can cause sleeplessness, and so may aggravate emotional instability and mental illness, frayed tempers, nervousness, palpitations, stomach upsets, nausea and tinnitus.

Drinking too much coffee also makes the kidneys work hard, although most regular drinkers seem to learn to tolerate it. A cup of coffee at bedtime might keep someone unused to it awake, but it might be no problem for someone who drank one regularly. So used do we become to our regular intake that we tend to have withdrawal symptoms like headaches if we reduce our usual level even a little.

In a survey done in 1990 by *Which?*, one in five people who had cut back drinking tea and coffee in the previous two years reported headaches, drowsiness, stomach upsets, irritability and depression. More than a third, however, said they felt better, often citing fewer headaches and better sleep. For many the pattern seems to be to feel worse for the first few days to a week, and better thereafter.

Not proven?

A problem that may have contributed to the inconclusiveness of various studies of caffeine consumption is that the studies tend to equate coffee, or sometimes tea, with caffeine when coffee and tea actually contain other active chemical substances. Nevertheless, decaffeinated products are a large and growing market.

Removing caffeine can be done in one of several ways. Organic solvents such as methylene chloride or ethyl acetate can be used to dissolve the caffeine out of green coffee beans. Another method is to put moistened beans in a chamber with liquid carbon dioxide, which has the ability to remove caffeine without affecting other natural chemicals in coffee or tea. Or, in what's called the Swiss Water Process, hot water can be used to wash out caffeine. A variant of this is the European Water Process, in which the caffeine-rich solution in the Swiss Water Process is treated with organic solvent. (Water processes are not suitable for removing caffeine from tea.) Manufacturers don't have to say which process they use but those who don't use organic solvents tend to draw attention to the fact.

Under European legislation, residues of methylene chloride in decaffeinated coffee have to be no more than five parts per million. Tests have shown that most decaffeinated coffee has a residue of less than 0.1 parts. Methylene chloride is also used in paint strippers, aerosols and dry-cleaning solutions and when it is inhaled at high concentrations can cause faintness, headache, skin irritations and even unconsciousness. There is no legal limit on the other organic solvent used for decaffeination, ethyl acetate.

A study in America a few years ago found a link between decaffeinated coffee and raised blood cholesterol. The researchers attributed the effect to the use of Robusta beans rather than the possible presence of solvents. But it would need a larger and longer study before the advice could be that people avoid Robusta beans.

Nevertheless:

- Generally, doctors recommend that you have no more than 400mg of caffeine a day – which means about six cups or four mugs of coffee.
- People with raised blood pressure, kidney disease, high cholesterol or a history of heart disease should have less.
- If you are suffering any of the symptoms listed above, you may want to try cutting out or reducing tea or coffee and sitting out any headache you get.
- If you are pregnant or breastfeeding you should restrict caffeine to about 60mg or one cup a day.

Alcohol

The case against

Drinking too much alcohol can do irreversible damage to your liver. It can also contribute to coronary heart disease, high blood pressure, heart failure, stroke and stomach disorders.

Drinking a lot can also make you fat. Alcohol is loaded with calories – twice as many per unit of weight as sugar. Makers don't have to give nutritional information on their labels, and the calorie count can vary enormously. Beers and lagers can have between 140 and 400 calories a pint. A standard glass of wine can have between 65 and 129 calories, and spirits clock up about 50 calories a measure. Mixer drinks also add to the calorie count – for example, a small bottle of tonic contains about 35 calories – unless you use a low-calorie version.

There are also short-term effects. Most of us think that alcohol helps us lose our inhibitions and gives us a feeling of well-being, but alcohol is actually a depressant. Its effect is to slow down messages travelling along the nerves to the brain, reducing coordination, lengthening reaction time, and impairing judgement, which is why even one unit of alcohol (defined below) will impair your ability to drive and three to five put you over the legal limit. Alcohol also makes it more likely that you will have an accident walking, cycling or working, even after just one or two units.

Drinking too much in a single binge also puts you at risk of alcohol poisoning or unsafe sexual practices.

And then comes the hangover.

Not everyone suffers as much and not all alcohol has the same effect. A hangover is a combination of the effects of dehydration and low blood sugar and comes also from congeners or poisons present in all alcoholic drinks, but particularly in darker ones like brandy and red wine.

What's the limit?

Because different drinks have different percentages of alcohol, a system of units is used to make it possible to compare one with another. A unit is 10ml or 8g of ethyl alcohol.

The formula for calculating the number of units in a bottle is to multiply the alcohol content as a percentage of volume by the volume of the bottle in millilitres and divide it by 1,000. So if you have a 75cl (750ml) bottle of wine with an alcohol content of 12 per cent, multiply 12 by 750 and divide by 1,000 and you will find that it contains nine units.

The current medical advice on sensible drinking is:

- Men should have no more than 21 units of alcohol in a week, spread over the week, but with one or two alcohol-free days.

Know your drinks

Alcohol intake is measured in units. **One unit =**

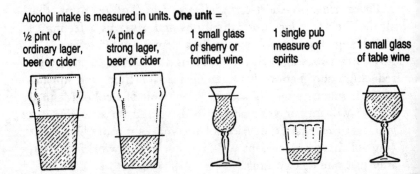

| ½ pint of ordinary lager, beer or cider | ¼ pint of strong lager, beer or cider | 1 small glass of sherry or fortified wine | 1 single pub measure of spirits | 1 small glass of table wine |

- Women should have no more than 14 units, spread over the week, but with one or two alcohol-free days.
- Individuals vary: these amounts will be too much for some people, while others could cope safely with more – the trouble with alcohol is that there is no point below which you can say with certainty that there is no risk.
- Alcohol has more effect on the young and the old – they need to be even more careful.
- Pregnant women and women hoping to become pregnant should have little or no alcohol – one or two units once or twice a week at most. Everything you drink when you are pregnant passes across to the foetus and alcohol has been associated with fertility problems and a higher risk of miscarriage.

Getting it badly wrong carries a price. Women with alcohol-related problems now take up one hospital bed in seven. Men

How much per week?

Units	Men	Women
below 14		
15–21		
22–35		
36+		

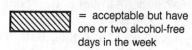 = acceptable but have one or two alcohol-free days in the week

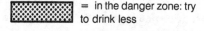 = in the danger zone: try to drink less

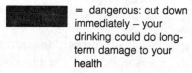 = dangerous: cut down immediately – your drinking could do long-term damage to your health

take up one in five. Unlike most other countries where such records are kept, women in Britain are almost as likely as men to die of cirrhosis of the liver. Elsewhere, the ratio goes from about half as many women as men contracting this incurable liver condition down to as low as a tenth.

If you need to cut down what you are drinking:

- Try low-alcohol or non-alcohol drinks instead of alcohol.
- Dilute alcohol with low-calorie mixers or mineral water or tap water.
- Try to drink more slowly – take smaller sips and pace yourself.
- Give your body drink-free days to recover.
- Give crisps and nuts a wide berth when you are drinking – they just make you thirstier.
- Don't use alcohol to slake your thirst.
- Eat before you drink.
- Don't be discouraged if you cut back on beer and find you become constipated – upping the fibre in your diet will help sort you out again.

If you are drinking more than the recommended limits and cannot cut back, or if you are worried about your drinking for any reason, there are a number of ways you can get help.

Contact **Alcohol Concern**, 275 Gray's Inn Road, London WC1X 8QF (071–833 3471) for information about a treatment or advice centre near you.

Alcoholics Anonymous or AA is the largest and best-known self-help group. Look under Alcohol in the phone book, or ring the central office on (0904) 644026, or write to General Service Office, PO Box 1, Stonebow House, Stonebow, York YO1 2NJ.

Al-Anon is a support group for families and friends of alcoholics in the UK and Eire, and **Alateen** offers similar help and support for their children. Both can be contacted on 071–403 0888, which is a confidential 24–hour helpline, or at 61 Great Dover Street, London SE1 4YF.

How does it work?
Alcohol passes quickly from mouth to stomach and small intestine, where it is absorbed into the bloodstream. Then it

circulates through the liver and on to the heart, lungs and brain. The faster it is absorbed, the higher the blood alcohol level; the higher the level the greater the effect.

The effect will be greater if:

- You are small, female, young.
- You drink quickly.
- You drink on an empty stomach.
- You add a fizzy mixer.

As the blood flows through the liver, the liver cleanses the alcohol out of it. But it is slow going – about a unit an hour. If you are drinking at a party, you could still be over the limit the next morning, and a lunchtime drink or two could have a top-up effect and put you over again. So just leaving your car at home when you go for an evening's drinking may not be enough to keep you on the right side of the law the next day.

A little of what you fancy . . .

The news is not all bad. It seems that, despite the dangers of over-indulgence, drinking a small amount of alcohol can do us good.

More than a score of studies in different countries in the 1970s favoured a moderate alcohol consumption over total abstinence. One was a ten-year study of 18,000 male civil servants in Whitehall, the result of which was published in *The Lancet* in 1981. It found that those who drank a little were less likely to die of a heart attack than those who did not, though the study found the benefit was cancelled out once people went over two drinks a day. A ten-year survey of 85,000 people in Oakland, California, also found a link between moderate drinking and lower incidence of heart disease. The Report of the Royal College of Physicians on alcohol, *A Great and Growing Evil*, published in April 1987, said: 'People who drink no more than 20g alcohol, who limit themselves to two standard drinks daily, have slightly lower blood pressures than teetotallers.'

Perhaps the most charmingly seductive case for the plus side of taking a tipple comes from a study reported by wine writer, Jancis Robinson, in her book *On the Demon Drink* (published by Mitchell Beazley). It took place when the Cushing hospital for the elderly, near Boston, Massachusetts instituted a cocktail hour at which patients were given beer and cheese and biscuits six days a week. Within two months, the percentage of patients needing sedation dropped from 75 to zero, and the percentage who were mobile went up from 21 to 75. And – though it is hard to be sure quite why – male incontinence dropped dramatically.

A little of what you fancy can, it seems, do you good – except for those for whom alcohol becomes a demon that turns on them.

CHAPTER 6

FOOD HAZARDS

HEALTHY eating also means having a healthy kitchen. Unless you know the hidden hazards and put safe procedures into practice, your kitchen can put you at risk of illness; it can become an accident just waiting to happen.

From the moment you get home from the supermarket with your shopping, the way you store your food can influence whether or not you get maximum nutritional value for your money.

In this chapter you will find the key points and practices you need to follow to ensure that your kitchen is a safe and efficient food factory.

Basic hygiene

Keeping yourself and your kitchen clean are essential to kitchen hygiene. You should also be aware that the food you bring into your kitchen is potentially contaminated and know how to make it safe and prevent it contaminating other foods. That is not as tall an order as it might sound. The trick is to identify the danger points in storing, preparing and serving food and to keep to a few simple rules to steer you through the hazards.

The first rule of kitchen hygiene is to wash your hands with soap and warm water before you handle any unwrapped food. Wash them again after handling raw food and before going on to touch anything else, and again every time you stop to stroke the dog, change the baby, go to the loo, blow your nose, touch your face or empty the pedal bin; in fact, wash them after anything that interrupts you whenever you are touching food.

Other rules you need to follow to ensure a safe, clean, healthy kitchen include:

- Cover any cuts or scratches on your hands with a plaster.
- Dry your hands on kitchen paper or a hand towel, but never on the tea-towel you are using for drying dishes.
- Don't 'taste' with your fingers.
- Don't smoke as you handle food.
- Never use the same board or knife, unwashed between, for raw and cooked food.
- To be really sure you are safe from food poisoning, use different coloured knives and chopping boards for different uses. For example, keep one colour for raw poultry, another for raw meat and so on.
- Wooden chopping boards tend to harbour germs. Scrub thoroughly every time you use them.
- Plastic chopping boards are easier to clean and can usually go in the dishwasher.
- Use a dishwasher or wash up in very hot – rubber-glove-hot – water with washing-up liquid, rinse in hot water, and let dishes drain on the draining board rather than dry them. (Polish drained glasses with a clean dry cloth.)
- The residual heat in the oven can be handy for drying washed pots and pans.
- Always wash up with hot soapy water everything that has been in contact with raw chicken or raw meat as soon as you have finished with them.
- The sooner you wash anything with food residue encrusted on it, the better – and easier.
- A nylon brush is safer than a dishcloth.
- Disinfect dishcloths regularly.
- If you use tea-towels change them often.
- When you are buying kitchen equipment, consider how easy it will be to clean. Does it have places where bits of food could get stuck and be difficult to remove?
- Make sure that any food left out of the fridge is in a well-sealed container.

- Wash the kitchen floor frequently.
- Bacteria, pests and vermin love rubbish. Keep waste well away from food and wrap it well before you put it in the bin. Keep all bins firmly closed and empty regularly.
- Don't let pets lick you or your plates.
- Don't give pets titbits in the kitchen (or from the meal table).
- Don't let cats walk over or sit on worktops or other working surfaces.
- If a pet urinates or vomits in or near the kitchen, clean up quickly and thoroughly and disinfect the area.
- Always follow the manufacturer's instructions on any disinfectant you use.
- Wash your hands again when you finish in the kitchen.

Safe cooking

Here are a few more simple tips to ensure that you aren't cooking up trouble in the kitchen:

- It not only makes cooking more efficient if you get out everything you need before you start to make a dish, but it can make it safer. It minimises how often you have to open the fridge or cupboard doors or rummage through the cutlery drawer when your hands might be contaminated.
- Pay attention to cooking times and especially temperatures in recipes. They aren't just there to help food pass the taste test, but also to ensure that bacteria are destroyed.
- Don't put complete trust in cookery books or other instructions either. Just because a piece of meat or a chicken should be thoroughly cooked by a certain time it doesn't necessarily mean it is.
- Meat needs to get to 75°C (a meat thermometer will check if it has) for all bacteria to be killed.
- Most food needs to reach, and cook for at least two minutes, at a temperature of 70°C in the centre.
- Poultry is cooked when you can stick a skewer right down to the bone and no blood flows. Any juices that run out should be yellow (clear).
- Don't start to cook frozen poultry or meat until it is thoroughly thawed.

171

- Always defrost in something that will catch and hold the drips, but where the food is not sitting in the drips.
- Always pre-heat the oven properly.
- It is dangerous to leave food sitting in a cooker in warm weather waiting for an automatic timer to start it up.
- Take special note of instructions on any chilled or frozen pre-cooked dishes. Warming them is not enough; go for piping hot.
- Don't prepare food, if you can help it, when you are ill with vomiting or diarrhoea, or for a day or two afterwards. If it is absolutely unavoidable, be meticulous about hygiene.
- Don't prepare food too far ahead and then leave it at room temperature before it is served. Bacteria will love it if you do.

Cooking, chilling and reheating food

Follow these principles for safe reheating from the fridge or freezer:

- Cool food when first cooked as quickly as you can (short of putting it in the fridge, which would then become too warm).
- When you want to eat, reheat the dish until not just warm, but really hot. Keep it above 63°C until serving.
- Don't reheat food more than once.
- Don't re-freeze defrosted food unless it is cooked or re-cooked between freezings.
- Catering for family functions is a bit of a minefield. Dishes like cold chicken under a sauce must not be allowed to sit around in a warm room or marquee – or you could serve up more than you bargained for.
- Sandwiches made with cold meat need to be kept in the fridge until the last minute.
- Everything must be covered from the minute you put it out until people are ready to eat.
- A big sit-down hot meal is even more difficult because the cooked food must be kept constant at a temperature of not less than 63°C.

Picnics and barbecues

- Picnics have their problems, too. Pack foods that should be kept cool in an insulated container.
- It is safer to keep fillings separate and let people assemble their own sandwiches or rolls on the spot, thus avoiding the 'soggy sarnie' syndrome, too.
- Be extra careful about cooking times when you barbecue. Make sure you cook chicken and burgers really thoroughly. If you have a microwave, it can help to part-cook food in the kitchen beforehand. (But if you do, don't let it sit around warm waiting to be grilled.)
- Keep pieces, especially chicken and burgers, small. Avoid the hottest part of the grill where it is difficult not to char on the outside while leaving the middle raw. And be careful not to contaminate what you have just cooked with the next batch of raw ingredients.

Microwaves

Microwaves are not only good news nutritionally (see **Chapter 4**) but they are also a boon for busy people. They thaw frozen food, reheat cooked food, and cook sauces (lump-free), soups, vegetables and fish beautifully. But the miracle workhorse of the 1980s has been failing to live up to some of its early promise, according to recent reports. Heat penetration is not deep or uniform, timers are not always reliable and microwaves have hot and cold spots.

The widely held view that microwaves cook from the middle outwards is quite wrong. In fact they cook by heat that penetrates from the surface inwards. The hottest spot is just a centimetre or two in – the maximum distance the microwaves affect by agitating the water molecules in food until they 'boil'. Beyond that, conducted heat (as in an ordinary cooker) takes over.

Similarly, when defrosting, you must always be careful that frozen food is completely thawed before you start to cook it. Otherwise, your cooking time will not be accurate.

The very cheapest microwaves may be of dubious value. They may cook at wattages as low as 400, which means few operations will have a time advantage over conventional cooking methods. If you are buying a microwave, consider a turntable, wave stirrer (a rotating antenna to help distribute the microwaves more evenly) and electronic touch-pad controls. Some mechanical clockwork timers are not accurate. You will get a more reliable performance, when you are using a clockwork timer for a short cooking time, if you turn it well past the setting you want, even right to the longest setting possible, and then turn it back again, rather than just turning it a small way to your chosen setting.

There are also differences in the way foods behave in the microwave. Thick soup, for example, needs frequent stirring because it heats up very quickly round the edges while the centre stays cool.

Don't forget:

- Check that heated food is hot right through to the middle.
- Anything you reheat should stay at 70°C for at least two minutes.
- Stir food during cooking to distribute the heat more evenly.
- If you are cooking pieces of food, rearrange them at least once.
- Turning food over a few times also helps distribute the heat.
- Round dishes encourage more even microwave distribution.
- Even if you have a turntable, turn dishes through 90° during cooking to minimise the effects of hot and cold spots (caused by uneven distribution of microwaves).
- Arrange uneven shapes (like chicken legs) with the thicker end out towards the circumference of a circle and the thinner facing towards the middle.
- Ignore standing times in recipes and makers' instructions at your peril.
- Don't cook food with clingfilm touching it.

Not all the recent criticism that cook-chill foods reheated by microwave can be unsafe is the fault of the microwaves. The food manufacturers have been coming under fire for inadequate and inaccurate information on some packets, too. Some now give more detailed instructions according to oven wattage and most have pledged to do so. If you are unsure what wattage your oven is, look on the front or back of the oven or in the instruction book or guarantee. Or phone the suppliers who will be able to check for you. Don't just rely on the instructions. If a dish is not hot enough in the time recommended, cook it longer.

Safe storage

The battle against bacteria begins as soon as you arrive home from the supermarket with your shopping. Here are a few useful general guidelines you might want to follow:

- Getting your frozen and chilled food (preferably bought last and carried home in a cool bag) into the fridge or freezer takes priority. Even an hour hanging around a warm check-out queue, car boot and kitchen can raise the temperature enough to encourage bacteria to increase.
- If you really cannot get chilled or frozen food home quickly, then an insulated container, or even a clean blanket wrapped around your shopping bags, helps keep it at the right temperature longer.
- Keep raw meat or poultry separated from cooked foods or foods that don't require further cooking.
- Make sure when you put raw meat or poultry in the fridge that it cannot drip on any other food.
- Rotate canned and packet foods. When you are unpacking from the supermarket, make sure the new ones go at the back.
- Canned food should be eaten within a year (except ham, which is better used within six months).
- Keep your storecupboard clean and tidy. Clean up anything that is spilled and keep flour or other dry ingredients in sealed containers.
- Watch out for any signs that rodents have been visiting – look for calling cards like droppings or gnawed packets. If you think you have a problem your local authority can help.
- Pack, handle and store raw and cooked food separately.
- Always wash your hands between handling raw and cooked foods.
- Much good advice on storing food before and after opening is now given on labels; check for advice like 'Once opened, store in refrigerator and use within one month'. Food products,

once opened, often have a much shorter life than the 'best before' date.

- A freezer pen, or any waterproof felt-tip pen suitable for writing freezer labels, is also handy to note on bottle labels the date on which they were opened.
- Both 'use by' and 'best before' labels apply only if you also follow any storage and preparation instructions given with them.
- Exceed 'use by' dates at your peril. Don't be lulled into a sense of false security by the fact that food still looks and smells okay.
- Store all food out of direct sunlight.
- Milk left on the doorstep loses its vitamin B2.
- Milk left outside is also vulnerable to attack by birds. Discard any that has obviously been damaged by birds or animals. There have been cases of disease introduced into the milk this way.
- Tea and coffee don't keep well. They lose their flavour within weeks, so don't buy too much at a time. The exception is instant or ground coffee in a vacuum pack, which will keep for up to a year. Ground coffee or beans keep well in the freezer.
- Throw away anything with mould on it.

Eggs

Eggs should be kept in the fridge to discourage any bacteria from multiplying. Use as soon as you can after buying, preferably within six to eight days, or follow the 'use by' dates.

Fats

Oils should be stored in a cold, dark place, as sunlight destroys vitamin E, turning the oils rancid. Under ideal conditions unrefined oils will keep for up to six months and refined oils for up to a year.

It may be tempting to buy whatever you use most in larger quantities for the sake of economy. If you do, it would be as well to decant some oil into a smaller bottle for current use and keep the larger container somewhere dark and cold to ensure it stays in good condition.

Fruit and vegetables

When you open a can of fruit or vegetables, put anything you don't use immediately into a fresh container. Once a can is opened, oxygen can start to react with the inside surface to release tin or iron into the food. Treat what's left over as if it were fresh – keep it in the fridge and use within a few days. The same goes for frozen produce once it has been thawed. Never re-freeze. Frozen vegetables are best cooked from frozen anyway to avoid vitamin loss.

Use fruit and vegetables that you buy fresh as quickly as you can. The longer you store them, the more nutrients will be lost. Until you are ready to use them, store them unwashed, unpeeled and uncut, away from heat and light. Remember:

- Potatoes are best kept away from sunlight to prevent them turning green due to formation of the poison solanine. (Cut off the green and any eyes and sprouts when you are preparing them for cooking. See under **Know the enemy** below.)
- Onions should not be stored touching potatoes or they can deteriorate faster.
- Apples and carrots should not be stored together or the carrots will turn bitter.
- Apples are best kept in the salad drawer of the fridge to prevent them becoming mealy.
- Pears ripen very quickly. Check daily, and put in a cool place when they are on the verge of ripening.
- Wash grapes as soon as you get them home and put on a cloth or paper towel to dry thoroughly. Eat within a few days.
- Melons should be stored in the fridge and covered well to prevent the scent permeating other food.
- Remove any damaged soft fruit from punnets and eat the rest within a day.
- Green vegetables keep best in the compartment at the bottom of the fridge, with lettuce in a plastic bag.
- Mushrooms should be kept cool and dry.

- The growth of mould on peaches and nectarines is inhibited if they are kept in the fridge.
- Root vegetables are best kept in a cool, dark place.
- Bananas are best kept out of the fridge or they go black.
- Keep oranges in the fridge but bring to room temperature or warm slightly in the microwave before squeezing for more juice.
- Store carrots, potatoes and parsnips in a cool, dark and airy place.
- Dried fruit keeps best in a sealed container and lasts for up to three months.

Fish

When you bring fish home, take it out of the shop wrappings and put it in a polythene bag or a rigid container to make sure that it does not taint other food in the fridge. Keep in the coolest part of the fridge for two days at most. Ideally, eat as soon as possible. Don't keep frozen white fish in the freezer longer than six months or oily more than four.

Shellfish are less suitable for home freezing than fish unless you have access to an absolutely fresh source and a fast-freeze control on your freezer. It is advisable to eat the day you buy fresh, or keep frozen at −18°C (0°F) or lower for no more than two months. Eat immediately once you thaw and never re-freeze.

Chicken and poultry

As soon as you get fresh or chilled chicken home, discard the shop wrapping and take out any giblets. Unless you intend to freeze the bird, put it on a plate, give it a loose cover of either foil or greaseproof paper so the air can circulate, and refrigerate. It should be cooked within two to three days. If you plan to freeze it, put in the freezer the day you buy it.

Giblets should either be cooked the day they are bought, or frozen for up to three months.

Thawing poultry is best done slowly in the fridge. Allow 24 hours for a 3lb chicken, 36 for a 4lb bird, 2–2½ days for 6–8lb in weight and 4–4½ days for an 18–20lb turkey. Thawing by submerging in cold water is risky because if the bird is contaminated with Salmonella, this increases the risk of food poisoning.

Thawing at room temperature is not advised either, but if you must do it, avoid defrosting in sunlight or a centrally heated room as these are the most dangerous ways.

Meat substitutes

Pre-packed **tofu** keeps for about a month unopened in the fridge. Once you open the pack, it has about four days' life, as long as you keep it in an airtight container full of water and change the water daily. It does not freeze well raw, but you can freeze it in a cooked meal.

Packets of dry **TVP** keep unopened for several months and can be frozen after being rehydrated. **Quorn** keeps for only a couple of days, but you can freeze it either raw or in a cooked meal.

Pulses

Store in airtight containers out of direct sunlight to avoid vitamin loss. Buy small quantities and ideally turn stock over regularly. Kept cool and dry they will last a year. Old pulses become hard, dry and more difficult to cook and digest.

Bread

Bread tends to develop two types of mould after three or four days in humid conditions. There is the highly visible blue mould and an invisible 'rope' mould which can make you quite sick. Once bread is mouldy, don't eat it.

Breads become stale when they dry out and their starch crystallises. The bread tightens up and hardens and its taste and smell change. Breads that are soft and moist to start with may *appear* to stay fresh longer because they do not dry out so quickly, but the starch is actually going stale at the same rate. The reason heat freshens bread up is that it reverses the crystallisation of the starch. The aim of good bread storage is to slow down the process as much as possible in the first place. So what are the options?

☺ A plastic bag will keep bread moist for a few days. Crusty loaves will become soft as the crust absorbs some of the moisture trapped inside the bag but you can harden the crust again in the oven. However, after a few days condensation could build up inside the bag and encourage mould.

☹ In the open bread will dry out more quickly. Crusty loaves may stay crusty – but only if the air is not too damp. If there is a lot of atmospheric moisture, the crust will absorb it and soften.

☹ The fridge is the worst place of all to store bread because the low temperatures speed up starch crystallisation.

☺ The freezer is actually the best place to store bread. Starch does not crystallise and mould does not grow below freezing point. Freeze bread already sliced so that you can take it out slice by slice as you need it.

Fridge sense

It is essential for safe food storage that fridges are kept cold enough – below 6°C. It is worth investing in a thermometer (which will also check the freezer).

To get the best from your fridge:

• Check the temperature by leaving the thermometer on the top shelf for a couple of hours. It should not be higher than 5°C there. If the fridge is working properly that will be the warmest shelf because hot air rises, but it is as well to check a few other spots as well. Check the temperature only after leaving the thermometer in the fridge for several hours and without handling or taking it out.

• Put fruit and vegetables in the bottom drawer where cool air, which can damage green leaf vegetables like lettuce, is not constantly circulating.

• Don't overload the cabinet or cold air will not circulate properly.

• Cool cooked food as quickly as you can, outside the fridge, before you put it in, otherwise it will make the fridge too warm for hours.

- Don't position the fridge next to your oven, radiator, dishwasher, washing machine (unless you always use the cold wash) or in any other place that is particularly warm.
- Clean and defrost the fridge regularly; when fridges are iced up they can't work efficiently.
- Check the rubber door seal from time to time to ensure it is not broken. Replace if necessary.
- Clean the dust and fluff off the housing at the back. It can trap warm air behind the fridge.
- A good general rule is to put dairy products on top, cooked meat in the middle and raw meat on the bottom shelf of the fridge (remembering to put raw meat on a plate or bowl so that it cannot drip).
- Don't keep anything in the fridge longer than five days. Play it even safer with pâtés and soft cheeses.
- Avoid opening the fridge door too many times or for longer than necessary. Never leave it open.

Freezer sense

Home freezing is unlikely to preserve as high a proportion of nutrients as commercial freezing because it is slower. But when you want to freeze to take advantage of a bargain, or to preserve produce you have grown or picked or dishes you have cooked yourself, you should bear the following in mind:

- Only use a freezer with a **** marking. Anything less is meant only for storing food that is already frozen.
- Use a fridge/freezer thermometer to check the temperature of the freezer: this should be −18°C or below.
- Use the fast-freeze setting to freeze as quickly as you possibly can.
- Freeze small quantities at a time.
- Never put warm food in the freezer.
- Always label food clearly with contents and dates.
- Pack and seal well to avoid 'freezer burn', which makes food dry and tasteless as well as destroying nutrients.

Recommended maximum freezer storage times

	Months		Months
beef	8–9	oily fish	2
pork	6–7	shellfish	3
lamb	6–7	bread and rolls	1
veal	6–7	sandwiches	1–2
sausages	3	cakes	6
mince	3	biscuits	6
bacon	1	pastries	3–6
poultry	6–9	stocks and soups	2–3
ham	3	sauces	2–3
pâté	1	mousses	2–3
cooked poultry	1–2	ice-cream, commercial	3
stews, casseroles	2–3	ice-cream, home-made	1
white fish	4		

- Defrost regularly for peak performance and maximum efficiency.
- If you have a power cut, insulate the freezer further with a rug or blanket and keep the door closed. How long you can safely keep the food varies. For example, a cabinet-style freezer unopened, insulated and full is good for about 35 hours or part-full for about 30 hours. Uprights are not good for as long without power. You may be in trouble with one after 10 or 12 hours. When the power is restored, put on fast-freeze for a couple of hours.

Know the enemy

Food poisoning is the general term for a number of different health problems that have their source in animals, birds or insects, in ourselves, in food, or in the way we handle, cook or keep foods.

There has been a dramatic rise in confirmed cases of food poisoning in the last ten years, but most people with food poisoning don't even go to the doctor and if they do, most doctors simply treat the symptoms without sending samples for analysis to establish the cause. In England and Wales 54,000 confirmed cases were recorded in 1989; it has been estimated that the official figures probably represent one in ten of actual cases. In the United States the official assumption is that reported cases are one in 100 of actual cases. So the true figure in England and Wales could lie anywhere between half a million and around five million cases a year.

Symptoms of food poisoning can come on as soon as an hour after eating contaminated food or as long as five days later. Possible symptoms include stomach ache and cramps, vomiting and diarrhoea and a high temperature. If you are only mildly ill, just take plenty of fluids and rest until you feel ready to eat solids again. But if the symptoms are painful or persistent, contact your doctor. If you think a particular food, shop, cafe or restaurant was the source of your food poisoning contact the environmental health department of your local council so that appropriate action can be taken.

Food poisoning is particularly serious for babies, the elderly, pregnant women and anyone who is already ill or has low resistance to infection.

Microbes are micro-organisms which include bacteria, viruses, fungi (yeasts and moulds) and tiny cells called protozoa, which have more in common with animals than with plants. Microbes are too small to see individually without a microscope.

What we generally refer to as food poisoning can be roughly divided up into:

- **Food-borne infections** such as Salmonella, Listeria, Shigella, Campylobacter and virus infections. They are a real hazard to the consumer because in many cases the organism actually grows in the food. Usually these food-borne infections take a few days after the food is eaten to make their presence felt.
- **Poisoning by bacterial toxins** or true food poisoning. The bacteria responsible include Staphylococcus aureus, Clostridium welchii, Bacillus cereus and Clostridium botulinum. These bacteria grow in food and produce potent toxins (poisons) which can often survive heat treatment even after the bacteria responsible for manufacturing them have been

destroyed. Illness caused by these toxins is often quite rapid. Symptoms appear within a few hours.

- **Direct food poisoning** is caused by adulterated food, poisonous ingredients like fungi, or food (such as kidney beans which need ten minutes' rapid boiling at the beginning of their cooking time) that have not been adequately processed. Some products become toxic if they are kept long enough to deteriorate, for example, green potatoes.

Below are enemies with which you are most likely to have a close encounter of a regrettable kind. The first word of the name records the genus or group to which the organism belongs and the second indicates specifically which member of that family they are.

Bacteria

Bacteria are the most widespread villains in the food poisoning story and the most common bacteria causing food poisoning are Salmonella and Campylobacter. Bacteria are either rod-shaped or spherical and can be detected as sticky slime on meat, fish or poultry that has gone off. They are so small that 50,000 would fit on the back of a stamp.

Bacteria-contaminated food does not have to be left at a warm temperature long for bacteria to multiply rapidly. One bacterium can become two in 10–20 minutes, and further divide into one million in around $3\frac{1}{2}$ hours. Because bacteria thrive in warmth the risk is greatest in hot weather. Bacteria-friendly environments include not only warm rooms, but car boots and our own bodies. They thrive at about the same body temperature – 37°C – as we do, but different types will grow right across the range from 5–63°C. Bacteria can live but cannot multiply in a fridge at a temperature below 5°C. In the freezer they go into a state like hibernation. Once thawed, they can go back into the dividing and multiplying business.

Besides warmth, bacteria generally (though see Bacillus cereus below) like food that is moist and high in protein – like meat, poultry, eggs and raw shellfish.

Bacteria do not grow well in food with high levels of sugar,

184

acid or salt, which are often used as preservatives in jams and pickles. But as the manufacturers cut down on these in response to consumer demand, the products need to be moved from storecupboard to fridge.

Bacteria causing food poisoning come in the following guises:

☹ **Salmonellas** – including Salmonella typhimurium and Salmonella enteritides. The main sources of the Salmonellas are raw meat, poultry, eggs and raw (untreated) milk. Infection occurs either because raw food is not cooked well enough or because cooked food is contaminated by bacteria from raw food.

☹ **Campylobacters** – the most troublesome of which is Campylobacter jejuni, which also comes from animals we eat. Contaminated water and raw milk can be sources too. Only a small amount of bacteria is needed to cause an infection, which is perhaps why it is the commonest recognised cause of infective diarrhoea.

☹ **Staphylococcus aureus** does not come from either plants or animals but from ourselves. We can all carry Staphylococcus bacteria on the skin and in the nose; they can cause such skin infections as boils. Not all strains of Staphylococcus aureus cause food poisoning, but since there is no easy way of telling one from the other we need to keep them all at bay. Staphylococcus aureus is a nasty one: when it multiplies it can form a toxin which is harder to kill than the original bacteria, because it can survive heating. It is this toxin that causes food poisoning. Poor hygiene in shops and kitchens puts food at risk.

☹ **Listeria monocytogenes** is widely found in the environment and one in 20 of us carries it in our gut without ever knowing it. We are all exposed to it from time to time and it is little or no threat to most of us. But a pregnant woman with listeriosis can pass the bacteria across the placenta to her baby to cause stillbirth or miscarriage. It can also cause a type of meningitis in the elderly and anyone, including transplant recipients and people with HIV, whose immune system is suppressed or damaged. So these groups are advised to avoid the foods which have been found to have the highest concentration of Listeria, which are ripened soft cheese and pâté.

Listeria grows slowly in the fridge, which is why recommended maximum temperatures for fridges have been revised (to 5°C or below) recently. Listeria has been found in small quantities on salad, herbs and vegetables – probably too low to be a hazard for most people. But it does suggest that the particularly vulnerable groups outlined above would also be advised to wash fruit and vegetables to be eaten raw and not to keep them for more than a few days in the fridge.

Small numbers of Listeria have also been found on pre-cooked poultry and cook–chill foods. It is particularly important that these foods are reheated thoroughly, all the way through to the middle. They must reach a temperature of 70°C for two minutes to be safe.

CAUTION – EGGS

The Government recommends that no one should eat raw eggs or uncooked dishes made with raw eggs. These include home-made mayonnaise and some home-made ice-cream recipes. It also recommends that the old, the ill, the very young, pregnant women and anyone with a damaged immune system should not eat lightly cooked eggs or dishes containing them, such as home-made hollandaise and béarnaise sauces and meringues. People in these categories should eat eggs only if the white and the yolk are cooked solid. (The shop-bought versions of all these foods are made either with eggs that have been pasteurised or with dried egg that has been pasteurised before drying or processed in a way that is similar to pasteurisation, so do not present the same risks to vulnerable groups.)

CAUTION – CHEESE

Pregnant women and anyone with low resistance to infection should avoid soft ripened cheeses such as Brie, Camembert or chèvre, as well as pâtés.

Spore-bearers

Spore-bearers are organisms that can wall themselves up in spores like tiny seeds when conditions don't suit them and stay dormant until they meet the conditions they like. They are widespread in animals and the environment and include the following:

☹ **Clostridium botulinum** is a food-borne spore-bearing bacterium that, like Listeria, causes illness but not diarrhoea and vomiting. Botulism is the most serious form of food-poisoning and is often fatal. Victims may feel dizzy and nauseous and have breathing difficulties.

Botulism poisoning has been caused by hazelnut yogurt (the hazelnut puree was not adequately heat-treated), smoked fish and badly canned or bottled foods. The Government is now recommending that home cooks who bottle vegetables should stop because of the risk. However, the bacteria will not grow in acidic foods so home bottling of fruit is safe. If you want to store vegetables, freezing is the safe way to do it. Clostridium botulinum does not like acidity or salt and many cured foods rely on their salt content to prevent botulism. Properly processed salt fish has a high enough salt content to prevent its growth.

☹ **Clostridium perfringens** is less dangerous than Clostridium botulinum. It survives, especially in meat, after cooking. When warm food is left standing the spores release the bacteria they were protecting and go straight into divide and multiply mode. Thorough reheating, all the way through to the middle of the food, will prevent a bad bout of food poisoning.

☹ **Bacillus cereus** is sometimes found on dry rice and spores will survive if the rice is not cooked thoroughly. Spores that survive boiling will germinate and multiply if the rice is left to stand at room temperature after cooking. (It should be refrigerated, then reheated thoroughly.)

Viruses

Not all food poisoning is bacterial in origin. Viruses differ from bacteria in that they need living cells in which to multiply and may pick some of ours to do it in. Suitable cells are reprogrammed to produce more viruses. Several hundred new virus particles can then burst out to look for other cells to repeat the process. Fortunately, cooking kills viruses. Unfortunately, it doesn't take many to make us ill.

Shellfish in contaminated water pick up viruses that stick to their skins and are harmful to humans; some of them cause us vomiting and diarrhoea if they are not destroyed by adequate cooking. Others cause hepatitis (jaundice). It takes only a small dose to cause an infection and these viruses can also be spread by people handling food.

Fungi

A number of people die every year in Europe from picking and eating poisonous mushrooms. Deaths are rarer in Britain because hunting wild mushrooms is not a popular activity here, although there is a growing interest. To be safe:

☹ Don't eat wild mushrooms unless you are absolutely sure you know what you are eating.

☹ Keep anything you haven't identified out of contact with the rest.

☹ Buy wild mushrooms only if you are absolutely sure you are buying from someone knowledgeable and reliable.

Alkaloids

Solanine and chaconine are two alkaloids (relatives of caffeine) found in potatoes. Eating green, sprouted or blighted potatoes can cause acute illness and even death. Symptoms are drowsiness, breathing difficulty and paralysis as well as stomach ache and diarrhoea.

Threadworm infection

Good hygiene can help to control the worldwide problem of threadworm or pin-worm. The worm is a centimetre long and its eggs are passed on contaminated hands to food and drink. Once swallowed, the eggs develop into worms in the intestine and emerge to deposit eggs on the skin around the anus. The irritation can cause sleeplessness.

When sufferers scratch the irritated skin they transfer the eggs on to their hands and potentially back into their and the family's food again. Regular and thorough hand-washing and short clean nails can break the cycle of infection.

Pesticides

Farmers use pesticides to help check diseases and insects in crops, to reduce weeds, and to discourage unwanted shoots on trees and mould on fruit. Pesticides are also used to keep stored fruit and vegetables in good condition so keeping more produce available for more of the year. The cheap, widely available fruit and vegetables we expect all year are partly due to pesticides. But is there a hidden cost?

In 1990, 28,000 tonnes of chemicals were used to grow and store food in the UK. However, nearly 500 insect species have developed some level of pesticide resistance and, as more pests become resistant, more toxic pesticides have to be used to achieve the same results. Pesticides also often kill beneficial predators such as ladybirds, so increasing the frequency of pest outbreaks. There is some concern about residues of herbicides in water supplies and pesticides inefficiently sprayed can drift from their target to damage other crops and wildlife. The long-term risk of pesticides is virtually unknown.

The Government's guidelines indicate 'minimal use', with a Code of Practice which states that farmers should use pesticides 'only when necessary in relation to efficient production, if the consequences of not using them significantly outweigh the risks to human health and the environment of using them'. It has set up a review of 130 of the 400 active chemical ingredients which are formulated into 3000 or more pesticide products for use on crops in the UK, but it will be least 20 years before the work is complete. Although the Government's Advisory Committee is moving towards more public disclosure, much information on the safety of British pesticides is not available in the UK – though the US Freedom of Information Act means it can often be obtained there.

Opponents of pesticides say:

- According to the World Health Organization, 3,000,000 people a year are poisoned by pesticide use and more than 20,000 of them die. (Most at risk are those who make or use them, not those who eat them in food.)
- Both the British Medical Association and the Royal Commission on Environmental Pollution have recommended a policy of reducing use.
- The Danish government aims to cut the use of pesticides by 50 per cent by 1997 and the Dutch by the same amount by 2000.
- Researchers in the UK have found that cutting pesticides by 75 per cent gave the same or a very slightly reduced yield on some crops without putting up the cost of the food. Using fewer pesticides actually saved money.

Pesticide action plan

If you are concerned about the level of pesticides in your food, here are a few things you can do to minimise it:

- Discard outer leaves which are likely to have the highest concentration of residue from greenhouse sprays.
- Peel fruit and vegetables to remove surface residues (but this will also reduce the fibre in your diet).
- Rub the skin of fruit and vegetables and you may get rid of a bit of surface residue.
- Scrub the skin of fruit and vegetables and you are likely to reduce the residue – and the peel – a bit more.
- Trim all visible fat off meat and poultry to remove low levels of persistent residues from pesticides in the animal's environment which tend to collect in fat.
- Wash fruit and vegetables to get rid of water-soluble residues on the surface (a good practice because it removes dirt and bacteria anyway).

Irradiation

Advocates of irradiation see the process, in which radioactive gamma rays zap food, as a safer alternative to fungicides and insecticides which may leave potentially harmful residues in food. They say that irradiation can reduce the bacteria in food, particularly Salmonella in poultry. It can also speed up fruit ripening and slow down sprouting in potatoes. It does not make food radioactive and some irradiation is permitted in 39 countries.

The British Government permits the sale of irradiated food but says it must be labelled, except where a very small proportion of irradiated food is used in a product. So, in theory, everyone has a choice as to whether to buy it or not. But there are loopholes.

The first is that compound ingredients don't have to be listed if the compound ingredient itself makes up less than 25 per cent of the finished food, such as a strawberry tart filled with jam made from irradiated strawberries, if the jam makes up less than 25 per cent of the tart. Also, 'herbs and spices' and 'mixed spices' can appear on labels instead of a list of specific herbs and/ or spices as long as they make up less than 2 per cent of the product. And if the ingredient is not named, then the fact that it has been irradiated isn't mentioned either. The current EC proposals, if accepted, would not close this loophole. Food manufacturers also favour irradiation, but so far the major supermarkets have been hesitant about selling irradiated food because of consumer resistance.

The anti-irradiation lobby says:

- In low enough doses to avoid taste and appearance changes it cannot be detected, so food manufacturers may be tempted to cheat on the labelling.
- Irradiation could be used to clean up unfit food. (Condemned prawns were known to have been treated in the Netherlands and sold in Britain.)
- Strict controls would therefore be needed but are difficult to enforce. There is no way to test food to discover if it has been irradiated.
- Irradiation could lead to nutritional cons – selling food that looks fresher than it is.
- Sterilisation of food requires doses above the legally permitted maximum.

- Irradiating some (but not all) foods reduces their vitamin B1 and vitamin E content.
- No one yet knows the long-term effects of eating irradiated food.

Consumers' Association has taken a close interest in irradiation and is not in principle against the process. But it believes that irradiation should not be permitted until outstanding safety and consumer protection issues have been resolved. It is pressing for the consumer's right to know when any irradiated ingredients are used no matter how small the amount. It is urging the Government to press for a change in EC law to ensure this.

Street food

Street food has a reputation for being chancy, but it may not be really deserved. How safe it is is discussed in more detail in the next chapter, **Healthy eating out**.

Eating abroad

There are considerable food hazards for travellers abroad, and the more intrepid the journey the greater the dangers are likely to be. You can also find out more about these particular health risks and how best to minimise them in the next chapter.

CHAPTER 7

HEALTHY EATING OUT

HOW important it is to keep health in mind when you eat out depends, in the main, on how often you do it. If a restaurant meal is a rare special occasion for you, then probably the best philosophy is – go for it. Have what you like. No once-in-a-blue-moon blow-out can make a significant difference to how healthy your diet is.

But increasing numbers of people eat out often. On average, we now eat more than three meals a week away from home. It might be business dinners or canteen lunches, fast food with friends after work or a work-out, regular wine bar suppers, a pizza after the pictures or a burger with the family. Whatever your habits, the more often you eat out, the more *where* and *what* become important ingredients in healthy eating, and the more the dishes you choose from the menu matter.

The subject is a complex and elusive one. Any advice on best selections has to be qualified. You can order something with the same name on the menu at two restaurants and be served two very different dishes. Recipes, tastes and cooking philosophy vary from chef to chef.

Comparisons between cuisines can't be much more definitive either, in part because of the wide variations within them. One French restaurant, for example, might serve Normandy regional cooking laced with cream and butter. A second might be Provençal in inclination and still high in fat but favour the healthier option of olive oil. Yet another might have espoused the modern trend towards lighter, cleaner flavours and less rich sauces and score highest of all on the low-fat healthy eating test.

So it is difficult to define 'a French restaurant' in any way that is useful for comparing it with, say, 'a Chinese restaurant'. Price may also be a consideration: to some extent, you get what you pay for.

Of course we can all exercise our rights individually and collectively to be assertive diners. Restaurant chains need to be as sensitive as any other retailer to consumer pressure. Their staying in business depends on giving us what we want. It is up to us to make sure they know what that is, something we can do only if we are clear about it ourselves.

If you eat out regularly, you can find restaurants that fit in with your lifestyle and price range, where they are prepared to give you information and listen to what you want. Take advantage of it. Ask whether there is cream in the dish if you want to know. Ask for steamed fish with lemon juice if you would rather have that than fried, swimming in a rich sauce. If you want wholemeal rather than white bread, say so. If you don't want butter added to your vegetables in the kitchen, point it out when you order. If you want an undressed salad, say so – and send it back if they forget. People often seem to accept treatment in restaurants that they would walk out on anywhere else. If you are paying the bill, you call the shots.

One way to find restaurants and cafes sympathetic to your healthy eating aspirations is to look out for those displaying the *Heartbeat Award* sign in England and Wales or the *Healthy Eating Circle* sign in Northern Ireland. They indicate that healthy food choices are provided and highlighted on the menu as well as no-smoking areas and a good standard of food hygiene.

Despite the qualifications and exceptions above, there are some general guidelines that can help you make more informed choices. If you bear them in mind you will generally eat more healthily than if you do not.

First, some good news for fast-food fans from research published in *Which?* (January 1993).

Better burgers

Burgers are fast and convenient and we spend a small fortune on them. Around £820,000,000 is rung up each year on tills at burger bars in high streets, off motorways and at railway stations, just for burgers. The fries and the milkshakes and so on bought with them add extra. So how healthy burgers are has an important effect on how healthy British eating is.

Happily, burgers, it seems, aren't as bad for us as we might have suspected. In general, *Which?* found the plain old burger lower in fat than we might have feared. The roll gives complex carbohydrates. The trouble only really comes when you add cheese and mayonnaise or a high-fat sauce or relish or when you make a meal of it – such as burger, fries, dessert and milkshake. Then a burger no longer passes the healthy eating test.

Which? found wide variations in the fat content of the same dish on different menus. Outlets do not have to give the sort of information that would help you make healthy burger choices but Burger King, McDonald's and Wimpy all do. At Burger King you will find it framed on the wall by the counter; Wimpy supply it on demand, and McDonald's take-away style.

What you might think are best choices tend not to be. Chicken and fish are a lower-fat starting-point than meat, but fish and chicken products often fared quite badly by comparison with beef by the time they were actually served, usually deep-fried in batter. One of the worst fast-food buys for fat content turned out to be chicken nuggets, cut so small they soaked up even more fat in the frier. Nine nuggets coated in batter and deep-fried could give 25g of fat, a third of the total daily recommended intake for a woman and nearly a quarter for a man. Worse still was a chicken sandwich (bun, a chicken burger and mayonnaise) from Wimpy, with 28g of fat.

Potentially healthy beanburgers, with their high offering of fibre, sometimes suffered similar fat-added problems. For example, Casey Jones' beanburgers have 27g of fat. Compare the fish, chicken and bean dishes with a beefburger (a 2oz patty and a bun), which had an average of around 10g of fat, and as little as 6g if you got it from McDonald's. So opting for something with chicken or fish or even beans in the name because it sounds healthier could turn out to be an unsound strategy. And bigger is certainly not better when it comes to healthiness of burgers, as the chart shows.

Which? found the worst burger buy from each of the chains was as follows:

Chain	Burger	Fat (g)
Burger King	Double Whopper with cheese	48
Casey Jones	Mighty Casey	43
Julie's Pantry	Half-pound cheeseburger	71
McDonald's**	Quarter-pounder with cheese	23
Snack Cafe*	Half-pound cheeseburger	60
Starburger*	Halfpounder	39
Wimpy	Halfpounder	51

* These chains were unable to supply *Which?* with nutritional information.

** McDonalds' burgers tend to be smaller and they don't do a half-pounder at all.

Figures were calculated from McCance and Widdowson.

Bear in mind that a medium portion of chips could add another 15g of fat to the meal, 21g if it was at McDonald's. Drinks can be high in sugar. A medium-sized cola has eight teaspoons of it and milkshakes nine, plus 6g of fat. Salt, too, is a worry. Some burgers contain more than the World Health Organization's recommended healthy limit of 6g a day and in addition Burger King, Casey Jones and McDonald's pre-salt their chips.

McDonald's is the largest fast-food chain in the world, with more than 12,500 outlets in 65 countries, including 450 in the UK. It scored best for low fat in most of the categories that *Which?* compared. It won the prize for the hamburger, cheese-burger, quarter-pounder, chicken sandwich and fishburger, but lost to Julie's Pantry beanburger and scored worst for chips. Their chips are fried in a mixture of vegetable oil and beef fat, boosting the proportion of saturates (though the company is doing taste tests as a preliminary to switching their frying oil). McDonald's burgers tend to be smaller – they don't do a half-pounder at all.

Wherever you buy, you'll do best with your burger if you

skip the cheese, resist the dollop of mayonnaise, go easy on sauces and relishes and give the chips a miss.

But if the burger has turned out to be not necessarily as bad a choice as most of us probably imagined, it could be much improved. Assertive diners might want to ask their burger bars how soon they can expect some even healthier options. Wimpy recently launched the new Lean Burger in response to consumer demand for more choice. It had 65 per cent less fat (11g) than Wimpy's regular quarter-pounder. Assertive diners might also point out that American fast-food restaurants usually offer salads with low-fat dressings, low-fat milkshakes and low-fat burgers as a matter of course. McDonald's US outlets offer the McLean Deluxe, the leanest big burger ever, with only 10g of fat. Why is it not on the menu in the UK? If burger chains can be convinced that consumers here also want healthier choices then they will have no choice but to follow that lead.

Sandwich bars

Hamburgers and chips are actually only our second-favourite way to eat out as a nation. Sandwiches eat up even more of our eating out budgets – around a third more, in fact. Fish-and-chips are third and pasta and pizza together fourth – which is pretty good news. With the guidelines advocating we fill up more on complex carbohydrates, a sandwich with the right filling can be healthy eating.

Chain retail outlets such as supermarkets increasingly sell sandwiches sealed for freshness, and with nutritional information printed on the pack so you can seek out the best buys for presence of fibre and absence of fat. If you aren't in the habit of reading it, you may be surprised to see how high the fat can sometimes be. Low-calorie sandwiches are often labelled too, for the benefit of slimmers. Generally in this context, low-calorie tends to equate with low-fat.

If you are buying from a sandwich bar, the burger bar advice above has a message in this context, too. Don't forget:

☹ Mayonnaise is a good thing to avoid.
☹ Watch out for the mayonnaise in which coleslaw is usually dressed and the mayonnaise used in coronation chicken.

☺ Salad cream is generally lower in saturates than mayonnaise but skipping the salad cream is healthier still.

☺ Ask your sandwich bar if they will do a reduced-fat or very low-fat mayonnaise or natural yogurt option.

☹ Bacon is a fat baddie, too, especially unless you know it is middle or back, carefully trimmed, grilled on a rack and well-drained and then blotted on kitchen paper – unlikely in a sandwich bar with a big turnover and staff working flat out. A bacon sandwich with a fried egg is worse.

☹ Sausage sandwiches have an unhealthily high saturates content, unless you are lucky enough to find a sandwich bar that seeks out lower-fat versions and grills out much of the fat.

☺ Brown and granary breads add more fibre to your diet than white. Wholemeal is even better. Ring the changes with baguettes or bagels.

☹ Full-fat cheese loads fat into sandwiches.

☺ Two rounds of single sandwiches are better than one triple-decker because of the better bread-to-filling ratio.

☺ Ask about low-fat bread spreads instead of butter. Or go without a spread. With many fillings you will not notice a difference.

☺ Cucumber, tomato and lettuce are a healthy way to add moisture and texture to a sandwich.

Fish-and-chip shops

The trouble with fish and chips is fat. Fish is a low-fat source of protein and potatoes are a low-fat source of carbohydrates and vitamins. Frying them is the problem.

If you eat fish and chips often:

☺ It's better to have some bread and cut down the quantity of fish or chips or both.

☺ Fish and no chips or a smaller portion of chips is better anyway.

☺ It pays to ask what oil a fish shop uses for frying and choose the one using vegetable oil, rather than one using beef fat or palm oil. (See **Chapter 3** for a guide to the healthiest.)

Pasta places

Pasta is a good source of complex carbohydrates. Pasta sauces can be a health trap. Even if a sauce is called tomato on the menu it can translate as tomato and oil; if you are lucky, the oil will be olive oil. Generally:

☺ Tomato or other vegetable sauces are your best bet.

☹ Sauces with cream or cheese or both as ingredients will be some of the highest in fat.

☺ A smaller plate of pasta, with bread or an undressed side salad or after a bowl of vegetable soup, beats a large plate of sauced pasta.

☹ Don't have too much cheese on top.

Pizza places

Pizzas are half-way to being a healthy choice – the bottom half. With the advice that we should eat more complex carbohydrates in the form of bread, a traditional pizza has a lot going for it. Unfortunately, the popular deep-pan versions, with a higher top to bottom ratio, are less good for us. So, paradoxically, are versions with a thinner, crisper base. Deep-fried pizzas are often very high in fat. Thin bases make less of a contribution of complex carbohydrates for the same amount of filling (and fat) as regular ones do. When you opt for pizza, remember:

☺ Choose the regular base. What you want is the highest proportion of base to top.

☺ Ham, tuna and prawns are better than peperoni, sausage or bacon.

☺ If you go for extra topping, healthier choices include tomato, onion, green pepper, pineapple, sweetcorn or other vegetables, chilli or olives.

☹ Don't ask for extra cheese, please.

☺ You might want to go for an undressed side salad to balance the meal up a bit.

☹ Garlic bread with melted cheese on it is even higher in fat than straight garlic bread.

☹ The non-diet versions of Coke and Pepsi have a lot more sugar in them than the diet versions.

Potato places

Jacket potatoes can be a good healthy option for eaters out. Just:

☹ Don't have a buttered potato.
☺ Choose a low-fat filling like baked beans, cottage cheese, tuna, chicken or even chilli con carne, rather than high-fat Cheddar cheese.

Steak houses

Steak houses have diversified and usually offer a lot more than steaks nowadays. Mostly, they have dropped the word steak in their name, too, to draw attention to the wider choices now on offer. They are increasingly catering for the health-conscious diner.

Look for:

☺ Melon filled with fruit as a starter.
☺ Vegetable soup.
☺ Prawn cocktail served with the sauce separate so you can control your portion size.
☺ Hot salads of beef strips or chicken breast with your choice of dressing.
☺ A salad trolley.
☺ Reduced-calorie dressings available for salads.
☺ Poached or chargrilled fish.
☺ Sauces served on the side with meat or fish dishes so you can take them, leave them, or just have a little.
☺ A choice of steak sizes.
☺ Jacket potatoes.

And don't forget:

☺ Leave the fat from the steak on your plate.
☺ The more well-done a steak is cooked, the more fat it sheds.

Salad bars

What could sound healthier than a salad bar? The reality disappoints, as *Which? way to Health* discovered when it investigated them in 1991. Most of the restaurant chains visited were found to offer single vegetable items like tomato and cucumber as two-thirds of their choices and the mixed salads that made up the remaining third tended to be dressed in a layer of vinaigrette or mayonnaise which added fat and calories. Few salad bars offer the option of a low-calorie dressing and even more rarely is nutritional information available. A suitable case for a touch of customer campaigning?

But salads can provide lots of vitamins, minerals and fibre. You can mix your own from the single ingredients so you have control of how much dressing you get. Or go for good choices such as bean and pasta salads, or grated carrot, red cabbage and so on, that are healthy as long as they do not have too much dressing. And have some bread to complete the meal, so taking in extra fibre and complex carbohydrate.

Hotels and catering chains

When *Which?* surveyed 30 of the largest hotel, restaurant and catering chains in the country in 1990, 18 organisations, between them responsible for 2,500 outlets all over the UK, replied. Most said they had noticed increased demand for healthier choices. A lot of them had responded by making at least some healthier choices available. Some made a positive effort to draw the attention of customers to those choices on the menu. Others simply waited to be asked. So it was often a case of assertive diners welcome – but you have to declare yourselves.

At the same time as the menu survey, *Which?* did further research that illustrates the difficulty of dining out healthily without the active cooperation of chefs, chains and restaurateurs. Researchers bought five samples each of lasagne, beef Madras and chicken with cashew-nuts from different restaurants and take-aways and compared them.

The lasagnes ranged from 16g to 25g of fat and from 7g to 13g of saturates per 300g portion. The beef Madras from five different Indian restaurants varied from 20g to 52g of fat and from 5g to 9g of saturates in the same amount. The 300g servings of chicken with cashew-nuts from five Chinese restaurants went from 21g to 51g of fat, with saturates varying from 5g up to 12g.

Despite the difficulties, there are tips worth knowing when you begin to pick your way through the menu minefield.

Chinese restaurants

The Chinese have a completely different definition of healthy eating from the orthodox Western view – so different that our thinking and theirs on the subject barely meet. Chinese diners will choose from a menu by assessing what they feel is their body's present state and then considering what would be healthy for them to eat at that meal. It might be meat if they feel there is too much cold in the body and it needs warming, for example. Besides this difference in attitude, there is another dietary consideration. The Chinese generally leave more fat on meat and cook meat in more fat than is recommended in the West, but they eat no dairy foods. As a result, they still have a lower total fat intake than people in the UK.

Here are some of the facts you need to bear in mind when you choose from a Chinese menu:

☹ Shanghai cuisine tends to use a lot of sugar in 'savoury' dishes, including in vegetables.

☹ Cantonese sweet-and-sour dishes in restaurants in Britain tend to have lots of sugar, too. As a rough guide, the cheaper the restaurant the higher the sugar content.

☹ Generally, the more you pay the healthier the food. Cheaper Chinese restaurants tend to use more fat and sugar in dishes and to use less healthy cooking methods.

☹ Spare ribs are usually loaded with fat. They often have untrimmed visible fat and are deep-fried in more.

☹ Dim-sum can be bad news. The savoury ones often have hot lard or fat poured over them. They are also often deep-fried. And the sweet ones can have a lot of added sugar.

☺ But some dim-sum are steamed. Go for them if possible.

☺ Steamed dishes, such as fish, can be good news. Unfortunately, you are more likely to find them at expensive restaurants than cheap ones. Some Chinese restaurants will coat the fish with fat to prevent it drying out while it is being cooked. The result can be delicious, but fat may. have been absorbed into the food.

☺ Dishes like beef with black beans and peppers have a sauce based on soy sauce and less fat or sugar than other options on the menu. (But watch the salt in soy. It's loaded.)

☺ Stir-fried food is healthy – but the real thing is rarely found outside more expensive restaurants because it is labour-intensive to prepare and it must be cooked at the last minute and served at once. You will often see stir-fry on menus describing dishes initially stir-fried but then braised, so that they will reheat. They are likely to have more fat and possibly sugar than a true stir-fry.

☺ Steamed rice is a healthy option. Pass over fried rice dishes to keep the fat content low.

☺ Noodles in or alongside a dish make it healthier by increasing the complex carbohydrate content in the meal.

☺ When you see 'pot' or 'bau' on a menu, it will be a casserole of fish or meat or bean curd, or some combination of them with vegetables, and is often a good choice.

☺ Bean curd is generally good news – until or unless it is fried. It is low-fat and highly nutritious.

☹ Monosodium glutamate or MSG is an artificial copy of a natural flavour-enhancing ingredient used in Chinese cooking and blamed – though without definitive proof – for Chinese Restaurant Syndrome. Sufferers develop swollen lips, eye irritation and vomiting, which are typical signs of (though not necessarily from) food intolerance. The cheaper the restaurant the more likely MSG will have been used freely (though again, not necessarily).

Indian restaurants

Sugar can be a problem in Indian restaurant food. Fat can be an even bigger one. But it is possible to find a healthy meal from an Indian menu. It helps to know:

☺ Tandoori dishes are a healthy eater's best bet, as they are cooked without any added fat or sugar. The name comes from the clay oven in which they were traditionally baked.

☺ The traditional accompaniment for tandoori food is a green salad, without dressing, and that's a healthy eating choice, too. But check as some Indian restaurants dress their salads because they think it will please Western customers.

☺ Choose boiled rice.

☺ Chapati has no fat in it, unlike nan which has a lot.

☺ Tandoori roti, a bread made thicker than chapati but from a similar dough, is also fat-free.

☺ Vegetable curries can have quite a bit of fat added in the cooking but they are still a better bet than the meat version of the same dish because the meat itself contributes more.

☹ Ghee is bad news. It is clarified butter and high in saturates, and some Indian dishes have an awful lot of it.

☹ Worst health choices tend to be the rich shahi dishes including pasandas, masalas and kormas, which can have both vegetable oil and ghee and a lot of added sugar as well.

☺ Some Indian restaurants use vegetable oil rather than the more traditional ghee in such curries as Madras and vindaloos and they don't usually have added sugar either.

☹ Healthy eaters should give poppadums a miss. The reason nibbling them gives you greasy fingers is that they have been deep-fried.

Japanese restaurants

Japanese food is not widely available in the UK and when you do find it, you can usually expect to pay a lot for it. The Japanese turn healthy vegetables into less healthy 'fritters' when they cover them with a delicate batter and deep-fry them for their popular tempura. Nevertheless, it is still one of the healthiest of cuisines. Japanese cooks may use a little more sugar in savoury dishes than Western ones, but on the whole it is a pretty healthy, nutritious and low-fat option.

Thai restaurants

If you go up country in Thailand itself, you will find one of the world's truly healthy cuisines. A typical Thai meal there might be steamed rice, raw or steamed vegetables, and nam prik, a sauce with fermented fish plus all sorts of delicious flavourings like lemon juice and garlic. It is almost as if the Thai diet had been designed in response to guidelines for healthy eating.

The popularity and influence of Thai cuisine in Britain has risen dramatically in the last decade. Generally speaking, the more authentic the restaurant the healthier. But there is still an enormous gap between an authentic dish in a restaurant and an authentic diet. A proper Thai meal might be hard to make a commercial proposition in Europe. Still, the more closely a restaurant sticks to authentic recipes, the more healthily you can eat there.

Recognising authenticity is the problem. It is not necessarily related to price, which is more likely to reflect decor, location and philosophy, but it can be a good indication if the menu is large and food comes slowly when business is not over-brisk and very slowly when the restaurant is busy. In Western cuisines, a large menu can mean a deep-freeze and a microwave out the back. With Thai it probably means that the restaurant is making everything to order. And that means the place is following the authentic Thai practice of cooking fresh and serving straight from the wok. A good Thai restaurant might offer 150 different dishes. So regard it as a good sign if your order has to take its turn in the queue.

It is worth remembering that:

☺ Almost all Thai restaurants cook to order – few reheat food.
☺ Thai salads are usually very healthy. They are made of raw or steamed or grilled ingredients and dressed with a mixture of chilli, garlic and Thai fish sauce.
☺ At authentic Thai restaurants most wok-fried dishes will be pretty healthy. If they are using the right equipment correctly, they will fry in oil at a very high temperature and little of it will be absorbed by the food.
☺ The steamed rice is a good bet.

☺ Thai soups are generally healthy, except for the ones that contain coconut.

☹ Coconut cream is used widely in Thai cooking. Coconut is high in cholesterol, and coconut oil, one step along the line from coconut cream, has very high levels of saturates.

☹ Thai curries usually have coconut cream in them, and so are usually best avoided if you are looking for a healthy option.

☹ Beware of steamed fish. Thai steaming is usually done by putting oil and then minced pork fat on top at the start.

☹ Non-authentic Thai restaurants will add about a teaspoonful of sugar to every dish that would have none in Thailand, because of the Eastern perception of Western tastes. Over a meal, that can add up.

How safe is eating out?

Of course healthy eating out also needs to be safe eating. Check whether the restaurant looks clean and see if the staff appear rushed off their feet. Being over-busy makes it more difficult to be careful about hygiene.

Have a look, too, at the length of the menu. If it is too long, the food may be coming from the freezer and straight into the microwave. That does not necessarily matter from a health point of view as long as it is hot enough, and hot enough right through, by the time it reaches you. But you may feel you wish to check if the prices reflect the fact that what you eat is not being cooked fresh to order.

Street food

With grazing increasingly becoming part of the pattern of our regular eating, eating out does not necessarily mean sitting down at a table and using a knife and fork. Seafood or hot dogs or burgers from a van on the street corner can be the most convenient way to bridge that gap. But how safe are they?

Meat and seafood are traditionally high-risk foods and street food is certainly potentially risky. It has often to be prepared in conditions that are unavoidably unhygienic. But when *Which? way to Health* investigated in 1991 the magazine found little evidence of street food causing illness and its own micro-biological tests were encouraging.

Of course, it is not necessarily easy to trace food poisoning back to street corner vendors. If a lot of guests at the same wedding reception become ill afterwards the common denominator is obvious. If a large number of people who buy hot dogs the same day from the same van go down with an attack of tummy trouble, it is less likely that the link will ever be established. Besides which, Environmental Health Officers rarely work late at night when many of the street food vendors are at their busiest and vans tend to move on from one local authority area to another, discouraging official attention. But on the plus side, the food does tend to be cooked and served hot, which gives some protection against bacteria. *Which? way to Health* found meat and meat products were mostly acceptable, but seafood bacteria levels less reassuring.

An interesting light is thrown on the question by a study at the Center for Disease Control in Atlanta where researchers reviewed 1500 food poisoning outbreaks throughout the USA. They concluded that only about 6 per cent were related to open-air foods. And more of them stemmed from foods served at picnics and church social events than from vans and stalls.

Here are some pointers to help you:

☺ Buy where the staff wear clean overalls or aprons and cover cuts or sores with a waterproof dressing.
☺ Buy where the staff cover their hair with a net or hat.
☺ Buy where the work surfaces look clean.
☺ Buy where rubbish is kept well away from food in covered bins or closed bags.
☺ Buy where ingredients are kept cold until they are cooked and then served hot.
☹ Don't buy where you see staff smoke, comb their hair or eat or drink on duty.
☹ Don't buy where you see scratches in a work surface. They can harbour bacteria.
☹ Don't buy where you can see dirt, grease, cobwebs or grubby teatowels.
☹ Don't buy where raw and cooked food are not kept apart.

Food on holiday

Even in the UK water doesn't even have to be dangerous to disagree with you. Just the presence of different bacteria from the ones you are used to can cause upsets, especially in young children. If you are staying down on the farm and your kids love the idea of milk straight from the cow you might be wise to resist. They could be far better off with pasteurised from the local shop. It might be unromantic, but it is safer, especially if it is what they are used to at home.

Food abroad

How safe it is to eat abroad depends partly on which country you will be visiting. Northern Europe, North America, Australia and New Zealand all have similar health standards to the UK's. Mediterranean countries and off-shore islands, where tourist development has been swift and has often outstripped the provision of treated water and sewage disposal, can have problems. Developing countries start off with different standards from ours anyway and you may find even lower standards of hygiene and technology the further you go from the bigger centres of population. The experience of many travellers is unfortunately reflected in the nicknames of such foreign exotics as 'Delhi belly', 'gippy tummy' and 'Montezuma's revenge'.

Unless you have reason to be confident that food handling standards are high, forget everything you have read so far about healthy eating. Forget low fat, low sugar, high starch and lots of fruit and vegetables as your primary healthy eating litany. Not becoming ill after eating must have a higher priority than longer-term health risks and nutritional benefits.

The safest food is food that is freshly cooked and served hot. Salads and cold food can be risky. Anything sitting around on a buffet for hours is likely to be bad news. It takes a bit of mental adjustment, but in developing countries where produce usually has an invisible coating of dried sewage, a plate of chips and a bottle of sugary soft drink can become the relatively healthy option and fruit and vegetables can represent the more unhealthy choice.

Besides using commercially bottled water for drinking (make sure you see the bottle opened) and even for cleaning your teeth, you should avoid ice made from local water.

High-risk holiday foods include:

☹ Salads – you will want to know if they have been washed in tap water anywhere you aren't drinking the water. And there can be a risk in some tropical countries of exposure from improperly washed vegetables to parasite roundworm eggs.
☹ Fruit – always peel fruit before you eat it. And do it yourself.
☹ Fruit juices from street vendors.
☹ Shellfish – it is safest to avoid shellfish altogether. By the time it had been cooked long and hard enough to be sure it was safe, you would no longer fancy it.
☹ Ice-cream – made from unpasteurised milk it may put you at risk from food poisoning.
☹ Uncooked or undercooked meat carries a risk not only of food poisoning but also of parasitic infections like tapeworm in some countries.
☹ Raw fish.
☹ Buffets, or anything else left out in a warm climate.
☹ Sauces and mayonnaise left out on the table.
☹ Food that has had flies on it or been reheated or handled a lot. (Regard anything canapé-like as suspect.)
☹ Anything free. Resist – or you could get more than you bargained for.

Here are some safer suggestions:

☺ Food that is fresh, cooked thoroughly, and served hot.
☺ Fruit, especially when it is easy to peel or slice open without contaminating the flesh inside (bananas, avocado, melon and paw-paw, for example).
☺ Commercially bottled water that you have bought unopened or seen opened in front of you.
☺ Packaged or tinned food.
☺ Freshly baked bread.
☺ Tea.
☺ Chips, if there is nothing that looks healthier on the menu.
☺ Ask for something like fried eggs that will have to be cooked

to order for you so that you know it will not have been sitting around encouraging bacteria to breed.

There are injections you may need before you travel to give you protection against diseases to which you could be exposed through food or otherwise when you are abroad. Check with your doctor at the very least two months, preferably three, before you are due to travel what is required for the country to which you are going. Check, too, if local mosquitoes carry malaria at the time of year you will be there. You may need to take tablets to reduce the risk of getting it.

If you are going to what you know is a high-risk and hot country, it is wise to carry medication to arrest diarrhoea and to prevent dehydration if you do come down with a bad bout of a tummy bug. There is a case for letting *mild* upsets just run their course, giving food a rest but avoiding dehydration with lots of sweet and salty (non-alcoholic) drinks unless the symptoms persist. But a serious bout can be extremely debilitating, and if you can't get a supply of trustworthy sweet and salty drinks you need to be equipped to take direct action.

Ask your doctor for something to take with you to arrest diarrhoea quickly and something else that will prevent dehydration if you do get diarrhoea. It is especially important to prevent dehydration in the very old and very young. (A cheap but effective home-made treatment is four heaped teaspoons of sugar and half a teaspoon of salt to a litre of clean water if all three are available. Drink lots of it.)

You may regret it if you decide not to give this first-aid kit luggage room. Letting your intestinal lining become damaged by prolonged, untreated, severe diarrhoea can cause malabsorption problems from which you could be months recovering. Even if you get only mild diarrhoea, convenience may be the overriding consideration. You may not want to face a long journey, especially on public transport, feeling weak and unsure how long you can go between visits to the lavatory.

One final word of warning: if you get diarrhoea accompanied by fever or bleeding it could be dysentery. Don't just treat yourself for it. You must see a doctor as soon as you can.

CHAPTER 8

EATING PROBLEMS AND PROBLEM EATING

FOR many people the perpetual pursuit of ideal slimness – often a quite unrealistic target – overshadows every meal they eat as they lunge between crash diets and bingeing. Everything consumed is taken with a side serving of guilt, while they deprive themselves in their constant pilgrimage towards the target that is always just out of reach. They live in the grip of the diet trap.

When researchers asked 33,000 American women what they most wanted out of life, more of them chose losing 10–15lb than success in work or love. No doubt a similar survey in the UK would not come to a significantly different conclusion: two-thirds of British women diet from time to time and 15 per cent are permanently on a diet.

Eating problems

Whatever degree of slimness these people do attain, the yo-yo effect almost always follows, when the weight lost too fast in a too-rigid calorie reduction bounces right back the minute they take the brakes off. Metabolism and psychology gang up to catch the stop-go slimmer on the rebound. Fewer than one in ten who lose weight keep it off permanently.

So, if you recognise the pattern and want to get off the merry-go-round and on course to a permanent solution to the problem of being overweight, crash dieting is out. Healthy eating – real healthy eating – is in. If you are carrying a few extra pounds they will not damage your health – the worst they will do is injure your vanity.

WHICH? WAY TO A HEALTHIER DIET

There is more potential mileage in coming to terms with the
fact that you are not a stick insect and will never become one
than in letting your weight cloud your life. If it helps, remind
yourself that the media-star models who earn more in a day than
most of us do in a year exhibiting their ribcages divide into the
naturally skinny and the ones who eat like a jockey before a big
race every day of their lives. Accepting that you are neither can
be liberating in ways that may surprise you. And the weight
bonus of deciding to kick the crash diet habit and settle for
sensible and steady healthy eating is that, over time, you may
well settle at a lower weight than you currently are anyway.

Are you overweight?
If you discovered when you read Chapter 1 that you are
overweight enough to be risking your health, you do need a
strategy for shedding some of that excess. Again, healthy eating
must be the theme. If you are genuinely overweight, healthy
eating should mean an eating pattern that will very gradually
get you into a healthier shape without setting up a rebound
effect. It should be an eating pattern that will help you stay a
healthy weight for the rest of your life.

Slimming diets can help you lose weight in the short-term.
They fail in the end if they have not changed the patterns and
habits that led you to gain it in the first place. So the way you
lose weight must have built into it good long-term habits if it
is to be a permanent solution to the problem. Below are some
pointers that may help.

To get yourself in the right frame of **mind**:

☺ Try to make friends with your body: for as long as you treat
   it as the enemy, weight loss is going to be a battlefield.
☺ Say nice things to it in the mirror. If you buy clothes, buy
   them to fit – not to be comfortable when you have lost
   another inch . . .
☺ Look at your lifestyle. Do you have some time for yourself,
   to do something that is for you, regularly? If not, now's the
   time to arrange some.
☺ Evaluate the other sources of pleasure in your life besides
   food. What – eating apart – do you do just because you enjoy it?

☺ Write a list of things you find enjoyable and relaxing, such as lying in a hot bath listening to the radio for half an hour, going for a swim, going for a walk in the park, going to a pottery class . . . Resolve to do at least one of them.

☺ Keep a food diary for a week or two. Write down literally everything you eat. Keep a chart with days across the top and times down the side, rule it into squares and record in them what you ate and what else was going on in your life at the time. When you have finished, study it in two ways. First, what does it tell you about the types and quantities of food you eat, and how do these compare with the healthy eating guidelines? Secondly, what does it tell you about when you turn to what sort of food? Is a row with your partner the trigger for a bar of chocolate, for example? Once you are more aware of what nudges you to eat, you can start looking for other ways to deal with those pressures.

☺ If you think there's a physical reason for your being obese, check with your doctor so that you can have appropriate treatment if necessary and stop kidding yourself otherwise.

To get yourself in the right frame of **body**:

☺ Use the guidelines in **Chapter 1** as your overall game plan.

☺ If you start to lose more than a pound or two a week you are overdoing it. Slow down.

☺ Never use laxatives as a slimming aid. Besides being dangerous for your health, they don't work for weight loss.

☺ When it says (in this book) semi-skimmed or skimmed milk, that means skimmed for you.

☺ Remember that getting a third of your calories from fat is the *maximum* recommended for healthy eating. You can reduce to very much less and still have a healthy diet.

☺ Really cut back the fat in your diet, but don't just do it negatively. Make a serious exploration of the hints and suggestions in **Chapters 3 and 4**. Try them and find the ones you like. There is no overnight cure for your problem. You need long-term commitment, so build in all the enjoyment you can.

☺ Don't forget that there are hints scattered through those chapters particularly for people with weight problems.

☺ Eat lots of vegetables and fruit and salads with low-fat dressings. They are nourishing, filling and can help retrain your taste.

☺ Fibre is a good friend to slimmers. It adds bulk without calories, making food feel satisfying and helping you feel fuller for longer.

☺ A big bowl of thick soup made of nothing but vegetable stock and loads of vegetables can be one of a dieter's best friends.

☺ Don't underestimate water. It makes fibre more effective, it can take the edge off your hunger, and your body needs lots of it to function efficiently.

☻ Be wary of alcohol – it consists of empty calories. A pre-dinner drink is not described as an aperitif (appetiser) for nothing. Alcohol can make you hungry. You may find that a glass of wine with a meal is less of a hazard than a glass on an empty stomach beforehand.

☺ Like everyone else, you should fill up on complex carbohydrates, without adding high-fat spreads, flavourings or sauces. But for you that doesn't mean you can eat as much of them as you like. You have to experiment to discover the right amount for you.

☹ Don't skip meals.

☺ Don't deny hunger – if you feel it, feed it. What creates weight problems is not eating when you are hungry but eating from habit and using food in an attempt to meet other needs. Success lies in what rather than when you eat.

☺ Try not to become too hungry. If you sit down to a meal ravenous, you will eat more than you need. And if you are starving and the next meal is too far away, that is when you are most likely to binge on pastry or chocolate or whatever your weakness is.

☺ You may have to re-learn what it is to be not hungry. If you don't think you have had a meal unless you leave the table feeling leaden, that may be part of what caused your problem. Once you know you can have a (sensible) snack when you need one, you may feel less compelled to keep eating at mealtimes as insurance against future hunger.

☺ Eat slowly, with pauses.

☹ Don't shop on an empty stomach.

214

☺ Try this trick. If you aren't sure if you want to eat something, close your eyes and imagine you have eaten it. Do you feel glad you did – or do you wish you hadn't? Go with your gut feeling.

☹ Don't be a slave to the scales. Don't weigh yourself more than once a week. And if you prefer to forget the scales and measure progress by how you feel in your clothes, that's fine, too.

☺ It is essential that you exercise while you are trying to lose weight. It increases your metabolic rate not only while you are doing it but for hours afterwards. That means you burn up more of what you eat and store less. It builds and protects muscle, and it can help you to learn to like your body better.

☺ If you have been doing no exercise, start with something gentle like walking. And start gently – 10–15 minutes a day to begin with.

☺ Don't exercise in the spirit of self-punishment. Find a form of exercise you really enjoy.

☺ Learn to forgive yourself. Tomorrow is always another day.

☺ And never say never. Don't tell yourself you are never going to have anything that you really enjoy ever again.

Are you underweight?

For some people, the problem is not being overweight but feeling that they are thinner than they would like to be. Paradoxically, much of the same advice applies to both groups. Like those who go through life forever dreaming of being thinner, those who feel underweight, too, might find that there is more mileage in getting to like themselves as they are now rather than letting an ideal future shape overshadow their lives.

But if you feel you are seriously underweight and want to increase your size, you should first check with your doctor to see if you are, and if there is a reason for it that needs treatment. For practical help, look at the slimming tips dotted through **Chapters 3 and 4** and turn them on their heads – with one proviso. You will need to make sure you don't overdo both total fat intake, and even more importantly, intake of saturates. Put plenty of carbohydrates – bread, pasta, grains, pulses – on your menu.

The other side of the scales

Obesity, anorexia and bulimia nervosa might seem to have little in common. Habitual over-eating, refusing to eat, and a compulsion to binge and vomit might seem unrelated. But they do share a common element – sufferers are not putting into practice what healthy eating really means. If being seriously overweight puts your life on the line in the long term, an eating disorder can put you at even more immediate risk.

Anorexia, untreated, is fatal. Anorexics, enslaved for complex underlying psychological reasons by the compelling but distorted body images that make them unable to evaluate their bodies realistically, can avoid food until it kills them. Anorexia has been reported in girls whose ages are not yet into double figures. Sufferers are prominently, though not exclusively, teens to twenties and female, and often highly intelligent.

Bulimics are people who binge-eat and then usually make themselves vomit after eating (though some alternate bingeing and fasting or use laxatives or diuretics). People suffering from **bulimia** experience as compelling the recurring cycle of splurging and purging. Some use vomiting to keep themselves seriously underweight. Some are obese, despite their regular vomiting. Some have weight swings. And yet others stay a normal and stable weight.

Because many succeed in keeping their weight down they can be, overall, the least visible group of the disordered eaters. But they are preventing their food nourishing their bodies, and storing up multiple health problems for the future. Bulimia, on average, starts slightly later than (and sometimes following) anorexia. It is widespread in women in their twenties and thirties, many of them hard-working, ambitious, intelligent and successful.

Anorexia and bulimia nervosa are both on the increase. Britain has an estimated 3,500,000 bulimics and anorexics, with 6,000 new cases being reported annually. It is anybody's guess how much bulimia remains unreported. Anorexics are also becoming younger all the time. Both conditions are complex and can become too serious for self-help alone to be enough.

You may need help if:

☹ You always feel guilty when you eat.

☹ You binge.

☹ You eat secretly.

☹ You eat a normal meal with other people, then top up alone.

☹ You surreptitiously eat a lot while preparing and serving family meals and then sit down and eat a normal meal with them.

☹ You look forward to eating on your own.

☹ You think about food a lot of the time, even when you are not hungry.

☹ You lie about what you eat.

☹ You don't believe friends you otherwise trust when they tell you how great you look.

☹ You feel threatened every time you get an invitation to eat out.

☹ You mentally calorie-count as you eat.

☹ You are bothered if you miss weighing yourself every day.

☹ You spend money you can't afford on food.

☹ You steal to buy more food.

It can be difficult to spot a young anorexic before the condition has run long enough to make it apparent from weight loss. It can be even more difficult to spot a young bulimic at all. Secretiveness is one of the symptoms of both illnesses. It can also be one of the clues.

Anorexia

Watch for these possible signs:

- Loss of periods.
- Irregular periods.
- Secretiveness about eating.
- Unwillingness to sit down and eat meals with the family, however apparently convincing the reasons and excuses.
- Possible lies about the amount eaten elsewhere.
- Preoccupation with weight and shape.
- An apparent interest in food – anorexics are often very interested in food and cooking as topics and skills, which can give false reassurance to their families that they are actually eating the stuff, too.

217

- A dramatic weight loss.
- Failing to put on weight and fill out in young teenagers.
- Not seeing friends as much.
- Constipation, stomach pains.
- Dizziness.
- Swollen face, stomach, ankles.
- Discoloured skin.
- Losing hair.

Bulimia
You may be alerted to a bulimic by:

- Dramatic weight swings or mood swings.
- Finding excuses to head for the bathroom after every meal.
- Missing money or missing food.
- Finding concealed food wrappers and containers.

Where to go for help
If you think you may have an anorexic in the family or are maybe anorexic yourself, your GP practice is probably the first place to start seeking help. Ask them about eating disorder clinics at hospitals in your area. Anorexia and bulimia may need both medical and psychological help, and therapy may need to involve the whole family.

Possible sources of help include:

- **The Eating Disorders Association**, Sackville Place, 44 Magdalen Street, Norwich, Norfolk NR3 1JE; (0603) 621414. This is an umbrella organisation which coordinates a network of local groups (many run by people who have suffered anorexia or bulimia) and provides information, telephone help and a newsletter.
- **Overeaters Anonymous**, PO Box 19, Stretford, Manchester M32 9EB. This is a self-help organisation for men and women with eating disorders that uses a 'twelve steps' recovery program modelled on that of Alcoholics Anonymous. They will put you in touch with the nearest of more than 100 groups countrywide.
- Your library may be able to give you details of self-help or support groups in your area. (Check their noticeboard, too.)

- Counsellors may help you sort out some of the underlying issues. Some counsellors are qualified to use more directly therapeutic approaches. Psychotherapists may also help you to work on symptoms and explore underlying problems. Contact **The British Association for Counselling**, 1 Regent Place, Rugby, Warwickshire CV21 2PJ (0788) 578328, who can put you in touch with counsellors as well as other therapists, including psychotherapists. Or contact **The United Kingdom Council for Psychotherapy** at Regent's College, Regent's Park, London NW1 4NS (071-487 7554).

Problem eating

Getting children to eat what and when you want them to can be a major cause of upset in families from a very early age. Parents with firm views about mealtimes and healthy eating for their children can find themselves on the losing end of a battle, with advertising guile, peer pressure and the child's tastes and preferences all ganging up on the other tug-of-war team.

A child watching commercial television for an hour after school and one on a Saturday morning each week could see 92 advertisements for food and drink, according to a survey done by the London Food Commission. That's nearly ten ads an hour. Almost 80 per cent of the ads were, the survey found, for foods high in fats, sugars or both. Only ten per cent of the ads could be considered as encouraging a healthy diet.

No wonder the advertising industry has children firmly in its sights. Research has shown that around 50 per cent of mothers say their children exert at least some influence on what they buy – particularly snacks, sweets, soft drinks and cereals.

Children's diets are certainly not all they might be. A 1990 study of British 11-year-olds revealed that in one week they ate on average:

- ☹ 4 packets of crisps
- ☹ 6 cans of soft drinks
- ☹ 7 bars of chocolate or other sweets
- ☹ 42 biscuits
- ☹ 7 puddings.

Further analysis revealed that few were choosing to eat fruit or vegetables and 40 per cent of their energy intake was coming from fat – that's 5 per cent more than it should be – with chips and sweets making up 20 per cent of their total diet. In addition it found that the number of children who were seriously overweight by that age had doubled in ten years.

Good nutrition in childhood matters for three reasons:

- Children need a good diet to meet their needs for growth and development.
- Food attitudes for life are laid down in childhood.
- High fat intake in childhood may lead to increased risk of coronary heart disease later, sugar intake to dental caries and low fibre intake to bowel disorders.

More than short-term nutrition and its long-term results are involved here. When meals start to become a battleground the war can escalate with both sides digging in. What children will and won't eat can become a source of constant anxiety for parents and pressure on their children. At best, that's an invitation to poor digestion. At worst, it is sowing seeds of deep discord in the family, and even of possible eating disorders later.

What should be a source of pleasure can become a hotbed of two-way friction and parental guilt. Here are some tips that might help you to prevent letting mealtime problems build up, or to defuse them if they already have:

- Take a leaf out of the advertising book. Give the dishes you want to promote names that will appeal to your youngster. Postman Pat pasta, for example, can be anything you want it to be in your own home, especially for the very young.
- If a child suddenly becomes a problem eater, ask for a medical check-up to ensure there is no underlying physical reason.
- Once you have reassured yourself about the child's health, check whether there is any underlying anxiety. If he or she is reluctant to tell you, a favourite toy might be able to say what the child can't or won't.
- If problem eating starts suddenly, see if you can work out what else could have been going on at the time. Bullying at school? Parental rows? It may be the problem that needs to be addressed is nothing to do with food.

- Check if your child is coming to meals hungry enough. Is there too much eating going on between meals or too close to mealtimes?
- Give children designer fun food – gravy in a central 'moat' on the mashed potatoes, for example – or faces – a spoonful of peas can be eyes, carrots can be hair, and so on.
- A sweet variation on the same theme – small pieces or slices of fruit or dried fruit can turn a pancake into a face. Giving it long hair can get lots more fruit into the picture.
- Sandwiches might appeal more if they are cut out in interesting shapes with biscuit cutters.
- Arrange food in the child's initials, or put initials on top of it.
- Some children might respond to the suggestion that vegetables 'build muscles'.
- Children love individual small packs, which are particularly useful for lunchboxes and picnic food for poor eaters, but there is nothing to stop you from using this ploy at the meal table, too.
- Involve problem eaters in planning, preparation and serving. Let them suggest meals.
- Serve meals back-to-front from time to time. Start with fresh fruit instead of leaving it until the end.
- Setting fresh fruit in jelly can give it more child appeal.
- Put in a special place in the fridge a selection of goodies that adds up to a day's good eating and let the child have it at any time and in any order he or she chooses.
- Be shameless about disguise. For example, sieved cottage cheese and low-fat plain yogurt would head few children's list of favourites. But they can be turned into a winning white sauce for lasagne by adding a little Cheddar to the mixture and topping the lot with a crunchy mix of broken crisps and a little more cheese before putting it in a hot oven.
- If your child has school dinners, liaise with the school. Make sure you know what he or she is getting there. Complain if you don't think it is healthy enough.
- Hold a tasting with 'yum' or 'yuk' ratings for various fruit, vegetables, toppings for bread and so on. It can be a good way to find out what children really like – for them and for you.

- You might also break a deadlock or a potential stalemate by asking the favourite toy what and how much the child would like to eat.
- This one's easier said than lived, but try to keep in mind that when children reject food you have prepared that they are not rejecting you or your love – even if that is how it can feel. They are only saying they don't want to eat something.
- Because not eating can arouse such anxiety in parents it can be a wonderful way for a child to get attention. The best tactic is to stick to giving rewards and praise for the behaviour you want to encourage and ignoring the undesired.
- Invite children who insist they do not want to eat anything to sit at the table with the rest of the family anyway. When they do, don't go back on the deal and press them to eat.
- Make sure that talkers at table take turns so that small children get their chance to be heard, too.
- Give the reluctant eater a turn at sitting at the head of the table.
- Let the child summon the family to dinner with a gong or a bell.
- Try providing a number of small dishes of, for example, salad vegetables, meat, cheese, raisins, fruit and letting the child create a mixture or salad of his or her own.
- Small children are often happier with little and often rather than bigger meals hours apart.
- Milk liquidised with a banana is nutritious and often very popular even with small children who are picky eaters.
- You can give rewards, including gold stars, bedtime stories and praise to children for eating what you want them to, especially when there is something on the menu they don't particularly enjoy.
- If the situation has become bad enough to warrant elaborate intervention, consider what psychologists call 'a token economy'. It means giving your child the chance to earn tokens for agreed good behaviour and cash them in for a reward when he or she has earned enough.
- Rewards can be whatever you decide, but for maximum effect involve the child in choosing them. You might want a list of them with rewards priced at different numbers of

tokens. Or perhaps you would like to have a screwtop jar full of agreed possibilities from which the child can take a lucky dip whenever he or she qualifies.

- Think about whether you really want to make it a rule that everything must always be eaten up. One thing common to many obese adults is that they seem not to know when they have eaten enough.

- Another is that they eat in a vain attempt to obtain forms of satisfaction other than nutrition from food. Maybe mealtimes will be more relaxed and less likely to set up destructive patterns for the future if you serve smaller helpings and offer seconds than if eating too much becomes associated with earning your approval.

- A good, balanced diet is the best source of healthy eating. But if you have an incorrigibly difficult eater, a multi-vitamin supplement might be a way to avoid poor nutrition for him or her and unnecessary angst for you, at least in the short-term.

- You may want to check that the problem is not in your own perception of what a healthy diet for a child is. Generally, it is what healthy eating is for an adult. But there are specific points of difference for different age groups. For a quick refresher course, have a look through the guide below.

Under-5s

Fat is an important part of the diet of young children because it gives a concentrated supply of energy while they are too small to have room to take in and digest large amounts of food. They need fat, too, for the absorption of the fat-soluble vitamins A, D, E and K and to supply essential fatty acids, which are the building blocks of all the tissues in the body. Under-2s should have whole rather than semi-skimmed or skimmed milk. Move them on to semi-skimmed milk after that. If you have a faddy, picky or difficult eater, you might want to keep them on full cream until they are 5.

Another danger for babies and toddlers is what dentists call fruit-juice caries – tooth decay caused by giving undiluted fruit juices or other drinks high in sugar in a bottle, which a child sucks for prolonged periods of time. Better to ensure that sugary solutions aren't left on and near the teeth for long periods and introduce teeth-brushing after a meal early.

Many parents depend largely or partly on ready-made baby food, but a recent Food Commission survey into 60 leading brands found many packed with starches, thickeners and sugar and with low nutritional values. So don't make assumptions about the contents without checking carefully the nutritional breakdown on the label. And unfortunately even that will often leave you guessing. Many brands do not break the carbohydrates down to indicate how much is starch and how much is sugar, though some do.

Children of this and later ages also need less fibre in their diets than adults do. If you fill them up with too much of it, there is a danger that they will not eat enough other food to get all the energy they need.

From 5 to 11

In some ways, healthy eating for this age group is easier. Children are not now growing as fast. It is easier for them to tell you, or to take direct action themselves, if they feel hungry. The downside is that parental control over what children are eating declines through this age group.

By this age, children need a lower proportion of their food to be fat because they have less of a problem with eating a sufficient volume of food to fuel their bodies. They can switch to semi-skimmed milk, and be encouraged to go for lower-fat bread spreads.

Tooth decay increases. Although sugar with meals is fine, because the other foods and drinks take it off the teeth with them and it is swallowed, eating sweets, biscuits, high-sugar drinks (including undiluted fruit juice) and fruit between meals can leave sugar round the teeth. Toffees and boiled sweets are the worst because they hang around unbrushed teeth the longest.

This area is one of the hardest for parents to win. A total sweets ban is likely to increase desirability, and you will probably find that a grandparent or neighbour or friend or other children are sanction-busting anyway. This has to be an individual decision, but many parents concerned about healthy eating opt for some sort of compromise like allowing sweets on one day a week only, or on special occasions only, and make it conditional on conscientious tooth-brushing immediately afterwards.

Soft drinks are another problem for parents. In hot weather, particularly, children need more fluid and want more fruit juice and soft drinks. Undiluted orange juice actually has no less sugar than fizzy drinks – both should be taken only in moderation. Steer them as much as you can towards water, diluted fruit juice and low-calorie soft drinks, and ideally those sweetened with aspartame rather than saccharin because aspartame is used in lower concentrations.

This is an age when some children opt to become the lone family vegetarian. Having what the rest of the family does minus the fish or meat is not enough. A healthy diet requires more. You will find tips on getting to grips with nutrition and cooking for a healthy vegetarian diet throughout this book. (Don't forget those good old standbys, jacket potato with baked beans and baked beans on toast.) If you are a vegetarian or vegan or are feeding one, you might want to have a look again at the advice in **Chapter 3** about vitamin B12 and iron, too. It's particularly important for children.

If your child becomes podgy now, look to the biscuits, crisps, cakes, sweets, ice-cream and high-sugar drinks to make the necessary cuts.

Adolescents

Now you can really have problems. Adolescents are using up energy like crazy. They need more than at any time in their lives. And food can get caught up in the battleground where teenagers are flexing emerging identities and where parents are struggling to keep hold of the reins.

Calcium and iron (see **Chapter 2**) become of prime importance now. Vegetarianism becomes even more likely in non-vegetarian families. Wholemeal bread, fruit, milk or cheese and eggs as well as vegetables and salads will help keep it a healthy option. For a teenager who opts to be vegan and avoid all animal products, it is particularly important to drink a fortified soya milk like Plamil or Granogen.

225

In later years

As we age we need less energy. But it is just as important that what we do eat gives us good nutrition. One of the biggest dangers for the elderly is not bothering to eat properly – living on tea and biscuits, for example. Cooking can be a chore for those not as physically able as they were, or for those having to cope with life changes like no longer having a partner with whom to share mealtimes, or a works canteen to supply the main meal of the day.

Remember:

☺ Meals on Wheels or a local luncheon club can be a way for some older people to improve their diets.

☹ The housebound get less sun and so may be at risk of going short of vitamin D.

☺ Old people who have lost teeth and whose sense of taste and smell are less acute than they were may want mushier and sweeter foods.

☺ Full cream milk can be useful for elderly people who do not eat well.

☺ Old people suffering from constipation – and many do – will benefit from eating wholemeal bread.

☺ Eating small and often helps fight off hypothermia, which is a particular risk in cold weather for the less mobile. Foods high in protein and carbohydrate beat those high in fat for increasing heat production.

Can food make you ill?

There is another group of both children and adults for whom healthy eating means something different still. Unlike those children whose behaviour problems are centred around the difference between their definition of a good meal and that of their parents, the children in this group are those for whom the food they do eat seems to be a direct cause of bad behaviour as well as other health problems. Healthy eating for them means discovering the food or foods to which they are allergic or have an adverse reaction and avoiding them. That is often not as easy as it sounds, for allergies that underlie such diverse symptoms or clusters of symptoms can involve detective work.

Possible physical symptoms of food allergy can include: swellings, sweating, fatigue, racing pulse, asthma, skin problems, headache, hay fever, catarrh, giddiness, mouth ulcers, bad breath, bloating after eating, bowel problems, frequent urination, impotence, menstrual disorders, aching muscles and joints, tension, panic attacks and anxiety, and depression. Any allergies in the under-5 age group tend to be inherited. The risk is increased by introducing foods too early into an infant's diet. More than a third of children who have an allergic reaction to a particular food at this stage have grown out of it by the time they are 3. Indications here can be skin rashes, runny eyes, asthma and just a general failure to thrive. If you suspect an allergy see your doctor.

One of the more controversial areas of the relatively new field of studying allergic and adverse reactions to food is how much it contributes to hyperactive behaviour in children. Many doctors have been slow to accept that it does. However, a major study of severely hyperactive children conducted in 1985 by the Institute of Child Health and the Hospital for Sick Children, Great Ormond Street, London, found that two of the main substances that provoked abnormal behaviour when they were withdrawn from the diets of these children, and then reintroduced, were the colouring tartrazine (E102) and preservative benzoate (E210). Dr Richard Mackarness, one of the pioneers of allergy diagnosis in the UK, said before he retired that the foods to which he most commonly found people allergic were cereals and sugars, instant coffee, tea, chocolate, eggs, milk and processed foods.

Parents who suspect that food allergy underlies hyperactivity in their child might find it helpful to contact **The Hyperactive Children's Support Group**, which was founded by Mrs Sally Bundy to help others in the wake of her own frustration trying to cope with her hyperactive son. There are support groups all over the country. To find out the nearest to you, contact 71 Whyke Lane, Chichester, West Sussex PO19 2LD; (0903) 725182.

ANSWERS TO QUIZ

1. Vegetable curries, chapatis and tandoori dishes all have less fat than the other choices. (See pages 203–4)

2. All but the stewed coffee. One or two cups daily of coffee that has been left to stew won't do much damage but half a dozen can raise harmful LDL levels. (See pages 41–2)

3. Calcium and iron. (See page 225, and pages 55–8 for where to find good sources of both.)

4. There isn't one. A low-fat butter substitute might have 40 per cent fat while a low-fat yogurt might indicate a fat content of only 0.5 per cent. (See page 69)

5. False: a Sturmer Pippin, for example, contains six times as much vitamin C as a Cox's Orange Pippin of the same weight. (See pages 82–3)

6. Grilling bacon under a hot grill is best, as more than a third of the fat is shed. Next best is frying it in a quarter-inch of hot oil (20 per cent of fat is lost), then in a quarter-inch of cold oil (15 per cent is lost). The least good methods are frying with only a little oil and microwaving. (See page 117)

7. The pressure cooker. (See page 129)

8. Labna is otherwise known as yogurt cream cheese, lower in fat than cream cheese, easy to make at home and eminently versatile. (See page 137)

9. About an hour, so if you drink a lot of alcohol at a party you might still be over the limit the next morning. (See page 167)

10. The fridge is the worst place as the low temperatures speed up starch crystallisation, which makes bread stale. The freezer is the best because mould does not develop and starch does not crystallise below freezing point. (See pages 179–80)

SOURCES AND RECOMMENDED READING

Much of the material in this book has been drawn from research carried out and published by *Which?* and *Which? way to Health* magazines, also published by Consumers' Association. Other material derives from three *Which?* Consumer Guides: *Understanding Allergies* by Mary Steel (1989), *Preventing Heart Disease* (1991) and *Understanding Stress* (revised edition 1992).

Other sources include:

Composition of Goods, Agriculture Handbook No. 8, Agricultural Research Service, United States Department of Agriculture, US Government Printing Office, Washington DC, 1975

Cooking with Mosimann, Anton Mosimann, Papermac, London, 1989

Diet, Nutrition and The Prevention of Chronic Diseases: Report of a World Health Organization Health Group, W.P.T. James (Chairman of Study group), World Health Organization, Geneva, 1990

Eater's Choice, Dr Ron Goor and Nancy Goor, Houghton, Mifflin, New York, 1992 (can be obtained from AA Books, 7 Hurst Lodge, Gower Road, Weybridge, Surrey KT13 0EF)

Eat for Life Diet, Janette Marshall and Anne Heughan, Vermilion, London, 1993

Eating for a Healthy Heart, Good Housekeeping with Coronary Prevention Group, 1988 (out of print)

Enjoy Healthy Eating, Health Education Authority, London, 1991

Feeding Time: How to Cope with Your Child's Eating Problems, Gillian Weaver, 1985

Food Sense; Food Safety; About Food Additives; Understanding Food Labels and Food Protection: guides from the Food Safety Directorate, Ministry of Agriculture, Fisheries and Food, London, 1991

The Food Revolution, Dr Tom Sanders and Peter Bazalgette, Bantam Press, London, 1991

Low Fat Cookery, Wendy Godfrey, Sainsbury's, London, 1985

On the Demon Drink, Jancis Robinson, Mitchell Beazley, London, 1988

The Low Fat Gourmet, Caroline Waldegrave, Sainsbury's, London, 1987

McCance and Widdowson's Composition of Foods, and supplements, A.A. Paul and D.A.T. Southgate, HMSO, London, 1978, 1988, 1989

Middle Eastern Cookery, Suzy Benghiat, Weidenfeld and Nicolson, London, 1984

Not All in the Mind, Dr Richard Mackarness, Pan, London, 1990

Sprouting Beans and Seeds, Judy Ridgway, Century, London, 1984

Your Food: Whose Choice?, National Consumer Council (Ed.), HMSO, London, 1992

Your Very Good Health, Rose Elliot, Fontana, London, 1981

INDEX